the
WOMEN's
DEVOTIONAL guide
to the Bible

the
women's
DEVOTIONAL guide
to the Bible

*A One-Year Plan for Studying, Praying,
and Responding to God's Word*

JEAN E. SYSWERDA

NELSON BOOKS
A Division of Thomas Nelson Publishers
Since 1798

www.thomasnelson.com

Copyright © 2006 by Jean E. Syswerda

All rights reserved. No portion of this book may be reproduced, stored in a retrieval system, or transmitted in any form or by any means—electronic, mechanical, photo-copy, recording, scanning, or other—except for brief quotations in critical reviews or articles, without the prior written permission of the publisher.

Published in Nashville, Tennessee, by Thomas Nelson, Inc.

Nelson Books titles may be purchased in bulk for educational, business, fund-raising, or sales promotional use. For information, please e-mail SpecialMarkets@ThomasNelson.com.

Scripture quotations marked NKJV are taken from the NEW KING JAMES VERSION®. Copyright © 1982 by Thomas Nelson, Inc. Used by permission. All rights reserved.

Scripture quotations marked KJV are from The Holy Bible, KING JAMES VERSION.

Scripture quotations marked NCV are taken from the NEW CENTURY VERSION®. Copyright © 2005 by Thomas Nelson, Inc. Used by permission. All rights reserved.

Scripture quotations noted NIV are from The Holy Bible, NEW INTERNATIONAL VERSION®. Copyright © 1973, 1978, 1984 by International Bible Society. Used by per-mission of Zondervan Bible Publishing House. All rights reserved.

Library of Congress Cataloging-in-Publication Data

Syswerda, Jean.
    The women's devotional guide to the Bible : a one-year plan for studying, praying, and responding to God's Word / Jean E. Syswerda.
      p. cm.
Includes index.
    ISBN 0-7852-1251-5 (hardcover)
    1. Bible—Devotional use. 2. Christian women—Religious life. 3. Bible—Criticism, interpretation, etc. I. Title.
    BS617.8.S97 2006
    220.071—dc22

                                      2006021424

Printed in the United States of America

06 07 08 09 QW 5 4 3 2 1

Lovingly dedicated to the memory of my granddaughter,

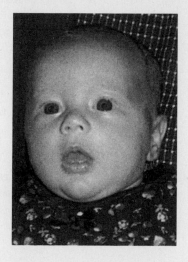

Ava Nicole Buck,

with us for three short months
and now safe in Jesus' arms.

MAY 5, 2005, TO AUGUST 1, 2005

Contents

Preface

When beginning a writing project as ambitious as this one, the months stretch out ahead, long but fulfilling and exciting. I began writing late in 2004, eager to work my way through God's Word and discover along with my future readers the beauty and depth of truth to be found there.

Prayer plays a big part in my writing schedule. I'd like to say it's always a planned and scheduled prayer each time I write. It's more often, however, a desperate plea for help when up against a blank page. My goal has always been to write what God inspires me to write. But even inspiration takes work and effort and rewriting and study.

I've worked in Christian publishing for many years. As an editor and publisher, then writer, I've spent countless hours in the Bible—studying, examining, presenting its truths to a variety of audiences. I know the process. Or so I thought.

One event on the first day of August, 2005, brought all I thought I knew to a catastrophic halt. On that terrible day, my three-month-old granddaughter died in her bed at home. I watched in horror as her mother, my daughter, performed CPR, and then turned our little girl over to emergency personnel. All to no avail. In the early afternoon, the unimaginable had happened. Our littlest family member was gone.

And with her went everything I had hoped and dreamed and thought I knew. Months later, when I went back to writing, I wrote from a position of brokenness and with my spirit crushed and crying. I went back through everything I had written before, reworking those pieces that I knew so much more about now, pieces on suffering and loss. And reassessing all I had said about a God I thought I knew but about whom

I discovered I had much more to learn. Now praying over what I wrote was the *only* way to get anything done. My cry was truly one of desperation, not because of an empty page but because of a broken heart.

So as you walk through the Scriptures in *The Women's Devotional Guide to the Bible*, I invite you to walk a road not just of suffering with me but a road of learning, a road that I pray will lead not just to knowledge but to peace and commitment to the God who grips our hands on a journey that holds suffering, yes, but also joy. As you read each passage and the materials that accompany those passages, I encourage you to do more than just read. Immerse yourself in the Word of God. Allow His truth to soak deep into your heart and mind. And enjoy the satisfaction and pleasure of a profound relationship with the God of the Bible.

Acknowledgments

So many people have given support and added their prayers to the work on this project, more so than usual because of the circumstances of my life when writing. First, last, beginning, and ending, I thank God, not just for His presence in writing this book but for His strength and comfort during life's most difficult times. My family also deserves my thanks for their love and support: my kids and grandkids, my mother and sisters, but especially my husband John. You're my rock. My small group from church provided in so many ways, but especially in praying, as I began to write again. A special thanks goes to my friend and prayer partner, Donna, for keeping me on track. To Ann Spangler and Linda Peterson, my thanks for continuing to work with me and believing in this book. To my editors at Nelson, Brian Hampton and Paula Major, go kudos for taking my efforts and refining and enhancing them in order to put out the best book possible.

Introduction

Have you ever wondered how the bits and pieces of the Bible—big books and little, poetry and prose, historical and theological—all fit together? Oh, you know that Psalms is in the middle, that Genesis is the beginning, and Revelation is the end. But what relationship do these books have with each other? What do Leviticus and Lamentations have in common, other than the fact that they both begin with the letter "L"? What are the Bible's overarching themes or purposes?

The Women's Devotional Guide to the Bible will provide you with a comprehensive overview of Scripture plus tools for in-depth study, reflection, and prayer. My hope is that this fifty-two-week program will make it easy for you to read, study, and pray the Bible on a daily basis. I also hope that it will lead you into a deeper understanding of the Bible as the whole Word of God so that you begin to see how its bits and parts fit together and how its message can provide inspiration and direction for your daily life.

The Women's Devotional Guide to the Bible uses a unique five-day approach to studying Scripture. Rather than taking a different passage each day and commenting on it, this guide focuses on an extended passage each week, giving you, the reader, a look at the passage from five different perspectives:

Monday offers a brief overview and summary information to help you understand the passage.

Tuesday gives helpful background information on the passage.

Wednesday provides a short Bible study that you can use by yourself or with a small group.

Thursday presents a chance for you to apply the passage to your own life.

Friday affords you an opportunity to pray based on the week's Scripture.

Monday's commitment to reading the Scripture as well as the summary information is pretty heavy duty. You may want to read the passages over the weekend if that works better for you. The Thursday and Friday readings have been purposely kept short so you have time to respond and pray.

The goal of *The Women's Devotional Guide to the Bible* is to give you an in-depth survey of Scripture. You'll get into every book of the Bible, you'll find truth in each passage, and hopefully, you'll see the overall beauty of the story of redemption that Scripture presents. If you're looking for a study that digs deep into Scripture, that provides profound teaching, and that gives you several ways to respond, this book is for you. But be sure to remember that it's just a *guide*. It's not intended to cover all of Scripture or present every truth of Scripture. It's also not necessary to stick to the five-day pattern. If working your way through each week takes you longer than five days, that's just fine. Use the study however it works best for you.

I hope and pray that *The Women's Devotional Guide to the Bible* will take you on an unforgettable journey, one that will not just provide great memories but treasures for your lifetime's journey with God.

An Incredible Beginning

Monday

Reading the Word
Genesis 1–3

THE STORY

With miraculous and spectacular action, God created, separating light and darkness, land and sea, earth and sky. No one watched. No one applauded. Only God knew what He had done and what was to come. With simple words and a creative energy that could only come from Almighty God, planets, sun, moon, animals, plants, birds, and fish appeared. Then on the sixth day, God's final creative plan unfolded as He formed a man, Adam, and then later a woman, Eve. Each day as God surveyed His work, He nodded His head in approval and said, *It is good*. For six days God worked, then on the seventh day He took a rest.

Soft breezes blew over rich soil and lush meadow. Luxuriant trees and plants grew with abandon as the sun shown down by day and the moon by night. In their private garden, Adam and Eve lived a life of perfection and intimacy with God, a life filled with pleasure and satisfaction.

Then, in the midst of that beauty and goodness, came an interloper—a liar who shattered peace and harmony by tempting Eve and then Adam to disobey God. And all was lost—or was it?

THE MESSAGE

This all-powerful God, who created your earthly home, is also all-loving. He recognized the sin of Adam and Eve, but He responded with loving action and careful punishment rather than heavy-handed vengeance.

THE MAIN POINT

Genesis 1–3 is the beginning, the story of firsts. The first chapters of the Bible record the first days of Creation, the first human beings, the first relationship between God and humans, the first husband-wife team, the first encounter with Satan and ensuing sin, and the first punishment for sin.

TAKE NOTE

Genesis 1—For centuries, scholars have debated whether God created the world in seven literal, twenty-four-hour days. Or are the days figurative for longer periods of time? The debate rages, with both sides making good points. Whatever your position on the issue may be, you can praise God today for making the miraculous, creative, and beautiful world in which you live.

Genesis 3:7—Have you ever given any thought to the sad words of Genesis 3:7? "They knew that they were naked" (NKJV). With the entrance of sin into the world came also the entrance of shame. Before they sinned, Adam and Eve were sweetly and totally unaware of themselves and their bodies as objects of embarrassment or indignity.

Tuesday

Reflecting on the Word
Genesis 1:27

You were created in the image of God. You were created to "look" like God. What good news that is! You weren't created to be the imperfect, bumbling, fumbling sinner that you know as yourself.

You are the only creature that bears God's image, the only one with spiritual as well as physical features. You are the only creature with a conscience, with a fully developed personality and will, the only one designed to live forever. Even more significant, you are the only creature God made to be in communion with Him. No other creature has a longing for God within, a vacuum that only God can fill.

Though you may feel like a poor imitation of God rather than a creature that fully bears His image, you are the only creature who can demonstrate godlike characteristics: God is just and calls you to be the same (Isaiah 30:18); He is holy and wants you to be holy (Leviticus 11:44–45); He is a righteous God (Psalm 111:3) and calls you to righteousness (Psalm 5:12).

The business of living the Christian life and growing in maturity as a believer is all about becoming more like God, more like Him than you were last year, last week, yesterday. Paul described in Colossians 3:1–17 what this looks like, what your part in this process is. And the apostle John wrote about that one characteristic of God that most fully describes Him and can be your highest goal in 1 John 4:16–17 NKJV: "We have known and believed the love that God has for us. God is love, and he who abides in love abides in God, and God in him. Love has been perfected among us in this: that we may have boldness in the day of judgment; because as He is, so are we in this world." That is, you were made, and live this day, in His image.

Wednesday

Studying the Word
Genesis 3

Reread Genesis 3, the story that describes the pathos of the human condition: the fall into sin and the need for a Redeemer. Alone or with several friends, answer these questions.

1. Satan, that sneaky snake, approached Eve with sort of a Groucho Marx shifty eyebrow aside and asked her something she quickly identified as a lie (Genesis 3:1–2). Why do you think he began this way?

2. Has the devil changed any since Eve's day? What sorts of tricks does he use to tempt people today?

3. Satan told Eve that if she ate the fruit she would "be like God" (Genesis 3:5 NKJV), a worthy desire. But how was he deceiving Eve this time? Who should she have spent time with if she actually wished to become more like God?

4. A big *oops* in verse 6. What did Eve turn toward instead of away from? Why was this a fatal mistake?

5. OK, Adam and Eve have both eaten what God had forbidden. What was the result (Genesis 3:7)? What did they see about themselves that they had not seen before?

6. In Genesis 3:14–15, Satan is now cursed. How does God reveal, even in this cursing, that all is not lost?

7. Compare husband/wife relationships before sin (Genesis 2:23–24) and after (Genesis 3:16). What has changed and how has it affected husband/wife relationships throughout history?

Thursday

Responding to the Word
Genesis 2:18

Many women—whether married or unmarried—read Genesis 2:18 with a shudder, finding difficulty with the word *helper*. Did God really mean *helper* the way most people think of the word, that women are somehow subservient and not quite up to par with men?

The Hebrew word here, *ezerl*, is used twenty-two times in the Bible. It is usually translated as *help* or *helper*. However, it is used to speak of God's power in Psalm 89:9, and three times the word is used to refer to God as a helper (Exodus 18:4; Deuteronomy 33:29; Hosea 13:9), all of which provide a clue to the fact that God does not intend a woman's position to be degrading or weak.

The woman who is a helper to her husband is not just *at* his side, she is *on* his side. She has her own distinct personality and gifts, her own abilities, her own interests. But above all, in the servant role so beautifully modeled by Christ, she is her husband's greatest advocate. Being his helper doesn't mean she follows behind him, picking up his dirty clothes and serving his every whim. It means she stands next to him as his equal, and they lovingly serve each other, with the full knowledge that at times serving might take the form of picking up those dirty clothes.

Reread Genesis 2:21–24, then take a little time to honestly assess yourself as a woman and, if you're married, as a wife. Are there aspects about being a woman that you find difficult? You can talk to God about it. He'll help you in those areas where you need to grow and change. If you're married, ask God to help you know what it means to be your husband's helper: his advocate, his lover, his friend, his servant, his most intimate companion. Whether you're married or unmarried, God can lovingly guide you in those areas where you relate to the men in your life—to your husband, to family members, to friends, to coworkers. Ask Him to help you to become the best you can be, a beautiful model of God's handiwork in a woman's life.

Friday

Praying the Word
Genesis 1:27

If possible, spend your prayer time outside today in order to enjoy the beauty of the world God created. Looking around you, praise God for specific parts of His creation: the trees, grass, water, flowers, mountains, and so forth.

Although you have inherited Adam and Eve's sinful nature, God has provided a way for you to become right with Him through His Son, Jesus. Bring to His loving attention any unconfessed sin.

Thank Him for the ways He has created you in His image as a unique female, with your own strengths, dreams, abilities, and potential.

Close your time of prayer by praying Genesis 1:27 back to God.

Creator God, You made me to be like You! How wonderful that is! And how much I fall short of Your image. Work in me day by day, Lord, to make me more like You so that I reflect the beauty of Your image to those around me.

Destruction and Salvation

Monday

Reading the Word
Genesis 6–8

THE STORY

Noah's wife plodded along the deck of the huge boat. She and her family had been saved from the flood in this rocking house on water. She knew they were fortunate, that God had seen her husband Noah's righteousness and had saved them from the destruction. But she had lost count of the days and weeks and months of rain and water and animals and their filth. Would it ever end? Or had they been saved from the flood waters only to die on this floating zoo?

As she turned a corner, she came upon her husband. He had a huge, almost silly grin on his face. She couldn't help but smile back. Noah held in his hand a dove. But what was unusual was what the dove had in its mouth. A green leaf! The dove had flown around, found dry ground where plants had begun to grow again, and brought back the evidence. Her mouth stretching now in a genuine smile, laughter bubbled up from deep within her. God had been true to His promise to save them. Life was beginning again.

THE MESSAGE

No matter how bad things get, no matter how deep you're dipping into sin, God provides a way out for those who seek Him. What a cause

| 7

for celebration! When *everyone* was doing evil *all* the time (Genesis 6:5), God found one righteous man, Noah, and used him and his family to preserve life.

THE MAIN POINT

In these chapters, where humanity's lowest of the low is recorded for all to see, God also appeared. It may not be the place you'd expect to see the high and holy God. But He's there, waiting for you, like Noah, to see Him and allow Him to pull you out of your sin and into His grace.

TAKE NOTE

Genesis 6:4—Giants. Huge men. Strong men. Men of influence. Princes and kings. Genesis calls these extraordinary people *Nephilim*. The spies sent to explore Canaan before the Israelites went in to conquer it also saw these giants and called them by the same name (Numbers 13:32–33). It's hard to say just how tall these giants might have been, but since the Israelites felt like "grasshoppers" (NKJV) next to them, they must have been of much larger than normal stature and strength.

Genesis 6:8—"But Noah . . ." (NKJV) Genesis ends its description of the horrors of sin that had permeated that culture with these two simple, but striking, words. God saw the bad, but He didn't overlook the good. And the good was Noah. Because of his faith and his life of righteousness in a world gone wrong, he found favor in God's eyes. And through him God saved a remnant of the human race to begin again.

Tuesday

Reflecting on the Word
Genesis 7:2–3

A misconception has been going the rounds for many years. It's propagated in the words of songs and rhymes about the flood. "Two by two." Or "The animals, the animals, they came in by twosies, twosies." From childhood on up, you're taught that the animals entered the ark by twos, one male and one female of each. There's a grain of truth here, but one that leads to a common misconception. Yes, *at least* two of each kind of animal entered the ark. But *more* than two of some kinds of animals entered the ark. So when you picture the animals prancing up the ramp—two elephants, two cows, two pigs, two zebras, two turkeys, two koala bears, two chickens—you'd be right only part of the time.

God told Noah to save two of each unclean animal and seven of each clean animal (Genesis 7:2). Does that come as a total surprise to you? Do you feel like you've heard and read the story of the flood a hundred times and missed this fact altogether? Well, join the crowd!

The command actually makes perfect sense. After the flood, Noah sacrificed some of the clean animals and birds as a thank offering to God. If only two had been preserved on the ark, then that animal would have been instantly extinct. Not God's plan at all.

What's just as interesting is that the distinction between clean and unclean animals isn't recorded in Scripture until much later, in Leviticus 11. Perhaps Noah and his culture had an early understanding of clean and unclean. Or perhaps God revealed the distinction to him as the animals were gathered and brought to the ark.

The beauty is in the details. So often a close reading of Scripture reveals something about God that you didn't recognize before. God's perfect plan to preserve the humans and the birds and the animals of His creation required close attention to detail, all of which He had worked out before He ever revealed anything to Noah.

Wednesday

Studying the Word
Genesis 8

Read through this story of the retreating flood, looking for those points of human interest with which you can connect as a person of faith.

1. "God remembered Noah" (Genesis 8:1 NKJV). Did God suddenly hit His head with the heel of His hand and say, "Oh, wow, Noah's out there in the flood! I better check in on him"? Do you think God actually forgot about Noah, then remembered him? If not, what other meaning could this have?

2. Put yourself in the place of Noah's wife. Replace your jeans and sweater for a robe and sandals. You've been cooped up on this boat for almost a year now. The only thing in sight, besides animals and the messes they leave behind, is water, water, and more water. Now try to imagine how you might have felt when the dove returned to the ark the first time (Genesis 8:8–9). How would your faith be tested in that moment? What would you say to Noah? To God?

3. Now describe how you might have felt when the dove returned with a fresh olive twig in its beak (Genesis 8:10–11). How would you act? What would you say to Noah? To God?

4. What seasons or incidents of testing have you experienced recently? What did that testing do to your faith? During that time, what did you say to God? To the others in your life?

5. Read Genesis 8:18–19 and think about the smiles that must have been on everyone's faces that day. More than anything, what did that open door and solid ground prove about God?

6. What has God proven to you about Himself during your difficult times of testing?

Thursday

Responding to the Word
Genesis 6:22

If Noah had a marker on his grave, perhaps Mrs. Noah would have had this verse engraved on it: *He did everything just as God commanded him.*

Did Noah realize that thousands of generations would read his epitaph in millions of copies of the Bible? Not likely. He just went about his daily life, living righteously in front of his less than righteous neighbors, measuring boards, gathering animals and food, and getting his hands black with pitch.

Not that Noah's daily life proceeded with ease. Obedience came at a price. The first price was looking foolish. Nobody but a nutcase would build a huge boat in the middle of a field, probably miles from any water. But Noah concerned himself more with God's opinion of him than with the opinions of those around him. So, he started pounding nails.

The second price Noah paid was walking into the unknown. His obedience required enormous faith on his part. Could he see what was coming? Not at all. But when God told Noah to build an ark because of an impending flood, he didn't ask, "What's a flood?" He simply obeyed.

People have all kinds of words and sayings etched on their tombstones. Sometimes those sayings reveal something of the person buried there. Perhaps it's a little ahead of the game to decide what you want engraved on your headstone. But it's never too early to think about what sort of legacy you're leaving your family and friends and neighbors. Would any of them say, "She did everything God told her to do"? Nothing would be greater!

Friday

Praying the Word
Genesis 8:20–21

Noah's first act after leaving the ark was to build an altar and offer sacrifices of praise to God. He and his family had obvious reasons to be thankful. As you look over the lessons of this week—God's holiness when confronted with sin and His loving preservation of Noah and his family—take a few moments to review your past history with God. Where has your sin offended His holiness? What about the sins of your family? Your culture?

In your prayer time today, confess those sins to God, asking Him for His forgiveness, and trusting Him to meet your need for freedom from your guilt. Then take it one step further. Ask God what role He would have you play in lovingly helping your family or your culture to recognize their sin. Whatever He asks you to do, be sure you are willing and ready to obey.

Then, as Noah did, thank Him. Thank Him for being a God of patience, a God of grace, and a God who loves to forgive those who come to Him in repentance.

Use God's own words in Genesis 8:21 to thank Him for His faithfulness and for keeping His promises.

God of faithful Noah, thank You for being my God as well. I pray that Your Spirit's touch will pierce my heart and reveal any sins that need to be confessed. I confess my great need for Your forgiveness, and I thank You for so freely offering it. Amen.

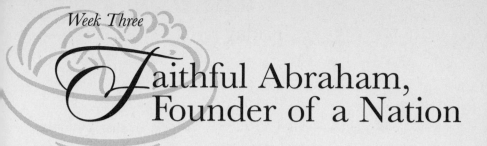

aithful Abraham, Founder of a Nation

Monday

Reading the Word
Genesis 12; 15:1–18:15; 21:1–22:19

THE STORY

Sarah stood behind the flap of the tent, leaning toward the sound of voices. Her husband Abraham was outside, talking with three visitors. From the look on Abraham's face, the news these visitors were bringing was a surprise to him. Sarah moved closer to the opening in the tent, hoping to hear more. One of the men was saying something like, "Sarah will have a baby next year." Sarah's laughter sputtered out of pursed lips. How foolish, silly even, to think that she and Abraham would have a child. They were just simply too old. It wasn't going to happen (Genesis 18:10–12). Sarah looked at Abraham, wondering if he believed something so absurd.

Little did Sarah know. Only a year later, her arms were wrapped around her baby son, Isaac. He was named after Abraham and Sarah's reaction to the promise of his birth (*Isaac* means "laughter"—Genesis 17:17–19; 21:3). Little Isaac would grow up and have a son, Jacob, who had twelve sons, who became the founders of the twelve tribes of Israel. Through God's promise fulfilled to a skeptical old woman and her husband, the nation of Israel was born.

THE MESSAGE

God often does the impossible, working through the unlikely, accomplishing what you might think is absurdly improbable. He doesn't do it just for fun. God always has a purpose. He wanted to make sure Abraham realized that Isaac's birth was miraculous and special, something only God could do. Look for that point throughout Scripture. More than some of the time, God does things in the oddest ways with the least likely people under the most implausible circumstances—all so that you will realize the work is fully His accomplishment and none of your own.

THE MAIN POINT

God knows what He's doing. Don't ever doubt it, even when it seems debatable. Look at the mess Abraham and Sarah created when they doubted. They took matters into their own hands and produced a son through Hagar. The resulting chaos had nothing to do with God's perfect plan to create a nation through another son, Isaac. As the story of Abraham demonstrates, waiting and trusting that God knows what He's doing is always the better option.

TAKE NOTE

Genesis 16:1–3—As crude and unappealing as it may seem today, Sarah's plan was not uncommon in her day. In fact, many in her day would have considered such an action a wife's responsibility. An infertile woman gave one of her servants to her husband in order to produce a family and remove the stigma of infertility. The children born of the union between the husband and the servant were considered to be the *wife's* children.

Genesis 16:12; 21:12–13—God told Hagar her son would be a "wild donkey of a man" (NIV). Not a very flattering description, and certainly not one most moms would want to hear. But Ishmael grew up to be a loner, a brute of a man who lived without friends. That didn't mean, however, that God didn't have plans for Ishmael. He promised Abraham that, though the nation of Israel would be established through Isaac, He wouldn't ignore Ishmael. A nation would be established through him as well.

Tuesday

Reflecting on the Word
Genesis 12:7

Abraham left his father's household and his homeland at the age of seventy-five, trekking from Ur to Haran to Canaan. Following the Euphrates River northward, he took the long way to Canaan but by doing so avoided crossing the vast and dangerous desert. The journey was long, and Abraham didn't know when it would end, when God would "show" him the land He had promised to him (Genesis 12:1 NKJV).

But that day did finally come. Abraham and his retinue arrived in Shechem, Canaan, where the Bible notes the "great tree of Moreh" grew. (Don't you find these small scriptural facts fascinating? What made this particular tree so significant that it deserves mention in the middle of the story of Abraham?) The town of Shechem was located a bit north and west of Jerusalem. God appeared to Abraham there and told him, "This is the place!"

In response Abraham built an altar.

Many ancient people, pagan as well as God-followers, built altars. Size, shape, and use varied, but most sacrificed animals on their altars (Genesis 8:20; Exodus 20:24–25; 24:4), symbolizing a gift to their gods as well as a form of worship. Altars were an important part of the furnishings of the tabernacle (Exodus 27:1–8) as well as the temple (1 Kings 6:20, 22; 2 Chronicles 4:1). For Abraham and the Israelite nation that followed, altars had even greater significance than they did for pagan worship. Altars were a symbol of communion with God, the burning of the sacrifice creating an aroma that pleased God (Exodus 29:18).

Altars also commemorated noteworthy events in the lives of the people. Noah built one when he left the ark (Genesis 8:20); Jacob built one when he was reunited with his brother Esau (Genesis 35:1–7); and Moses built one when the Israelites defeated the Amalekites (Exodus

17:15). Joshua built one when the Israelites returned to Canaan after their slavery in Egypt (Joshua 8:30).

Christians still build altars today. Perhaps there is a rail in the front of your church where you can go to pray or to participate in the Lord's Supper. Maybe you recall some other spot in your church where you gained a significant spiritual victory. Perhaps you have a favorite place where you go to commune with God. All of these places are altars. In fact, any location that offers you a sense of separation from your everyday life and a closer communion with God is an altar.

Wednesday

Studying the Word
Genesis 22:1–19

The story in these verses shows the remarkable depth of Abraham's faith and the extent to which God might go to test those who claim to believe in Him. Read the story of Abraham and Isaac, then answer these questions as honestly as you can:

1. Genesis 22:1 states pretty clearly what God was doing here. Why do you think He wanted to test Abraham? Why would He test anyone? What is He trying to accomplish? For reference see also Job 23:10; James 1:2–3; 1 Peter 1:7.

2. God asked Abraham to give up the son whom He had promised to use in building a nation. Why was one so dear to Abraham chosen to test him? What has God used or could He use to test you?

3. How quickly did Abraham obey God (Genesis 22:3)? What do you think was going through his mind on this trip? What would be going through your mind?

4. In Genesis 22:6–8, Isaac questioned the plan. Do you think he had any idea what was going on? Explain your answer.

5. Just as Abraham clenched a knife in his surely shaking hand to kill his son, God intervened. What did God provide for the sacrifice instead of Isaac (Genesis 22:13)? Compare this sacrifice with the sacrifice of Christ on the cross, noting the parallels between them.

6. Note in Genesis 22:14 the name that Abraham gave this place. What does the tense of the name tell you about Abraham's faith and what he'd learned?

7. What did God promise to Abraham because he had passed the test (Genesis 22:15–18)?

8. What confidence can you gain from Hebrews 12:5b–11 when you are tested?

Thursday

Responding to the Word
Genesis 18:9–15

Sarah laughed. It's not so funny when you think about it. She didn't laugh at something she thought was "ha-ha" funny. She laughed at something she thought was "how-ridiculous" funny. She laughed because she didn't believe God was capable of fulfilling the promise He had just made.

Her laughter was tinged with more than a little bitterness too. Notice the sarcasm in her words: "After I have grown old, shall I have [this] pleasure, my lord [Abraham] being old also?" (Genesis 18:12 NKJV). God had promised to fulfill Sarah's most treasured dream. And instead of rejoicing and believing, Sarah laughed.

While it's pretty easy from this end of the timeline to judge Sarah harshly for her imprudent reaction, God didn't. That's right. God didn't reject Sarah and didn't withdraw His promise. Until she lied and said she hadn't laughed, He didn't even reprimand her. He just repeated His promise, adding one rhetorical question, a question that asks it all: "Is anything too hard for the LORD?" (Genesis 18:14 NKJV). Sarah's only possible answer? "No . . ."

Is there anything too hard for the Lord? Can He really accomplish anything He pleases? Cure the sick parent? Return the prodigal child? Heal the scarred emotions? Open infertile wombs? If Sarah were to arrive today to speak to you personally, she would shout her assurance along with her laughter: "*Yes! He can do everything He says He can do! Believe it!*"

Friday

Praying the Word
Genesis 12:1–9

If you don't already have an altar, a special place where you spend time alone with God, create one now. It doesn't have to be anything extravagant, just a place where you can remove yourself from your everyday life and turn your focus completely on God. It might be a special chair in your family room. Or a corner of your bedroom. Or perhaps a spot in your office. Have your Bible and other study or devotional tools close at hand. You might want to have music to play or candles to light. Whatever helps you bend your mind and your ears to hear God rather than the cacophony of earthly living.

Commit to spending regular time at your altar. Sit or kneel in God's presence, talking to Him honestly about all that you have on your mind—your blessings, your troubles, your needs. Reread the story of Abraham and Isaac and the name Abraham gave the altar (Genesis 22:1–14). Think about the truth of God's work and provision in your life, and then perhaps name your altar something that reflects that truth.

God's words to Abraham in Genesis 15:1 are His words to you also as you face your life with its struggles as well as blessings. Use His words to pray your thanks back to God for His strength and protection.

I need You in my life, Lord. I need regular communication and communion with You. I confess my lack of faithfulness in seeking You. Make my hunger for You so great that my only response can be falling on my knees before You. Amen.

Abraham's Family

Monday

Reading the Word
Genesis 24; 27:1–30:24; 31; 41; 45; 49:29–50:26

THE STORY

Joseph rubbed his face with his hands, quickly wiping away any evidence of the tears that kept filling his eyes. He looked out again at the men gathered in front of him. The youngest, Benjamin, looked up at him with large, innocent eyes that reminded him of their mother. Joseph and Benjamin were brothers, sons of Jacob and Rachel. Joseph watched his half brothers, sons of Jacob and Leah, wondering if they had changed at all since they sold him into slavery. Turning to Benjamin again, Joseph felt his control slipping and quickly left the room. He ran into his private office and sent everyone away. There he collapsed, sobbing for all that was lost.

Joseph's mind twisted and turned, memories flashing—his mother, his father, the years of slavery and being in prison, and now his position of power in Egypt. He could do anything he wanted to these brothers of his. Anything. How could he face them? These men who had only wanted his death? This younger brother whom he barely remembered?

Then Joseph recalled why these men were here. Food. They had none. He had plenty. They were hungry. Joseph's *father* was hungry. Squaring his shoulders, certain now of his direction, Joseph returned to his brothers. He looked at them, remembering the promise God had made to their great-grandfather Abraham to make them into a great nation. Despite any lingering anger, Joseph had a job to do. These men were, after all (bumps and warts and sins and jealousies notwithstanding), the founders of a nation, God's nation of chosen people, Israel.

THE MESSAGE

God used these very ordinary, not-so-perfect men and women to accomplish His purposes. It's easy to look back at these stories and think these people were more faithful and followed God's direction more easily than you do. But a close reading of the stories reveals just what God wants you to know: these men and women, these founders of the nation of Israel, were no more perfect than you are. They wavered and sinned against God and each other and wondered if God knew what He was doing. God used them in spite of themselves, just as He'll use you in spite of your not-so-perfect self.

THE MAIN POINT

God always keeps His promises. Even when scheming (Rebekah) and deception (Jacob) caused alienation from the rest of the family; when jealousy caused separation, slavery, and brushes with death (Joseph); and when famine struck (Joseph's brothers in Egypt), God used those destructive circumstances to fulfill His constructive promises.

TAKE NOTE

Genesis 24:2—This ancient custom of putting a hand "under" (NKJV) the thigh, near a man's sexual organs, demonstrated the deep level of trust that existed between Abraham and his servant. It sealed their agreement, similar to a handshake or a signed document in today's society. The only other time it is mentioned in Scripture is in Genesis 47:29, when Jacob made an agreement with his son Joseph.

Genesis 28:22—Following his grandfather Abraham's example (Genesis 14:20), Jacob promised God a tenth of all that he gained financially. Ancient peoples paid a tithe, which has historic roots in the word *tenth*, to rulers as well as religious figures. The first mention in the Bible of such a practice is in Genesis 14:20, when Abraham gave a tenth of the spoils of victory to the high priest Melchizedek. Moses established the tithe as a law of God that continued throughout Israelite history (Leviticus 27:30) and is still practiced as a structure for giving in many churches today.

Tuesday

Reflecting on the Word
Genesis 31:22–35

Rachel's theft of her father's household gods could mean one of two things. Either she thought they would increase her claim to an inheritance from her father, or she felt that she and Joseph and Leah and their families needed the supernatural help these gods might offer.

Whatever her motive, Rachel's actions reveal a deficiency in her faith. No matter what she thought these idols could accomplish for her or for her family, she was mistaken. Like holding on to a rope that's attached to nothing, Rachel held on to these false gods that had no power.

And she wasn't about to give them up. Can you picture her coyly crossing her slim legs, then raising her reddened face to her father and simpering, "I'm so sorry, Daddy, but I can't get up. I'm having my period." She knew her father would never expect her to move, nor would he touch what she was sitting on—blankets, furs, gods, whatever. Her period made all she touched unclean and effectively kept her father from discovering her robbery.

But be careful how quickly you criticize Rachel for trusting in something so powerless. What rope do you cling to that has no real power? A retirement fund that could disappear with one downturn of the market? A friend who could turn against you? A paycheck that could end tomorrow? The only rope that's sturdy and won't let go or fray is God. Cling to Him.

Wednesday

Studying the Word
Genesis 29:14*b*–30:24

Like two cats that just can't seem to get along, hissing and scratching whenever they come into proximity, Jacob's wives, Rachel and Leah, spent most of their marriage fighting for first place in their husband's heart. Their battles only caused grief for them and their families. Answer these questions to get at the heart of their problems as well as some possible solutions.

1. Genesis 29:16–18 tells why Jacob was in love with Rachel but not with Leah. What does this tell you about his character as a young man? Why do you think people so quickly judge others based on outward appearances? How can you combat this tendency in yourself?

2. What does Genesis 29:31 tell you about God? Name some specific ways He has shown His love for you in your life circumstances.

3. What did Leah want more than anything (Genesis 29:32)? What did Rachel want more than anything (Genesis 30:1)?

4. What does Genesis 30:8 tell you about Rachel's character and about her relationship with her sister Leah? What does Genesis 30:15 tell you about Leah's character and about her relationship with her sister Rachel?

5. Genesis 30:22 NKJV says God "remembered" Rachel. Does this mean He had forgotten her? What other meaning could it have?

6. When have you felt like God forgot about you? How has He shown you that He never forgets and always cares (Nahum 1:7; 1 Peter 5:7)?

7. If you're married, with whom, or what, do you share your husband? Another woman? A career? A hobby? Whatever it is, what can you learn from Leah and Rachel?

Thursday

Responding to the Word
Genesis 50:15–21

Joseph was broken. Not only had his long-lost father died, but his brothers still didn't trust him. So they stuck with their usual modus operandi, and lied. They told Joseph their father had said something he *might* have said, but didn't. Joseph probably looked at his brothers and realized how much they had changed from when they were young and so jealous that they sold him into slavery. But he also realized how little they had changed. They assumed Joseph would respond as they would have responded. With revenge.

Did Joseph now think it was time for long overdue paybacks? Not at all. Joseph showed just how much he *had* changed. Rather than the arrogance and superiority of his youth, Joseph offered his brothers only one thing: forgiveness.

Forgiveness. Perhaps the hardest thing to freely offer anyone. Had Joseph forgotten what his brothers had done to him? Unlikely. He was enough of a realist to remember. Was he no longer hurt by the years of separation from his father and family? Doubtful. Rather than looking at his past circumstances, however, Joseph looked at God. And what he saw there was a revelation. All that his brothers had done to him out of hatred and envy, God had used to bring safety and protection. So he chose to forgive his brothers.

Did you catch that? He *chose* to forgive.

In his book, *Experiencing God's Forgiveness,* Luis Palau tells a remarkable story about forgiveness. Clara Barton, who founded the Red Cross, ran into someone who had once done a vicious thing against her. But she acted like she had no memory of the action. When a friend reminded her, saying "Don't you remember it?" Barton responded, "No, I distinctly remember forgetting it."[1]

---

[1] Luis Palau, *Experiencing God's Forgiveness* (Sisters, OR: Multnomah Press, 1984).

That's forgiveness.

Is it easy? Never. Will the one who wronged you always seek forgiveness? Probably not. Will the hurt continue? Most likely. Will there be scars? Usually. If you're struggling with forgiveness, you're not alone. But God's call is to forgive anyway, just as He forgave you.

Colossians 3:13; Romans 5:8—Meditate on these two Scriptures, pray them to God, and since you don't have the strength to forgive (Joseph probably didn't either), ask God to give you His.

Friday

Praying the Word
Genesis 41:51

After the horrors Joseph had experienced at the hands of his brothers as well as the Egyptians, he had the wisdom and grace to move forward instead of wallowing in the past and its pain. The first evidence in Scripture of Joseph looking to the future instead of the past is in Genesis 41:51, where he names his first son "Manasseh," which sounds like and may be derived from the Hebrew word *forget*.

Spend your prayer time today placing the past and its pain and difficulties before God. Ask Him to give you the same wisdom and grace He gave to Joseph. Tell Him how much you hurt, how angry you are, and how scarred. Then ask Him to give you what you need in order to stop viewing your life from the rearview mirror.

He loves to answer such requests, you know. He delights in giving you a bright future in spite of your past. Check out Jeremiah 29:11 for His promise.

Father, I give You all my past, and I ask You to bring me healing from the hurts that are there. I thank You for Your promise not just of a future, but a future with hope. Give me the wisdom and grace of Joseph to walk out of my past and into a future that's bright because You're in it. Amen.

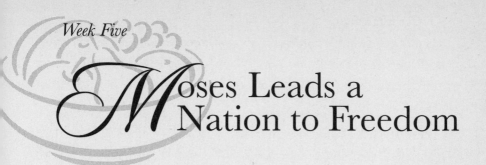

Moses Leads a Nation to Freedom

Monday

Reading the Word
Exodus 1–4:21; 5:1–6:12; 7–12

THE STORY

After years of herding sheep in the desert, protecting them from wild animals, finding water and grass for them, Moses wasn't afraid of much. But this was a curious and rather frightening sight. He approached a bush that was on fire but didn't burn up. As he stole closer to examine this oddity, a voice spoke from within the bush: "Moses, take off your sandals. You're standing on holy ground." Moses' hands shook as he removed first one, then the other sandal. The voice went on to tell Moses that the miserable slavery of the Israelites in Egypt had not gone unnoticed. God wanted Moses to go back to Egypt and lead the people out.

Moses knew all about the conditions of the Israelites. After all, he had watched their rough treatment from his safe position in Egypt's palaces. Though he was an Israelite, he'd been raised as Pharaoh's son. He'd been on the run from Pharaoh for killing an Egyptian slave driver. Now God wanted him to go back to Egypt? And lead the Israelites? Him? What was God thinking? He wasn't a leader! He couldn't speak to his own children without his tongue getting all tangled up in his words, much less to the king of Egypt!

Eventually Moses had to obey. God tolerated only so much argument, and then made it clear He wasn't *asking* Moses to assume this leadership position, He was *commanding* it.

THE MESSAGE

Freedom! That's what the story of Exodus is all about. Between the last verse of Genesis and the first verse of Exodus, about four hundred years passed—years when the people of Egypt forgot all about Joseph and how he had saved their nation from famine. Joseph's family had grown from about a hundred to millions, and the Egyptians now viewed them as a threat. So they forced the Israelites into slavery. God saw their misery and sent His ambassador, Moses, to Pharaoh. Freedom didn't come without a price, however. Ten plagues whipped through Egypt, breaking the people and their Pharaoh until they practically thrust the Israelites out of their country.

THE MAIN POINT

God has a great memory. When He makes a promise, He keeps it. He had promised the land of Canaan to Abraham and his descendants. Those descendants were now living far from Canaan in Egypt. Exodus 2:24 states that God remembered His promises to Abraham and began His work to keep them. The principle doesn't apply only to the Israelites. God keeps His promises to all of His people. If you belong to Him, that includes you!

TAKE NOTE

Exodus 3:5—Moses met God for the first time at the sight of a bush that was on fire but didn't burn up. As if that weren't curious enough, God told Moses to take off his sandals because the ground there was "holy" (NKJV). In many cultures, even today, removing footwear when entering a home is a sign of respect. Perhaps God's command was as simple as asking Moses to show proper respect in His presence. As a sinful, sullied human being, Moses needed to remove the very article that was most in touch with the defiled world he lived in—his sandals.

Exodus 7:10–12—Moses and Aaron had just strutted their miracle stuff before Pharaoh, only to have his magicians duplicate the same acts. Most would probably stand there stupefied, thinking, *What's up with that?* But Moses and Aaron were likely already aware of the powers behind these sorcerers' acts—occult, demonic power. As difficult and disappointing as it may have been for them to see these sham magicians duplicate the power of God, the game wasn't up yet. God's power had the final say when Aaron's staff-turned-snake gobbled up the snakes made by Pharaoh's magic men.

Tuesday

Reflecting on the Word
Exodus 4:21

Throughout the story of the Israelites' bid for freedom, the book of Exodus mentions ten times that God "hardened" Pharaoh's heart and ten times that Pharaoh "hardened" his heart (Exodus 4:21; 7:3, 13–14, 22; 8:15, 19, 32; 9:7, 12, 34–35; 10:1, 20, 27; 11:10; 13:15; 14:4, 8, 17). Those verses that speak of Pharaoh hardening his own heart pose no problem, of course. What else would one expect from a heathen, diabolical ruler, one who wanted to keep his slaves rather than free them? Pharaoh and a hard heart go together as naturally as bacon and eggs.

But what about those verses that say God hardened Pharaoh's heart? Doesn't that sound like something that God wouldn't (or at least shouldn't) do?

Make no mistake. Pharaoh had no intention of following God's will or obeying Him. In the first five plagues, the king hardened his own heart. In the following plagues, God hardened his heart. God didn't force a hard heart upon Pharaoh against his will. Pharaoh willingly and willfully did all he could to thwart God's will rather than to promote it.

In his letter to the Romans, Paul conveys the same truth. Given enough resistance (as in stubbornly refusing to give in during the course of five plagues), God will let people dive as deeply into sin as they wish (Romans 1:24, 26, 28). Dangerous territory!

Looking at these passages from the perspective of the ancient writer also helps in understanding it. The writer would have found no contradiction between the two statements: God hardened Pharaoh's heart; Pharaoh hardened Pharaoh's heart. God is involved in some way in all of history's events. God's will and Pharaoh's actions are entwined into one, with little or no distinction between who did what or who caused what.

Wednesday

Studying the Word
Exodus 3:1–4:14

If you've ever doubted your abilities for a particular task, this study is for you. Moses was sure he was *not* God's man of the hour. Answer these questions and discover what happened.

1. Why was Moses herding sheep on the "back of the desert" (Exodus 3:1), that is, deep into the desert? What had happened to Moses' early efforts to come to his people's aid (Exodus 2:11–15)?

2. Why do you think God used a "great sight" (Exodus 3:3 NKJV) to get Moses' attention? What sorts of things does God use today to get your attention?

3. What was Moses' first excuse for not taking the leadership role God was offering (Exodus 3:11)? After his upbringing in Pharaoh's household (Exodus 2:10), why would Moses answer this way? What was God's response to Moses' excuse (Exodus 3:12)?

4. What was Moses' second excuse (Exodus 3:13)? What was God's response (Exodus 3:14–15)?

5. What was Moses' third excuse (Exodus 4:1)? How did God answer (Exodus 4:2–9)?

6. What was Moses' fourth excuse (Exodus 4:10)? What was God's response (Exodus 4:12)?

7. After all of God's promises in response to Moses' excuses, what did Moses dare to tell God (Exodus 4:13)? How did God respond (Exodus 4:14–17)?

8. After all his wavering and excusing, what did Moses become and how did God use him (Hebrews 11:24–28)? Where does the writer of Hebrews say Moses got the strength to accomplish all of this?

9. How often today do people (do you) ask God—either by action or inaction or words—to send someone else? What do you think God

might be able to accomplish with a people who willingly and wholeheartedly accept His call to action?

Thursday

Responding to the Word
Exodus 12:31–42

The plagues on Egypt progressed. Each one heaped more misery on the Egyptians than the one before it. Several of the plagues demonstrated God's power over Egypt's primary gods (Hopi, god of the Nile; Ra, god of the sun; Apis and Hathor, just two of the Egyptians' cattle gods; Heqt, frog god). Then the tenth and final plague arrived, visiting horror on every house that didn't have blood on its door (Exodus 12:7). Pharaoh and the Egyptians did a total about-face, no longer resistant but now eager to see the Israelites on their way. The people didn't just stand in their yards, waving as two million Israelites left the land. They were so eager to see these people leave that they willingly gave the Israelites goodies to take along the way, gold and silver and rich clothing.

Not only were the Israelites now out of Egypt and free from slavery, they were rich!

Long before Moses' meetings with Pharaoh, long before the plagues, God had promised this would happen. He told Moses that His people would eventually leave Egypt, and they wouldn't go "empty-handed" (Exodus 3:21–22 NKJV). He told the same thing to Abraham, more than five hundred years before (Genesis 15:13–14).

As usual, God kept His promises and then added icing to the cake. Never a God of stingy or meager ways, He heaps on unexpected (and usually undeserved) blessings while He's keeping His promises.

Paul expressed God's generosity this way: "Now to Him who is able to do exceedingly abundantly above all that we ask or think, according to the power that works in us, to Him be glory in the church by Christ Jesus to all generations, forever and ever. Amen" (Ephesians 3:20–21 NKJV).

Try as you might, you can never imagine all the good God has planned for you if you belong to Him. Abraham discovered that. So did Moses and Paul and thousands of others on their faith journeys. He keeps His promises, then heaps on even more blessings. What an incredible God!

Friday

Praying the Word
Exodus 6:6–7

"Free at last!" Martin Luther King's words on the steps of the Lincoln Memorial in 1968 are an echo of God's words through Moses in the book of Exodus. After four hundred years of slavery in Egypt, they are free at last.

But God here was offering so much more than deliverance from physical slavery. He would not only free them from Egypt, but He would be their God, offering them His love and His protection. Over and over again in Exodus, He called them "my people," then later in the story defined them as His "special treasure" (Exodus 19:5 NKJV).

As you review the story of freedom recorded in these passages, recall your own release from the slavery of a sinful and destructive life. What has God saved you from? What has He given you that is more than you could ever imagine? Spend time in prayer today thanking Him for His great goodness. If you wish, use the words of Psalm 106:1 in your prayer: "Praise the LORD! Oh, give thanks to the LORD, for He is good! For His mercy endures forever" (NKJV).

You are good, Lord, and I do praise You! You have freed me from what sin could have produced in my life. You have called me Your special treasure. Help me to live each day with Your view of me in mind. You are good, Lord! You are good!

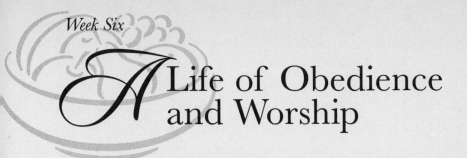

A Life of Obedience and Worship

Monday

Reading the Word
Exodus 19:1–20:21; 32; 36

THE STORY

A cloud of dust rose from the thousands of sandaled feet slapping the desert floor. The first flush of freedom had passed, and the drudgery of daily travel had begun. The people kept their eyes on the cloud of smoke or the column of fire that moved in front of them and led the way. And they began the slow transformation from slaves to free men and women. As Mount Sinai loomed ahead, the column of smoke stopped. With sighs of relief, the weary people dropped their belongings in the sand and began to set up camp.

Some time later they watched from a distance as Moses climbed the mountain to meet with God. On the mountain Moses would receive the Ten Commandments as well as many other laws by which the nation would be governed.

The people sat in the desert waiting patiently, then not so patiently, for Moses' return. He stayed up on the mountain with God for so long that they thought he was gone forever. When Moses finally did return, he found the people dancing, a golden calf idol clear confirmation of their inability to faithfully follow and obey God. Moses listened as God outlined His plan to destroy these disobedient people, then begged God to reconsider, even going so far as to offer, in an act of love and supreme sacrifice, his life for theirs.

| 35

THE MESSAGE

God wants to be involved in every aspect of your life. The Ten Commandments given in Exodus 20 cover many different areas of life, from relationships with God to families to husbands and wives to communities. Other laws in Exodus and Leviticus reveal God's direction for even the minutiae of life. God doesn't want your life to be devoted to worrying about each law and your obedience to it. Rather He knows what's best for each part of your life and wants you to know it too.

THE MAIN POINT

God will be your companion on the journey of life. As the Israelites journeyed through the desert, He gave them instructions for building a place to meet Him in worship. The tabernacle was an intimate space, a symbol of God's close presence with the Israelites. That same desire for intimate companionship with His people continues yet today as God responds to those who hunger for Him (Matthew 5:6).

TAKE NOTE

Exodus 19:11, 18, 20, 23—In a beautiful twist of providence, Moses returned to Mount Sinai, also known as Horeb, the place where he first heard God's call to lead the people of Israel (Exodus 3:1). In the midst of His call to service, God told Moses that after he led the people out of Egypt they would return to this same place. Now in Exodus 19 that promised event took place.

Exodus 32:4—What's so special about a calf? Why would the Israelites worship something that looked like a mere calf? No strong bull or rich, milk-giving cow, but a young calf? The Israelites had watched as the Egyptians worshiped their idols, including the fertility worship of calves. These false gods were thought to aid in the fertility of the land as well as the people, and worship included sexual immorality. Aaron made the calf, then proclaimed a feast, a day of revelry that included eating and drinking and "play" (Exodus 32:6 NKJV), which might have included sexual indulgence as part of the celebration.

The Women's Devotional Guide to the Bible

Tuesday

Reflecting on the Word
Exodus 32:7–14, 31–32

Moses, the reluctant leader (I can't do this, I can't talk, send some-one else, yada yada yada—Exodus 3–4), now showed just how capable and selfless he had become as the captain of the Israelites. Moses met with God on Mount Sinai. He'd been there almost six weeks (Exodus 24:18). The Israelites quickly lost faith and figured Moses was gone for good. And (can you believe it?), God with him. So with Aaron's help, they collected gold and silver, made a calf idol, and worshiped it.

God noticed their activity, of course. He roared His displeasure to Moses, along with His plan to destroy the Israelites and build a new nation. Moses stepped in with calm and reasoned argument. Astonishing, isn't it? First, that Moses would defend these people; after all, he'd experienced their weaknesses (Exodus 14:10–12; 15:23–24; 16:1–3; 17:1–4). And second, that he would dare to point out the flaws in God's plan to annihilate the Israelites.

Moses went down the mountain to deal with the people and their sin. When he saw their revelry and heard their singing, his own anger broke out in full force. He threw down the tablets with the Ten Commandments written on them. He ground the golden calf into a fine powder, spread it on water, and made the people drink it. Then he sent God-fearing Levites out with swords to kill those who had foolishly followed this false god.

Those were the actions of a true leader, meting out justice when it was required. But then Moses took a step up to a higher level of leadership. He went back to God and begged Him to forgive these people, even though Moses realized they had committed a "great sin" (Exodus 32:31 NKJV).

As if that was not enough, Moses took still one more step. He told God, "If you can't forgive them, punish me instead. Blot me out of the book of life instead of these people" (Exodus 32:32, author's para-phrase). Sit up and take notice! God had accomplished great things in the life of this reluctant leader. Moses offered his life for the lives of the Israelites in the ultimate act of servant leadership. And, in so doing, he gave a clear picture of the Savior who would come thousands of years later and offer His life to pay for the sins of the world (Mark 10:45).

Wednesday

Studying the Word
Exodus 20:1–17

Take a close look today at the famous Ten Commandments. Under attack in secular America, but still relevant nonetheless, these ten rules cover most aspects of life and give straightforward instruction. Read through them once, then come back to this page and answer these questions.

1. Although the Ten Commandments are given in a negative form ("You shall not . . ." NKJV), there are definite positive implications. If you shall not do this, it means you *shall* do this instead. Begin today by phrasing each of the commandments in positive language.
2. How does God identify Himself to the Israelites before giving them the Ten Commandments (Exodus 20:2)? Why do you think He uses this particular information about Himself?
3. What relationship do the first four commandments deal with (Exodus 20:3–11)?
4. The first commandment (Exodus 20:3) is pretty clear. What sorts of false gods did the Israelites worship? What sorts of false gods do people today tend to worship? What false god do you struggle with? Be honest here!
5. The second commandment (Exodus 20:4–6) records the sin of making something to physically represent God, who has no physical nature. People in today's culture seldom bow down to idols

made of wood or stone, but they do worship physical objects. Can you think of what those might be?

6. What does the third commandment (Exodus 20:7) prohibit? What does it mean exactly to take God's name in "vain" (NKJV)? Check out other translations for clues. You can also review Jesus' take on it in Matthew 5:33–37.

7. The fourth commandment (Exodus 20:8–11) deals with the Sabbath. What two reasons does God give for His command to rest on the Sabbath? (See Exodus 20:11 for the first and Deuteronomy 5:15 for the second.) What applications does this command have for a society where most people observe the first day of the week as their day of rest?

8. What relationships do the next six commandments deal with (Exodus 20:12–17)? Review each one, recording specific ways it could and should be lived out in your life today.

Fifth—Exodus 20:12
Sixth—Exodus 20:13
Seventh—Exodus 20:14
Eighth—Exodus 20:15
Ninth—Exodus 20:16
Tenth—Exodus 20:17

Thursday

Responding to the Word
Exodus 36:1–7

Fickle people, those Israelites. Or, perhaps not fickle but convicted?

After the debacle of worshiping a golden calf idol, Moses outlined God's plans for building the tabernacle, a place for worshiping the one true God. Moses asked the people to donate the materials to build this worship center. (If you're wondering where a bunch of freed slaves got all these riches, check out Exodus 12:33–36.) And the people of Israel obeyed. Day after day after day, they obeyed.

They brought their gems, their gold and silver, their purple and scarlet fabrics. And then they brought some more. And some more again.

Finally those working on the tabernacle had to tell the people to *stop*. They had "much more than enough" (Exodus 36:5 NKJV) to build the worship center. The people had to be "restrained" (Exodus 36:6 NKJV) from bringing more. How about that? A restraining order on offerings!

Were they just capricious people, blown about by the winds of whatever project was in front of them—golden calf, tabernacle, whatever? Or were they convicted people, recognizing the error of their ways and showing God the depth of their sorrow? Perhaps the Israelites were just generous people, holding their new possessions lightly, and willing to give liberally to the God who had freed them from slavery.

Which just naturally begs the question: What's wrong today? How many churches do you know that have *too much*? Have you or anyone you know ever given so much that you were told to stop?

Paul wrote the Corinthian church about giving generously and cheerfully in 2 Corinthians 9:6–7. As you read about the Israelites' generosity in Exodus 36 and Paul's description of merry giving, examine your offerings as well as your spirit as you give those offerings. Does the level of your generosity reflect the level of your thanks to God for freeing you from slavery?

Friday

Praying the Word
Exodus 20:2–3

The stories of the Israelites—their liberation from slavery, their worship of a calf idol and its consequences, their generosity in bringing gifts for building the tabernacle—all reveal something about them. But more than that, these stories reveal something about God. He is compassionate and will come to His people's aid when He sees them suffering. He is holy and punishes sin. But He is also loving and will not destroy completely. He is clear about expectations. And He expects total devotion.

When you think of all that you've been saved from (and that is quite a lot when you sincerely reflect on what your life could be and what it is), you'll probably quickly agree that God doesn't just expect, He *deserves* your total devotion.

Thank God today for saving you and freeing you from what you could have become, then dedicate yourself wholly and unreservedly to Him.

Holy God in heaven, Lover of my sinful self, I offer all that I am in total devotion to You. You have my love, my belongings, my future, and my past. You gave Your whole self to me freely, nothing held back, not even Your life. How could I do any less? It's all Yours, loving Lord, freely given, nothing held back. Amen.

Obedience, Disobedience, Consequences

Monday

Reading the Word

Leviticus 26; Numbers 11; 13:17–14:25; 20:1–13; 21:4–9;
Deuteronomy 6

THE STORY

Caleb watched and listened as the men with whom he had spied out Canaan described what they had found there. "The land is rich! Lush vineyards and fertile fields and beautiful cities." Caleb smiled his agreement. He watched as the people sampled the fruits they had carried back with them. His smile turned to a scowl, however, when he heard the next part of the report. He and Joshua exchanged glances of dismay as the other spies warned that the people in Canaan were huge and strong and too mighty for them to conquer. "The people will devour us if we go in. We're like little grasshoppers next to them!" (Numbers 13:27–33, author's paraphrase).

Wait a minute! Caleb shouted. He couldn't believe what he was hearing! Did they think God would bring them this far, out of Egypt and through the desert, only to abandon them now? *We can surely conquer them and take the land!* Caleb, and Joshua with him, understood what the others had missed: God would do the conquering.

THE MESSAGE

The Israelites continued to struggle with obedience. Like little children who test their parents' restraints, they pushed and prodded, testing the limits of God's patience. God told them that obedience would bring blessing and that disobedience would bring punishment. But they continued to grumble, fight, complain, and argue. They simply could not get it straight.

THE MAIN POINT

Disobedience has consequences; obedience brings blessing. Although the correlation may not be as direct as you might like (disobedient people still prosper; obedient people still suffer), the general truth holds. In the end, those who follow God and obey Him win!

TAKE NOTE

Leviticus 26:41—What in the world is an "uncircumcised heart" (NKJV)? The writers of the Bible used this terminology (Jeremiah 9:26; Ezekiel 44:7, 9; Acts 7:51) to describe those who hadn't cut wickedness out of their hearts and lives.

Deuteronomy 6:8-9—The people of Israel took God's instructions here literally, writing words of God on their doorposts as well as recording them on parchment and putting them into little leather boxes called "phylacteries" (Matthew 23:5 NKJV), which they tied to their arms and heads. The practice seems to have come into vogue later in Israel's history, probably after the return from captivity in Babylon. Jesus criticized the Pharisees for wearing God's words on their bodies but not carrying them in their hearts (Matthew 23:1-6).

Tuesday

Reflecting on the Word
Numbers 13:26–14:8

What serious trouble the ten spies and the Israelites who listened to them got into when they viewed their situation through their own eyes rather than from God's perspective. When the spies went into the Promised Land, they saw exactly why God had promised it to them: the produce grew rich and plentiful; the cities were large and well protected.

Just one problem, however, and not a small one. In fact, it was a giant problem. The people there were huge. "Giants," the ten spies called them (Numbers 13:33 NKJV). They felt like little grasshoppers next to them. And they figured the giants looked at them like little insects, too, easily stepped on and crushed.

The ten spies only saw what they saw.

Two spies, however, looked at the situation from a different angle. Caleb and Joshua saw God in all the circumstances: the fertility of the land and the ability to conquer it. They didn't see the giants through their own eyes and feel small. They saw the giants through God's eyes and knew those huge soldiers weren't invincible. Caleb and Joshua assured the people: "[God] will bring us into this land and give it to us" (Numbers 14:8 NKJV).

It's pretty easy to do, you know—forget the God factor. Your life is falling apart around you and you wring your hands, wondering how you'll escape, how you'll ever get back to "normal." A loved one dies, a job is lost, a child rebels, a husband leaves—whatever you're facing, do your best to view it not just through your own troubled eyes, but through the eyes of your Lord, who promises to be with you (Joshua 1:9) and who promises to bring something good out of it (Romans 8:28).

Wednesday

Studying the Word
Numbers 21:4–9

This short story of more trouble in Israel takes only six verses to relate but includes some great lessons as well as symbolism for today. Read those six short verses and answer these questions.

1. Why did the people complain (Numbers 21:5)? Before you think you wouldn't have participated in the grumbling, picture yourself in the situation. You are hungry, thirsty, worn down. Even worse, your little ones are hanging on your robe, begging you for water and crying out because their tummies are empty. What would you have to say to God in such a situation?

2. Were the people actually and truly going hungry? Or were they just dissatisfied with the food God had provided for them?

3. What sorts of things do you complain about most quickly? Why? What does your complaining accomplish?

4. How did God punish the Israelites for their complaints?

5. Why do you think God punished them so severely for merely complaining? What deeper problem did their complaining reveal?

6. What does your grumbling reveal about you?

7. What does verse 7 tell you about the people of Israel? About Moses?

8. God didn't send away the poisonous snakes; rather, He provided a way of healing from their bites. What did He tell Moses to do?

9. What does this snake on a pole foretell about another future Savior?

Thursday

Responding to the Word
Deuteronomy 6:4–6

The words of these verses, known as the *shema,* which literally means "hear," were some of Moses' most eloquent and often quoted. Remember, this is the same Moses who told God he couldn't possibly lead the people of Israel; after all, he was "slow of speech and slow of tongue" (Exodus 4:10 NKJV). God had certainly delivered on His promise to Moses to "be with your mouth and teach you what you shall say" (Exodus 4:12 NKJV).

Israelites in past history, as well as Jews today, recited the *shema* regularly, professing their faith in God: "Hear, O Israel: The LORD our God, the LORD is one!" (Deuteronomy 6:4 NKJV). They wrote these words, plus others, on the door frames of their houses and on scraps of paper that they enclosed in little leather boxes and tied on their arms and foreheads. These served as a constant reminder of God's place as first in their lives.

Even more important, Moses told the people to impress and record these words on their hearts (Deuteronomy 6:6), so filling up their beings that they were a natural part of life's everyday events, at home, on the road, in bed, rising in the morning. Moses instructed the people to use these everyday occurrences to teach their children about God and His goodness and holiness.

Let it spill over, run out, bubble up. So fill your life and heart with God and His words that they are just naturally transmitted to those around you. What an effortless way to instill such important truths in your children! As you go about the normal activities of life—driving in the family van, cooking a meal, playing in the yard, reading in the evening—the truths of God and His love will infuse your conversation and your way of living. Your children will grow up not only understanding God but also loving Him.

Friday

Praying the Word
Deuteronomy 6:4–5

Use the words of the *shema* to frame your prayers this week. Each day, start out your prayer time with the words God spoke to the people of Israel through Moses: "Hear, O Israel: The LORD our God, the LORD is one! You shall love the LORD your God with all your heart, with all your soul, and with all your strength" (NKJV).

Spend time one day meditating on what it means to love Him with all your heart, another day meditating on loving Him with all your soul, and a third day, with all your strength.

Father God of all, You are the Lord my God. You are the one true God. I love You, Lord! I love You with all my heart, with all my soul, and with all my strength. Amen.

Joshua Leads Israel into the Promised Land

Monday

Reading the Word
Joshua 1–4; 6; 23–24

THE STORY

Joshua ran his hand along the wall of Jericho as the people of Israel marched around it again. This was their thirteenth time around, once each day for six days, and today, the seventh day, seven times around. They were on their seventh time around now. Joshua's heart beat heavily in his chest, and the band holding his hair grew damp with sweat. He'd seen miracle after miracle in the last forty-plus years, yet each time anticipation made him nervous, uncomfortable. But then he remembered what God had told him: "Be strong and of good courage; do not be afraid, nor be dismayed, for the LORD your God is with you wherever you go" (Joshua 1:9 NKJV).

Joshua took a deep breath as they neared the completion of today's seventh time around the wall. He was waiting to hear the long blast of the trumpets, getting ready to lead the people in shouting, as God had commanded.

Then he heard it. The long, clear sound of trumpets blowing together! He raised his fist in the air, opened his mouth, and shouted at the top of his lungs. All the people joined in until the sound of voices raised in obedience to God reverberated through the air. Joshua turned to face the wall of Jericho, no longer apprehensive but now certain of what would happen next. As they shouted another sound joined their voices. A rumble. A roar. Then a shaking of the ground beneath their feet as the wall of Jericho began to shake, then quake, then fall with a thunderous crash. Once again, God had fulfilled His promise to go with the Israelites into the Promised Land and make it their own. Joshua ran forward into the exposed city, leading the men into battle and victory.

THE MESSAGE

Joshua's leadership took the Israelites into the Promised Land and into victory. His strength of character (remember, he was one of the original spies who urged the people to go into the land—Numbers 14:6–9), his trust in God's promises, and his tutelage under the great leader, Moses (Numbers 11:28), made him God's choice (Numbers 27:18–22) to lead the people as they entered Canaan. His leadership of Israel had as much to do with God as with his gifts or abilities. As with all great leaders, Joshua recognized that, and consistently relied on God for direction and strength.

THE MAIN POINT

"Be strong and of good courage; do not be afraid, nor be dismayed, for the LORD your God is with you wherever you go" (Joshua 1:9 NKJV). It just doesn't get any better than that! God's promise to Joshua is also His promise to you. Whatever you face—enemies, walls, discouragement, defeat, tragedy—God will be with you and will give you courage. And—hallelujah!—ultimate victory.

TAKE NOTE

Joshua 2:18—The spies told Rahab to tie a scarlet cord in her window to let them know where she was in Jericho so they could save her and her family on the day of battle. The red cord was probably just a length of rope that had been reddened with a common dye made from an insect. Since Rahab was known to be a prostitute (Joshua 2:1), some think she may have used this scarlet cord to advertise her profession, similar to a red light district today. Actually, no historical evidence exists to prove it. Rahab's scarlet cord, however, can be compared to the lamb's blood brushed on doorposts in Egypt, when the angel of death passed over those homes (Exodus 11). Her blood-red rope caused the Israelite soldiers to pass over her house and spare all those within it.

Joshua 6:5—Most towns of any size in ancient Israel had walls built around them. Mizpah's wall in central Israel was almost thirty-five feet tall and fifteen to twenty feet thick. These walls provided a defense against the marauders that were so prevalent at that time. Citizens from surrounding areas ran to the safety of walled cities when their enemies were on the prowl.

Tuesday

Reflecting on the Word
Joshua 3:14–17

These verses record a true act of faith on the part of the priests of Israel. They didn't have the luxury of Moses' staff parting the waters before stepping through (Exodus 14:16). No magic wands waving, no leader going before them. Just God's simple instructions. Step into the water, and it will part.

This event took place during flood stage of the Jordan River rather than in the heat of summer's dry periods (Joshua 3:15). And the people had been ordered to stay at least two thousand cubits, which is about one thousand yards, behind the priests who carried the ark. So these daring men were out there in the flood waters, alone. Can you imagine carrying the heavy Ark of the Covenant on poles, then stepping out into a river that is deep and rushing, perhaps raging? It took an obvious leap of faith on the part of these priests!

God often works that way. He gives what you need only exactly when you need it. Not before. So, the priests plunged into the river and saw God's promises at work. As soon as their feet touched water, the river stopped flowing, and the people could cross on dry ground.

Do you ever feel like you've been thrown into the *middle* of a river of difficulty or hardship or trauma? No tiptoeing into it on the edge. A belly flop right in the middle. But if you assess your situation, you'll find you're not out there alone. You would have gone down long ago if you were totally alone. God, Himself or in the form of a friend, a relative, a pastor or counselor, is there with you. Just as He was with the priests when they stepped into the water, so He is with you when life's tough situations rough you up. Hang on to His promise that if you follow Him "you will know which way to go, since you have never been this way before" (Joshua 3:4 NIV).

Wednesday

Studying the Word
Joshua 4:4–9

This story of a memorial structure, the first one built by the Israelites in their new homeland, offers great instruction as well as encouragement in remembering the work of God in your life. Read the story, and then answer these questions.

1. How many stones were used to build this monument (Joshua 4:3)? What did each stone signify?

2. Where did the men pick up each of the stones? What might the fact that these stones came from the "middle" (Joshua 4:3 NKJV) of the river tell you about where your best materials for a monument to God's faithfulness can be found?

3. What was the purpose of this memorial of twelve stones? What were the Israelites supposed to say when they were asked about them?

4. What sort of memorial could you build to a time when God delivered you or gave you courage or supported you during a difficult time? What would be the purpose of such a memorial? What could you tell others if they asked you about it?

5. These stones were still standing when the book of Joshua was written (Joshua 4:9). This could have been just a short while if Joshua wrote the book. However, if Samuel wrote it, as some think, the memorial could have already been centuries old. Why is long-term recall of what God has done important? In your life? In the church's life?

Thursday

Responding to the Word
Joshua 24:15

The people of Israel had reached the proverbial fork in the road. They had conquered much of the land of Canaan, settled in its cities and towns, and harvested its fruits and grains. Joshua was getting old and knew his death wasn't far off. He called the people together at Shechem to remind them of God's faithfulness in leading them out of Egypt and into Canaan (Joshua 24:1–13). He knew from experience that the people of Israel were unpredictable, easily swayed away from God to worshiping idols. His goal was to present them with the truth, giving them a chance to decide which way they would go.

Joshua's striking final words to the people of Israel have gone down in history as a clear call to decision-making. Whom will you serve? You can't sit on the fence. You must make a decision, declared Joshua. Then, true to his character throughout his long life, he plainly and resolutely announced his decision to follow God alone.

The call goes out still today. Whom will you serve? The gods of your culture? The idols of society? Or the one true God who has so faithfully remembered His promises to you, sending Jesus Christ as a substitute for your sins, offering life instead of death?

Picture yourself standing in a crowd, listening to the great leader, Joshua, call for your decision: "Now therefore, fear the LORD, serve Him in sincerity and in truth . . . choose for yourselves this day whom you will serve . . . But as for me and my house, we will serve the LORD" (Joshua 24:14–15 NKJV).

Friday

Joshua reviewed with the Israelites all the ways God had helped them crush the people of Canaan and take the land, just as He had promised. Joshua realized the importance of the past, of recalling what the Lord had done, of committing to memory the faithfulness of God.

What was true for the people in Joshua's time is still true for you today. Spend some time today recalling and recording what God has done in your life. Look back over the long term, reviewing where you were and where you are now and how God got you there. Remember events in your life where God fulfilled His promises to save you, to protect you, to give you hope, to be your strength, to bring healing. Record those times in your life that reflect God's promise-keeping character. Then use the words of this verse to pray your thanks to God for His goodness.

I do know, Lord, and I do affirm with all my heart that not one of Your promises to me has failed. Not one! How grateful that makes me! Help me always to notice how You're working in my life and to remember Your good promise-keeping character. I love You, Lord! Amen.

Judges Rule the Land

Monday

Reading the Word
Judges 4; 6–7; 13–16

THE STORY

Deborah stood high on Mount Tabor, General Barak beside her. The sight in the valley below frightened and thrilled them at the same time. The valley rumbled with their enemy Sisera's nine hundred iron chariots and thousands of soldiers. The view frightened them with its power. But a thrill accompanied that fright because God had promised Deborah and Barak victory over Sisera. This was the day Israel would gain freedom from twenty years of oppression at the hands of Sisera and his brutal armies.

Deborah tore her eyes from the view below her to the view behind her. Ten thousand Israelite soldiers were gathered, ready to fight. Yes! God was going to give them a great victory today!

Deborah filled her lungs with the fresh air of Mount Tabor, then ordered Barak: "Up! For this is the day in which the LORD has delivered Sisera into your hand. Has not the LORD gone out before you?" (Judges 4:14 NKJV). With a roar and an uplifted fist, Barak led his soldiers down the mountain to certain victory.

THE MESSAGE

Each story of each judge in the book of Judges reveals again the fickle nature of the Israelites and human beings in general. Do you see yourself in them—even a little? When times are good, you slip into your old independent patterns and your need for God doesn't seem quite so acute. You get complacent. But let hardship come into your life, and immediately you cry out to God for help. You need Him in your life. Now! That's the story of Judges, a continuous cycle of blessing, complacency, hardship, repentance, and deliverance.

THE MAIN POINT

Without apology the book of Judges conveys God's readiness to do anything to draw His people to Him. Hardship in the form of wars and famine and oppression eventually turned the Israelite people away from their sin and idol worship back to the God of their fathers. In the New Testament, Hebrews 12:1–13 gives a clear picture of how God continues to use discipline to bring His people closer to Him.

TAKE NOTE

Judges 13:5—Even before he was born, Samson was designated as a Nazirite. The word *Nazirite* has its roots in the Hebrew word for "vow" or "consecrate." Most Nazirites took a temporary vow in order to consecrate themselves to God for some special purpose for a set period of time. The Bible records three men, however, who were Nazirites their entire lives—Samson, Samuel, and John the Baptist. Three practices marked the Nazirite vow (Numbers 6:1–21). First, they drank no wine and ate no produce or juice from grapes. Second, they did not cut their hair for the time of their vow of separation. And third, they did not touch a dead body. While Nazirites didn't live lives of separation from their families, the evidences of their vow were quickly apparent to those living around them.

The Women's Devotional Guide to the Bible

Tuesday

Reflecting on the Word
Judges 4; 6–7; 13–16

As you read the Old Testament, are you ever bothered by the extent of the violence recorded there? Murders, wars, wholesale annihilation of entire cities and nations? At some point most people grapple with the atrocities recorded in the Bible.

Two main points are crucial. First, the Bible is no pretty picture book, revealing God's grace and love while glossing over His justice and punishment. The realities of life in Old Testament times are clearly depicted. The sins of individuals are presented without trying to put a positive spin on them. The battles and wars are recorded with the huge loss of human life they brought about. God is interested in making people His own and in showing how desperately they need Him. While not condoning violence in and of itself, the Bible records the truth of ancient history.

Second, when cities or nations were slated for destruction, the cause was always their appalling sinfulness, the debauchery of their ways, their complete disregard for God and His commandments. Often God used the Israelites as the means for punishing them. But with the Amorites, God demonstrated patience. Occupying the land promised to Abraham, the Amorites' continued wickedness eventually brought God's judgment, following the Israelites' release from Egyptian bondage (Genesis 15:16).

Violence and war are no less a part of today's culture than they were of the cultures of the Old Testament. Terrorism has brought the realities all too close to home. What of the peace that Jesus offered in John 14:27? "Peace I leave with you, My peace I give to you; not as the world gives do I give to you. Let not your heart be troubled, neither let it be afraid" (NKJV). His peace does not offer freedom from war or conflict. He was facing the crucifixion when He spoke these words! Jesus' words, instead, offer something far better: faith in God and His promises, confidence in Him when trouble does arise, and a sense of security that only He can provide.

Wednesday

Studying the Word
Judges 6:10–16, 36–40

The story of Gideon, like the story of Moses, reveals God's fondness for using unlikely people to accomplish His most difficult tasks. The Midianites had tyrannized the Israelites for seven years, so much so that the people had abandoned their houses and fields and were living in caves in the mountains (Judges 6:2). Read this part of Gideon's story and think through your answers to the following questions.

1. Based on what the Midianites had been doing to the Israelites, why would Gideon thresh his grain inside a winepress (Judges 6:11)? (A winepress was a big container where several people could stomp on grapes to produce the juice for making wine.)
2. What do you think this revealed about Gideon—ingenuity or cowardice? Explain your answer.
3. Why do you think the angel called Gideon a "mighty man of valor" (Judges 6:12 NKJV) before he had ever gone into battle?
4. What is the answer to Gideon's question in verse thirteen? Had God truly "forsaken" (Judges 6:13 NKJV) them?
5. What excuse does Gideon give for questioning God's choice of him to lead Israel (Judges 6:15)? What other Bible people used such excuses with God? Why do you think God chooses people who have so little confidence in their own abilities?
6. Some people think "putting out a fleece" as Gideon did (Judges 6:36–40) shows a lack of faith. What do you think about Gideon's fleece? What do you think about people today who try to discern God's will by putting out a fleece?

The Women's Devotional Guide to the Bible

Thursday

Responding to the Word
Judges 14–16

Samson spent a lot of time flexing his great muscles, physically and psychologically, before the people of Israel and their enemies. His need to prove his strength only proved his weaknesses. He used his power as much for personal revenge on those who had offended him (Judges 15:3, 7) as for God's punishment on those who were oppressing His people.

Early in Samson's life, God's Spirit moved in him (Judges 13:25), giving Samson the power he needed in order to judge or rule the people of Israel. God's purpose in giving Samson his incredible prowess was to punish the Philistines, who had been tyrannizing the Israelites for forty years (Judges 13:1). But rather than coming out wielding the power of God, Samson came out swinging the jawbone of a donkey, killing anyone who got in his way. Rather than letting God's Spirit rule his life, Samson's passions ruled his life.

And yet . . .

Here's the beauty in a story of violence and self-indulgence: Samson is listed in Hebrews 11:32 as a hero of the faith! Does that surprise you? Perhaps it shouldn't. God has no problem using the imperfect people of this world to accomplish His perfect will. In fact, every person He has ever used, in Bible times or today's times, was or now is *imperfect*.

Spend some time today reflecting on that truth. Ask Him how He wants to use your imperfect, often weak self. Then go out wielding the strength of His Spirit within you.

Friday

Praying the Word
Judges 13:8

When Manoah received the news that he and his wife were going to have a baby after years of infertility, he had just one thought, and it was a good one: Lord, come and teach us how to raise this child that you have promised. Raising children is one of the greatest and most difficult tasks of human existence. You can read all the books in the world and listen to all the experts and still there will be times when you throw up your hands in surrender, admitting you have no idea what is the best course of action to take. For that reason, every parent, aunt, uncle, cousin, grandma, grandpa, friend can offer one true thing to aid parents in raising their children. And it's exactly what Manoah did. He prayed.

Bathing the raising of children in prayer will provide more help and strength for the task than any other one thing. Whether praying for your own children, for nieces and nephews, for grandchildren, or for the children of friends, you offer the parents and the children a gift of enormous value.

Father, we know from Your Word that children are loved and important in Your sight. Help us, Lord, as we bring children up before You. Give us wisdom and strength for the task. And let us see our children through Your eyes, as beings of value and tremendous significance. Make us more aware each day of the importance of immersing the task in communion with You. Amen.

An Israelite Love Story

Monday

Reading the Word
Ruth 1–4

THE STORY

Ruth reached up to push her hair back under her head covering. She was wet with sweat from working in the hot sun. But her sack was full of grain that would keep her and her mother-in-law, Naomi, from going hungry. Looking around, Ruth sighed. Everything seemed so strange. She was glad she had come to Israel from her home in Moab. She couldn't leave Naomi alone. But she did feel as if her life had taken a turn she hadn't truly expected.

Little did she know her life was about to take another unexpected turn. A shadow fell across the field in front of her as she worked. Ruth looked up to see a stranger. Silly that she would think of him as a stranger—everyone here was a stranger except for Naomi. The man introduced himself as Boaz, the owner of the field. Then he spoke so kindly to Ruth that she felt tears start in her eyes. His kind words soothed her feelings of loneliness and strangeness. Ruth didn't know it, but that day she met her future husband and the father of her son Obed. Her future in this strange new land was secure.

THE MESSAGE

It's nice to think of this as a love story, although love between Boaz and Ruth is never mentioned. The story does, however, reveal much about the love and concern of God. God's love followed Naomi to Moab and back to Israel. His love provided her with Ruth, who loved Naomi and was better to her than "seven sons" (Ruth 4:15 NKJV). His love supplied Naomi with a grandson, one who became the grandfather of King David and a link in Jesus' family line (Matthew 1:5–6).

THE MAIN POINT

Redemption, a word rich with meaning and portent, fills the book of Ruth. God redeemed Naomi's grief over the loss of her husband and sons by giving her a grandson and a continuation of her family line. God redeemed Ruth by bringing her out of her heathen family and nation and making her part of His own people and a part of the family of His Son, Jesus. God redeemed a situation distorted by sorrow and bitterness and offered fulfillment and joy in its place.

TAKE NOTE

Ruth 1:4—Naomi's sons were not condemned for marrying foreign women, even though God had forbidden it (Deuteronomy 7:1–4). Discovering why involves digging a bit deeper. The Moabites were descendants of Abraham's nephew Lot (Deuteronomy 2:9). Therefore, although they were not Israelites, they were distant relatives and not part of God's command through Moses to refrain from marrying foreign women.

Ruth 3:1–13—Does the story sound a bit like a romance novel? A late-night seduction scene? Not a bit. Boaz slept on the threshing floor to protect his grain and woke in the middle of the night to find something else to protect. A woman. And a young one at that! Naomi led Ruth to these actions, and Boaz quickly understood them as a request not just for the protection he could provide but also for marriage. No sexual escapades are implied.

Ruth 4:7—Pass the sandal, please. Passing a sandal was a way in early Israelite culture of sealing a bargain, similar to a handshake or a signature on a document today. The practice is mentioned in other ancient documents as well as the Bible. If a man refused to marry his brother's widow, the widow was allowed to take one of his sandals and spit in his face. From that day on his family was to be known as "The Family of the Unsandaled" (Deuteronomy 25:7–10, author's paraphrase).

Tuesday

Reflecting on the Word
Ruth 2:20

The story of Ruth and Boaz tickles the romantic funny bone of those who read it. But Boaz's actions go far deeper than any romantic interest he may have had in Ruth. Boaz acted as Ruth's "kinsman-redeemer," according to the laws Moses gave the Israelites after they left Egypt. The kinsman-redeemer had a number of responsibilities. He was the closest in relation to the dead relative (unless, as in Ruth's case, the closest relative deferred to another). He took over the property of the dead relative, so it would stay in the family (Leviticus 25:25). That meant he also took over any debt that came with the property. He avenged the wrongful death of a relative (Numbers 35:19). And he married the widow in order to continue the family line of the one who had died (Deuteronomy 25:5–10) and to support her and save her from the destitution that was the fate of many widows in Israel.

When Boaz first met Ruth, he realized that she was his relative. He began to take an interest in her, offering her the protection of working in his fields, giving her bread to eat, and telling her he admired her for all she had done for his relative, Naomi. Was he romantically interested in the young woman? The Bible gives no indication. The greater point of his attention is the spotlight it puts on Boaz as a good and godly man, one not only able but suitable to marry a woman like Ruth and carry on her dead husband's family line as kinsman-redeemer.

Did you know that you have a kinsman-redeemer too? You do! As your brother (Hebrews 2:12), Jesus came to avenge all that sin had done to harm you. He came to save you from the destitution of continuing to live in sin, which is the fate of all unbelievers. Ruth and Naomi found incredible joy and relief from a dark future when their kinsman-redeemer acted on their behalf. That same joy and relief from a dark future, in even greater measure, are yours when you accept Jesus as your Kinsman-Redeemer.

Wednesday

Studying the Word
Ruth 1

The story of Ruth begins with Naomi's journey to Moab with her husband and their two sons and her return after their deaths. Her sorrow and bitterness at the turns her life have taken only increase as she leaves Moab for her homeland in Israel.

1. What was characteristic of the "days when the judges ruled" (Ruth 1:1 NKJV) in Israel (Judges 21:25)? How might that situation have contributed to Naomi's family troubles?
2. Why did Naomi decide at this point to return to Israel (Ruth 1:6)?
3. Why do you think Naomi insisted that her daughters-in-law return to Moab rather than accompany her to Israel (Ruth 1:8–13)? What sort of reception would these young Moabite women likely get in Israel?
4. Why was Naomi bitter (Ruth 1:13)? Were her circumstances God's fault? Was God responsible for her bitter spirit? What sorts of things cause bitter spirits in people today?
5. Ruth's response to Naomi has become famous in its inspiring selflessness (Ruth 1:16–17). Name at least three things that Ruth's words reveal about her character.
6. Which of these characteristics is most absent from your life? How can you go about developing it?
7. What do you suppose made the women of Bethlehem exclaim, "Can this be Naomi?" (Ruth 1:19 NIV)?
8. Naomi asked that they call her "Mara," which means "bitter," instead of Naomi (Ruth 1:20–21). What does Naomi's statement reveal about her character?
9. Do you feel or have you ever felt bitter about the troubles or tragedies in your life? What causes not just sorrow over life's trials but bitterness? What does Jesus offer in its place (Isaiah 26:3; Romans 5:1–5)?

Thursday

Responding to the Word
Ruth 4:13–15

Naomi, who had lost her husband and her two sons in Moab, could only look at her losses. She told her friends not to call her Naomi, which means "pleasant," but to call her Mara, which means "bitter." She didn't see clearly the blessing of her daughter-in-law Ruth or the compassion of old friends who greeted her eagerly when she returned from Moab to Bethlehem.

But God hadn't forgotten old Naomi-Mara. He was getting ready to make some radical changes not only in her life but also in her character.

When life throws darkness and disaster your way, God has the same plan in mind. He isn't the author of your troubles, contrary to what Naomi asserted in Ruth 1:21. But He is eager to use them to upgrade your character.

For the believer, all of life's events have purpose. God carefully orchestrates the good and the bad into a design that builds beauty and grace into a believer's character. (See Paul's affirmation in Romans 8:28.) If the believer allows it and trusts God to do it, that is.

If you respond with anger and bitterness toward life's circumstances, whatever they are, your name may as well be Mara. Your bitterness will twist your countenance, your relationships, and your personality into a caricature of what God intended for you to be. If, however, you *choose* (note that word!) to look at life as God's classroom, one where He's teaching and molding you into His planned design for you, your countenance, your relationships, and your personality will be awe inspiring, a thing of grace and beauty.

Friday

Praying the Word
Ruth 2:11–12

Each step of the story of Ruth reveals a little more about her outstanding character—her tenderness toward Naomi, her willingness to endure living in a foreign land, her hard work in the fields, her compassion, her humility—all excellent traits in anyone.

Boaz's words in Ruth 2:11–12 reveal that Ruth's qualities had come to the attention of more than just her mother-in-law. Those in the town were also aware of what a gem she was and were talking about it.

Question 6 in Wednesday's study asked you to identify one of Ruth's qualities that you would like to develop more deeply in yourself. In your prayer time today, focus on that attribute, seeking God's help in developing it. Ask Him to reveal to you where you are lacking and where He wants to help you grow.

I need Your help, Lord, to become all that You intended me to be. Develop me where I'm lacking, especially in this one specific area. The harder I try, Lord, the more I realize I can't do this on my own. I need You! Amen.

Week Eleven

Samuel the Prophet and Saul the King

Monday

Reading the Word
1 Samuel 1; 3; 9–10; 13; 15

THE STORY

Samuel's thin legs shifted uneasily under the warm robe that covered him. This had been one sleepless night. Three times he had heard a voice calling, "Samuel!" He assumed it was the old high priest, Eli, needing his help. So he quickly got up from his bed and went to Eli. But Eli had been sound asleep and hadn't called. Only after the voice had called Samuel's name three times did Eli realize what was going on. God was calling to the boy. The fourth time Samuel heard his name, he knew that it was God calling to him, and he answered as Eli had instructed, "Speak, LORD for your servant hears" (1 Samuel 3:9 NKJV).

The Lord had spoken. And now Samuel was wide awake, wondering how he would give the bad news to Eli. Samuel loved the old priest and had no wish to hurt him. But God's message had been one of judgment for the evil shenanigans of Eli's sons. God told Samuel that the events would be so severe that the "ears of everyone who hears it will tingle" (1 Samuel 3:11 NKJV). How Samuel dreaded telling good Eli the terrible news. But it was what God had asked him to do, so the boy rose from his bed to fulfill his mission.

In the years that followed, Samuel saw the fulfillment of God's message when Eli's sons as well as the Ark of the Covenant were lost in battle with the Philistines. When old Eli got the news, he fell over with shock and died. Samuel then ruled Israel until God answered the people's cry for a king "like all the nations" (1 Samuel 8:5 NKJV), giving them first King Saul and then King David.

THE MESSAGE

The government of the people of Israel was in transition during the times of Samuel and Saul. The time of the judges was receding; the time for kings was arriving. The man Samuel was a prophet of God but also a divinely appointed judge and ruler of Israel. He brought the people's request for a king to God and anointed the first two kings who would rule Israel—Saul and David. The beauty of the story is not in the form of government but in the continuity that God's control over events brought. No matter what was going on in Israel—judge, no judge, king, no king, unrest or peace—God was over all and in all.

THE MAIN POINT

God can be trusted. When His people turned away from Him, again and again, He could be depended on to stand firm and loyal. When Samuel recounted the years of his judgeship over Israel, he reprimanded the people for their capriciousness in following God. But he also reminded them that God would forgive and would never abandon them (1 Samuel 12:20–25), even if He punished them for their rebellion.

TAKE NOTE

1 Samuel 10:1—People as well as objects were anointed in ancient times as a sign that they had been set apart for God's special use. Jacob slept with his head on a stone when he ran from his brother Esau. He anointed that stone when he awoke because God had met him in that place (Genesis 28:18–19). Moses anointed the priests (Exodus 28:41) and the furnishings of the tabernacle (Exodus 29:35; 30:26–29) as sacred objects before the people began to worship there. Samuel anointed first

Saul and then David as kings over Israel. Anointing symbolized cleansing and setting apart for God.

1 Samuel 13:22—Evidently as another tactic in their plan to totally subdue the people of Israel, the Philistines confiscated the most deadly weapons that could be used against them, the spear and the sword. Then they went a step further and put out of business or deported all blacksmiths, and with them their abilities and their knowledge. The Israelites had to fight the Philistines with whatever weapons they could find, plus one more thing, of course: God. When God went with them into battle, weapons or no weapons, losing just wasn't an option.

Tuesday

Reflecting on the Word
1 Samuel 1:11, 24–28

Hannah's godly character is revealed more fully in the one act of sacrifice recorded in these verses than in any other. Surely her mother's heart was breaking when she gave her son to the Lord while he was still very young (1 Samuel 1:24). When Hannah had prayed and asked God to open her infertile womb and give her a son, she promised that son would belong to God "all the days of his life" (1 Samuel 1:11 NKJV). She kept little Samuel close to her at home as long as she was breast-feeding him. But when she weaned him to regular food, at about the age of three, she knew the time had come to fulfill her promise to God.

Close your eyes and picture the scene. Hannah looked her boy full in his little round face. His eyes looked back at her, trusting and loving. She held in a sob as she remembered what she had promised God if He would give her a son. Never had she realized how difficult keeping that promise would be. Never had she realized the depth of the love she would have for her son. But now the time had come. Without equivocation, but not without grief and tears, Hannah kept her promise and delivered Samuel to the house of the Lord and Eli.

Hannah knew that promises were made to be kept. So she kept them. It was that simple.

In the New Testament, Matthew quotes Jesus' teaching on vows. He cautioned His listeners not to make vows lightly. And He kept it as simple as Hannah did when He said, "Let your 'Yes' be 'Yes,' and your 'No,' 'No'" (Matthew 5:37 NKJV).

Promises are meant to be kept, whether they're made to God, to a coworker, to a subordinate at work, to a friend, a relative, or a small child. Just as God has kept every promise made to you, He wants you to take every promise just as seriously.

Wednesday

Studying the Word
1 Samuel 13:1–15

King Saul and his soldiers were quaking in their sandals, watching as the Philistine army prepared for battle. As leader, Saul's preparations proved to be all wrong.

1. Compare the numbers of Philistine soldiers with the numbers of Israelite soldiers (1 Samuel 13:2, 5). How did the men (and presumably their families with them) respond when they realized the difference in these numbers (1 Samuel 13:6–7)? How did the army of Saul and Jonathan respond (1 Samuel 13:7*b*)? How do you think you would respond in a comparable situation?

2. What did the soldiers forget in their fear (Deuteronomy 31:5–6)?

3. Why was Saul waiting for Samuel? (Compare 1 Samuel 10:8 with 13:8.) Why do you think Samuel was late?

4. How did Saul's soldiers respond to the threat of the Philistines and the waiting for Samuel (1 Samuel 13:8)? How serious were these desertions (1 Samuel 13:15)?

5. What did Saul do when Samuel didn't show up (1 Samuel 13:8–9)? What were Saul's other options? What do you think you might have done?

6. Why was it wrong for Saul to offer this sacrifice (1 Samuel 13:13 and also 15:22)?

7. What punishment did Samuel prophesy for Saul's disobedience (1 Samuel 13:14)?

8. Why was Saul's action such a big deal for a king? Didn't he have a right to do what he thought was best? He was king, after all! What is this story's whole point and the lesson for Israel and for you?

Thursday

Responding to the Word
1 Samuel 15:22

Saul, Saul, didn't you learn from your first lesson about obedience?

Saul went into battle with the Amalekites, following God's command to do so because of the Amalekites' mistreatment of the Israelites when they had traveled from Egypt to the Promised Land (1 Samuel 15:1–3). God's orders were to destroy everything. *Everything.* While that order may be as hard for you to stomach as it seemed to be for Saul, the command was meant to be obeyed.

Did Saul bother to do so? Nope. Just as when he was supposed to wait for Samuel before sacrificing and fighting the Philistines (1 Samuel 13), Saul decided he knew better than the commands of God. Rather than destroying everything as he had been told, he saved out the best of the sheep and cattle. Bigheaded, pigheaded Saul. Arrogant with victory, Saul boasted, "We saved them 'to sacrifice to the LORD your God,'" when Samuel confronted him with his disobedience (1 Samuel 15:15, author's paraphrase).

Perhaps Saul's intentions weren't so bad. Perhaps he was actually serious in his desire to sacrifice these animals to the God who had given him victory. But all the "perhaps" in the world don't diminish the fact that saving these animals from destruction was an act of disobedience.

Samuel's response is one that has gone down in history as the bottom line against which all actions can be measured:

> Has the LORD as great delight in burnt offerings and sacrifices,
> As in obeying the voice of the LORD?
> Behold, to obey is better than sacrifice,
> And to heed than the fat of rams. —1 Samuel 15:22 NKJV

No matter how good the action, no matter how pure the motive, only obedience counts. Only obedience.

Friday

Praying the Word
1 Samuel 15:22

These words of Samuel are worthy of another day of study and meditation. As you approach your time of quiet prayer today, focus on the obedience quotient of your life. How in line are you—not only in actions but also in spirit—with the loving obedience God wants?

If you're having trouble in an area or two, recognize that all the good intentions and willpower in the world won't produce an obedient lifestyle more effectively than strengthening your connection to the power source, Christ. In Him you'll find what you need to live a truly obedient life, one that looks obedient on the outside because of the heart obedience on the inside.

As you pray today, talk to God about your need for His help to live as He commands.

Thank You, Lord God, that I don't have to rely on my own strength or abilities to follow You truly and faithfully. Give me a clear vision of Your will and way for my life, then give me the strength—and the burning desire—to follow it. Help me to remember that no good deed can ever take the place of an obedient heart. I love You, Lord. Amen.

Week Twelve

David's Early Years

Monday

Reading the Word
1 Samuel 16–20; 25

THE STORY

David closed his eyes as he felt the silky oil soak his hair and trickle warmly down his face. When he opened his eyes, the prophet Samuel filled his vision. David's handsome young face reflected the questions that were racing through his mind and heart. He knew what anointing meant. The anointed object or person was set aside for God in some special way. But what did this mean for him? What response was required? What should he do? He had no idea.

David's eyes fixed on Samuel's. Though he knew all about Samuel and the work he had done for the Lord, David had never met him before. David knew, too, that this event was not Samuel's doing but God's. And he knew God would reveal the implications of the event in His good timing. Through his years of caring for his father's sheep—years alone out in the desert—David had developed a deeper understanding of God than many young men of his age.

Rather than pounding Samuel with questions, David stood and quietly waited, waited for what Samuel would say, what God would do. And as he waited, God's power and an assurance of God's presence filled David, giving him the patience and the confidence to wait and to follow only when and where God led.

THE MESSAGE

What Saul was missing, David had. Heart. A heart that loved and followed God fully. David was just what God was looking for, "a man after His own heart" (1 Samuel 13:14 NKJV). Saul's actions betrayed the emptiness of his heart. While David's actions weren't always perfect, his heart remained in tune with God's.

THE MAIN POINT

God is looking for people whose hearts are in tune with His. Those are the people, no matter how good (or bad) they might look on the outside, that God can and will use. You can fix up the exterior of a car and it will look great. But if the motor doesn't run, the car doesn't fulfill its purpose. You can clean up your act, fix up your exterior deeds, modify your exterior behaviors, and still have a heart that doesn't beat along with God's. All the exterior spit shine in the world doesn't take the place of becoming a person after God's own heart.

TAKE NOTE

1 Samuel 17:40—When you think of David and his sling, don't picture a Huck Finn character with a twig and rubber band apparatus in his back pocket. David's sling was a deadly weapon, as he so effectively revealed when he fought Goliath. A sling was a long band of leather with a wider space in the middle to hold a stone. The stone was probably about the size of a common baseball today. The two ends of the sling were held together and swung around the head. Then, with the target in mind, the slinger would release one end and send the stone to its mark. In the time of the judges, the tribe of Benjamin had a contingent of seven hundred left-handed fighting men who could "sling a stone at a hair's breadth and not miss" (Judges 20:16 NKJV).

1 Samuel 25:4–11—During times of feasts and festivals, custom and hospitality demanded payment, usually in the form of food, to those who had provided protection in recent months. David's men had defended Nabal's men and flocks from wild animals and roaming bands of out-

laws. Rather than offer the payment that David had every right to expect, however, Nabal thumbed his nose at David's men and sent them away empty-handed.

Tuesday

Reflecting on the Word
1 Samuel 17

One of the Bible's most loved and most repeated stories is that of David and his battle with the giant Goliath. Too young to be a soldier, too needed at home to be with the army on a regular basis, David came to the battlefield, saw the threat, and realized that not only Israel's but God's honor was at stake (1 Samuel 17:36).

When ancient armies fought, at times they presented their champions for battle rather than whole armies with the huge loss of life such battles produced. Each army would choose the best, biggest, strongest soldier to fight. The winner took all—the land, the produce, the people of the conquered army. This is exactly the scheme Goliath shouted from the valley each morning and evening for forty days.

Rather than busying themselves with finding God's champion, however, Israel's army quivered in fear. Until young David arrived.

David didn't look at Goliath and see a giant who was nine feet tall and a seasoned soldier. He saw an enemy of God almighty. Can't you just picture David (strong, yes, but still a youth), standing before Saul (an older, rougher, veteran soldier) like a young boy in a classroom raising his hand as high as he could and shouting, "I'll do it! I can do it!"

Saul immediately realized that sending David out to fight Goliath would mean not only David's death but defeat for Israel. David didn't argue that the match was uneven. So was the match between him and the lions and bears that he had killed while herding his father's sheep. Just as God had saved David from the paws of wild animals, He would save David from the hand of this bully, Goliath.

Read 1 Samuel 17:45–47 slowly. You'll discover there the source of David's strength for this battle as well as all those to follow. No chest-beating boasts for David. No hurled threats about his strong arm and well-aimed sling. Actually, the words contain very little about him at all. David directed the focus away from himself toward God, who was the true champion of the day. The root of all of David's successes as a ruler can be found in these words.

Wednesday

Studying the Word
1 Samuel 16:14–23

Saul's struggle with anger and depression dogged him throughout his latter years. Read this passage, and then answer these questions to discover where he, and possibly you, might find relief from these emotions.

1. Begin by comparing 1 Samuel 16:13 and 14. Whom did the Spirit of God enter? Whom did He leave?

In the Old Testament, the Holy Spirit came in power on those God wanted to use for some special task or service. God's Spirit was not available to every believer until after Christ's death and return to heaven (John 14:26; Acts 1:8).

2. Why did the Spirit leave Saul?
3. What effect did the Holy Spirit's presence have on David's life? What effect did the Spirit's absence have on Saul's life?
4. What prescription for his troubles did Saul's servants suggest (1 Samuel 16:16)?
5. How do you think this servant of Saul knew so much about David (1 Samuel 16:18)? What does his description tell you about David?
6. What happened when David played his harp for Saul (1 Samuel 16:23)?
7. What part does music play in the life of a believer? One who is going through difficult times? One who is enjoying good times?
8. How can you use music to soothe your emotions or to express them?

Thursday

Responding to the Word
1 Samuel 18:1

The Hebrew word used here of the friendship between David and Jonathan speaks of a friendship that goes deep and includes a lasting and loving relationship. David and Jonathan didn't just share an acquaintance and enjoy each other's company. They *loved* each other. Their souls were knit together in close relationship.

What makes this friendship so remarkable isn't that two men who were both warriors, both young and gifted, both strong and virile formed a bond. What makes this friendship so remarkable is that in most circumstances it would never have happened. Jonathan was heir to the throne of Israel. David was usurper to the throne of Israel. The Bible doesn't go into detail, but somehow Jonathan recognized David as God's leader of choice. And, rather than grabbing and holding on to his royal rights, he relinquished them in a demonstration of great character. That in itself was an act of humility and grace on Jonathan's part. As if that weren't enough, however, he took one more leap of character and formed a friendship with the man who should have been his enemy, a friendship that has gone down in history as one to be admired and imitated.

Often friendships require sacrifices, sometimes as significant as the one made by Jonathan. He gave up his rights as heir to the throne in order to form a friendship with David (1 Samuel 18:4: giving his robe to David signified his surrender of the throne). You might have to defend your friend against attack, as Jonathan did when his father attacked David (1 Samuel 19:4; 20:30–34). You will have to sacrifice your privacy, your need at times to keep things to yourself, sharing them instead with your friend (1 Samuel 20:41–42). You might have to sacrifice your love of self in order to love your friend enough to form a true bond (1 Samuel 20:17).

Do your best to continue to develop and nourish your friendships. They're precious and not to be taken lightly. If you don't have such a

The Women's Devotional Guide to the Bible

friendship, make work of developing one. That's right! True friendship doesn't just happen. You may feel an instant bond or connection with someone, but deep friendship only develops when you're willing to give of yourself and work at being a friend.

Friday

Praying the Word
1 Samuel 16:7

Today, focus your attention more than usual on your inward spirit rather than your outward appearance. Focus your attention on what God sees, rather than on what those around you see. Focus your attention on being authentic, on being *real*. Don't just put on a good face, put on *goodness*.

As you get ready for your day, put on a gentle spirit with your makeup. Put on self-control with your clothing. Put on kindness with your shoes. With each step of your morning routine, think of a godly attribute that you can develop. See Galatians 5:22–23 for a list of those attributes and for the source of power to make them part of your character.

And, of course, as you get ready for your day, spend time in prayer, asking God to help you be authentic, to be on the inside the image you try to project on the outside.

Dear God, I know how far short I fall of focusing on what is truly important. Help me always to remember what is important to You—what's inside rather than out-side—and then give me the power through Your Spirit to develop those inward charac-teristics that please You. In Your name today, Lord, I put on gentleness and kindness and patience and self-control and all the rest. Thank You for what You're accomplish-ing in my life already. Amen.

David as King

Monday

Reading the Word
2 Samuel 1–2; 5–7; 11–12

THE STORY

The excitement of the day expanded David's heart within his chest until he felt like he would burst with the emotion. He looked just ahead of him at the Ark of the Covenant as it moved along the road into Jerusalem. The sun glinted off the golden wings of the cherubim on its top. The priests who carried it walked as though the box was almost weightless, the excitement of the event obviously affecting them as much as it did David.

Without much thought, David stripped off his heavy kingly robe and tossed it to a nearby servant. Clad now only in a lightweight undergarment, David felt a marvelous freedom from the weight of his royal robes as well as his royal duties. David's arms and legs were released to express all he was feeling.

A huge smile crossed David's face as he realized what today's events signified. Today the ark would take its rightful place in the center of Israel. Today God's presence would again be known and felt in the center of His people. "Glorious!" David shouted aloud. The people around him responded, "Hallelujah!"

God's promises were coming to fulfillment. And he, David, was blessed to witness and be part of it. David's feet began moving in a dance of joy. He raised his arms and threw back his head. He hurled his body back and forth in an abandoned dance of praise.

As David's sun-darkened legs leaped and whirled, his eyes moved up to a nearby window. There, standing in the shadows, David saw his wife Michal. Even before her face came fully into view, he knew what he would find there. Only disapproval. Michal never seemed to approve of David; he didn't think enough of his royal position, she said. At this point, David just didn't care. He met her glare with a smile and a skip of joy.

THE MESSAGE

Throughout David's reign he would do many things without truly considering the consequences—sometimes good, sometimes bad. Dancing with abandon before the Ark of the Covenant was one of the good times. Without a thought for what others might think, without a consideration of the royal and exalted position he now held, David forgot everything but praising God with all his being.

THE MAIN POINT

This incident is just one incident in a life filled with abandoned love and service to God. David's life illustrates, perhaps better than any other in Scripture, the beauty and usefulness of such a life. Have you ever expressed your praise of God's work and goodness in your life as thoroughly as David did here? Today, do your best to abandon all your self-awareness and selfishness in order to offer up a sacrifice of praise to God that is wholly and fully expressive of your love for Him. Who knows? Maybe you'll even begin to dance before Him with "all [your] might" (2 Samuel 6:14 NKJV).

TAKE NOTE

2 Samuel 5:6–10—For the first time, the people of Israel had fully conquered and settled the city of the Jebusites, Jerusalem. David's army defeated this city in central Israel, and then David moved there and made it his capital. The city was on a hill surrounded by deep val-

leys, a natural fortress. Although located in the territory of the tribe of Benjamin, it was near David's hometown of Bethlehem, in the territory of his family's tribe, Judah. By moving the government to this newly conquered city in Israel's heartland, David united the tribes who had been loyal to Saul, a Benjamite, with those loyal to him, thereby fortifying not just a city but his place as ruler over all the tribes of Israel.

2 Samuel 11:4—The bath that Bathsheba took while David watched was a ritual bath taken after a woman finished her monthly period. During the time of a woman's flow, she was considered unclean (Leviticus 15:19ff). When her period was finished, a cleansing bath restored her to clean hygiene as well as religious cleanliness. This note in Scripture makes it plain that Bathsheba was not pregnant by her husband Uriah when she went to David's bed.

Tuesday

Reflecting on the Word
2 Samuel 6

With thirty thousand men following, the Ark of the Covenant rolled on its cart toward Jerusalem. It seemed like a beautiful scene, a wonderful day—until the oxen stumbled. Then, Uzzah, the son of the family where the ark had been housed for fifty years, reached out his hand to protect the ark. And he died for his consideration.

Years before, after the ark had been captured in battle by the Philistines (1 Samuel 4:1–5:12), God sent illness and death to each Philistine city it visited. When the Philistines decided to get rid of it, they sent it on a cart into Israel (1 Samuel 6). The ark's arrival in Israel prompted excitement. But not respect. When some of the men looked into the ark, God put them to death (1 Samuel 6:19). Thinking just like the Philistines, the people decided the ark was the problem—not their own behavior—and put it in Abinadab's house with his son as guard. There it stayed throughout Samuel's final years and King Saul's reign.

Unlike Saul, who didn't seem to understand its significance, David recognized that the ark represented the actual presence of the Lord in Israel. He had established Jerusalem as his military and political headquarters. Now he wanted to establish it also as the religious center of the country. And to do that, he needed the ark.

But, rather than checking the rules Moses had established for moving the ark (Numbers 4), David followed the Philistines' lead, built a new cart, hitched up a couple of oxen, and the ark began to roll toward Jerusalem. Only after Uzzah's sudden and frightening death did anyone think to check the rules.

The next time David and his people moved the ark, they moved it the way God had commanded. The event sparked as much joy and dancing as the first, with a much better outcome.

Wednesday

Studying the Word
2 Samuel 12:1–15

Read again the story of David and Bathsheba in 2 Samuel 11, then answer the following questions about sin and forgiveness based on 2 Samuel 12:1–15.

1. How did Nathan approach David? How does Nathan's approach help you in how you might approach someone who is sinning and needs to be confronted?

2. Who was the rich man in Nathan's story? The poor man? The lamb? What does this tell you about the role of each person involved in this situation (2 Samuel 12:1–4)?

3. How did David respond to the story (2 Samuel 12:5–6)? Did he recognize himself in it? Why not?

4. What approach did Nathan take next (2 Samuel 12:7–11)? What lessons about God's gifts and expectations can you discover by reading these words?

5. When David realized that Nathan was confronting him about his sin with Bathsheba, what was his response? What does this response show you about David? About how you could (should?) respond when confronted with your sins?

6. Why do you think the sin David tried to keep secret would be punished in such a public way (2 Samuel 12:10–12; 16:22)?

7. Turn to Psalm 51 and read there the hymn of remorse and forgiveness that David wrote after this incident. What assurance for your own sinful self can you find there?

Thursday

Responding to the Word
2 Samuel 11:1–5

Rather than looking away from temptation, David looked again. His surrender to temptation didn't happen within minutes. The longer he contemplated, the longer he dwelled on Bathsheba and her beauty and his desire, the harder it became to resist.

David had stayed home from the spring battle with the Ammonite city of Rabbah. Some say he should have been with his army. Others note that he easily could have directed the battle from the safety of his palace since Rabbah was only about forty miles from Jerusalem. Often, ancient armies kept their highest ranking generals in the relative safety of the rear lines or a nearby fortified city.

Whatever David's reason for staying in Jerusalem, he got up one night, perhaps restless with being safely in Jerusalem rather than with his men in battle. Walking around on the roof of his palace, he saw Bathsheba bathing. Then, rather than looking away, giving Bathsheba the privacy she deserved and giving himself the chance to resist, he looked again. He would have done well to take Job's advice about how to look and *not* to look at the opposite sex (Job 31:1).

The best time to resist temptation is the first time it appears. Rather than looking again, look away, right away. The longer you look, the more you contemplate, the harder resisting becomes.

The New Testament has quite a lot to say about temptation. Jesus' example when He was tempted in the desert illustrates the use of the truths of the Scripture against the devil's deceit (Matthew 4:1–11). Don't ever think this was an easy test for Jesus to ace—that He just whipped out those verses and walked away from Satan. He wrestled with His desire to surrender, just as you do. The beauty of the struggle is that it gives Jesus compassion when you are tempted. He fully understands your battles with temptation (Hebrews 2:18; 4:15).

The Women's Devotional Guide to the Bible

The apostle Paul understood temptation and its hazards as well. But he also understood God's place in the tempest. In his letter to the Corinthian church, he ends a long list of temptations and sins with a promise of God that you can hang on to. First, you aren't alone. Any temptation you face has been faced already by someone else. Second, you aren't without resources. God has promised that no matter what the temptation, He'll provide a way for you to resist. You just have to take it (1 Corinthians 10:13).

Friday

Praying the Word
2 Samuel 7:18–22

After hearing Nathan's words about what God would accomplish through David and his family, David responded in a prayer of thanksgiving that provides an excellent structure for your own prayers of thanksgiving. Spend some time today reflecting on how God has blessed you and your family. Be specific. How has He blessed you in good times? How has He sustained you in times of suffering? What have you learned during the good times? During the difficult times? What ways has God used you in other people's lives?

As you pray today, use your reflections to offer your thanks to God for His involvement in every part of your life.

Sovereign Lord, David's God and mine, I am as amazed as David that You would love me and care to attend to my needs. I thank You for all that You've done. There is no one like You, O Lord! Amen.

Solomon and Rehoboam Rule

Monday

Reading the Word
1 Kings 3; 4:20–34; 6; 8; 10:1–12:24; 14:21–31

THE STORY

King Rehoboam tapped the floor with his golden scepter as he listened to the people's complaints. His leg jiggled in rhythm to the scepter's taps. He covered a tired yawn with his hand as the yammering of Jeroboam and his cohorts continued.

Rehoboam had no idea the people had been so unhappy with his father Solomon's policies. He shook his head in disgust. His father's reign had been a time of peace and prosperity in Israel. And the people had the audacity to complain about a little work.

Rehoboam turned bored eyes toward his advisors. He knew even before they spoke that they would disagree on the best way to handle this situation. All he wanted, he thought, was to be done with it all. A lot of nerve these people had, complaining to him, the king! Making life miserable for him, the king!

Without much thought, and certainly no consideration for what God would have him do, Rehoboam took the advice of his younger advisors. "This is how it will be," he spoke firmly, his scepter thumping the marble of the floor forcefully with each word. "You think life was hard under my father's rule? You haven't seen anything yet . . ."

THE MESSAGE

Rehoboam's biggest mistake was not who he listened to. It was who he didn't listen to—God. He went to his advisors, which was good and proper. But he didn't add God to the equation at all, which was a big mistake. And he and the people paid for it in rebellion and division, war and conflict.

THE MAIN POINT

You can't make a much bigger mistake than not listening to God, not consulting God when decisions need to be made. Whether you're considering how you'll "rule" your business, how you'll run your household, how you'll raise your children, how you'll respond to difficulties—whatever your decision, big or small—God is interested and has input. He knows your past and your future, and He has your ultimate good in mind.

TAKE NOTE

1 Kings 6:7—Solomon built a temple for God that was roughly the same plan but twice as large as Moses' desert tabernacle. Even more interesting, no hammer or chisel or other tool was allowed at the temple site. The builders cut all the stones before bringing them to the temple site. Without the loud sound of iron tools, workers were able to maintain a worshipful quiet even while the temple, a place of worship, was going up.

1 Kings 10:27—Can you imagine it? So much silver in Jerusalem that it was as common as stones? Like picking up a couple of stones to buy groceries? The description in this verse sets up the image of Solomon's great wealth better than any other. Note also that much of Solomon's wealth came because those seeking his wisdom brought rich gifts to his kingdom (1 Kings 10:24–25). So in His usual way of giving more than you ask (Ephesians 3:20), God used the wisdom that Solomon requested to give him the riches he hadn't asked for (1 Kings 3:1–15).

Tuesday

Reflecting on the Word
1 Kings 8:27–30

After all the time, effort, stone, wood, bronze, gold, and silver put into the temple building, Solomon stood before God to dedicate it. And he admitted it wasn't enough. Such a meager building—though magnificent in human eyes—could never hold the God of all creation. Yet, Solomon asked God to look down on the temple and the people gathered there, to hear their prayers, and to respond. When you read this passage, it may sound like praying from or toward the temple in Jerusalem is important in getting God to hear your prayers. It's really not.

While a special place of prayer can be beneficial, can stimulate reverence, it's not actually required. In Old Testament times, God was present in the tabernacle and then the temple in a very special way. But He wasn't restricted to them. God heard prayers offered at a burning bush in the desert (Exodus 3), from the belly of a whale (Jonah 2:1), from a dungeon (Jeremiah 37:16–17), and from a window in Babylon (Daniel 6:10). Today, God may meet you in some special place of worship, whether a church or a favorite quiet time location. But He's just as present and listens just as closely when you pray with your hands in soapy water at your kitchen sink, while you're seated in your car or on a plane, or as you're soaking your pillow with your tears.

All that Solomon said of God is still true today. All of the earth and the heavens are not large enough to hold Him (1 Kings 8:27). No church building today, no matter how large or splendid, can contain Him. God hears your prayers today wherever you are, just as He heard Solomon's prayer from the temple. He hears your prayers, just as He heard the prayers of the people of Israel, when they prayed from Jerusalem or from some other location. And He still forgives.

Wednesday

Studying the Word
1 Kings 3:5–15

Have you ever felt totally, completely, absolutely, and utterly inadequate for some task? Perhaps something your boss asked you to do? Or perhaps in a situation with one of your children? Or how to best respond in a situation of suffering? You can read books and go to seminars and learn a lot. But there's only one place to find true wisdom. Solomon knew the Source and found his wisdom there. So can you.

1. Why do you think God appeared to Solomon? What made him a good candidate for an audience with God (1 Kings 3:3)?

2. Do you think the Lord would have given Solomon anything—*anything*—he asked for? Why or why not?

3. Solomon said he was only a "little child" even though he was actually around twenty years old when he became king (1 Kings 3:7 NKJV). Why do you think he felt this way? Why might he have felt inadequate to rule Israel?

4. What did Solomon ask the Lord to give him (1 Kings 3:9)? Why do you think this pleased God (1 Kings 3:10)?

5. If God came to you and said He'd give you anything you asked for, what would you request? Be honest here! Would your request please God? Why or why not?

6. Read 1 John 5:14–15. How does the truth of this verse affect your answers to question 5?

7. What three things did God promise to give to Solomon besides wisdom (1 Kings 3:12–14)? Which of these three things came with a stipulation (1 Kings 3:14)? Why?

8. Think of ways God has answered your prayers in the past. What does recalling answered prayer from the past do for your prayer life in the present?

9. Read Ephesians 3:20. How might the truth of this verse change your prayer life? How might it add to your confidence in bringing your requests to God?

Thursday

Responding to the Word
1 Kings 9:4–6; 11:1

The chapters before 1 Kings 11 relate all the successes and riches and wisdom that God gave Solomon during his reign. Riches that make even today's wealthiest people look needy. Wisdom that even today's most well educated can't match. Palaces and temples and cities and stables and ships that make even today's largest enterprises seem small. And all given to him because he asked God for wisdom (1 Kings 3:5–15).

Then 1 Kings 11 brings the first hint of darkness. With one word—*however*—the picture changes. All was not right in the kingdom. Solomon's love for women was his weak spot.

Have you ever heard of the "slippery slope" logic? Perhaps your mother or a teacher or minister used it on you, "The path of sin is a slippery slope." Take one step toward sin and you'll slide down that slope until you're mired in it. You may laugh. You might make jokes about it. It even might not always be true. But in a general way, when talking about sin in your life, it is true. It's a slippery slope.

Early in his reign, Solomon strengthened his relationship with Egypt by marrying one of Pharaoh's daughters. It was a common way to build alliances between countries. He didn't stop there, however. He also married women from countries that God had specifically told the Israelites to stay away from, nations that worshiped many foreign gods. In fact, Solomon married so many of these women (see 1 Kings 11:3 for the astounding tally), and he enjoyed their company so much, that they gradually (that's the slope coming in there) turned his heart away from total devotion to God.

Your mother warned you when you were a child. One lie leads to another, bigger lie. One misdeed leads to another, bigger misdeed. One little sin—nothing big, not much to worry about—can so easily lead to more. Before you know it, you're like Solomon, who went from avidly showing his love for the Lord (1 Kings 3:3) to letting his wives turn his heart away from God so that he was no longer totally devoted to Him (1 Kings 11:4).

Did it happen overnight? Of course not. Gradually, little by barely noticed little, Solomon's heart turned away from God toward his women and their gods. That's the slippery slope in a nutshell. You don't go careening down it. One small and seemingly insignificant decision leads to another and another, until you're further away from God than you could have ever imagined.

Like Solomon, all along the way, you have choices. You can choose to stay on the path toward God and wholeness, or you can choose to move further and further away from Him and His goodness. Each step is usually a small one. But each step adds up to a lifetime of living one way or the other. Read about Solomon in these chapters and take his lessons to heart. Don't let anything—people, money, fame, success, family—lead you anywhere but closer to God.

Friday

Praying the Word
1 Kings 8:23–24

Picture in your mind the grandeur of the scene. All the people of Israel were congregated together in Jerusalem for the dedication of the new temple. The structure astonished them with its beauty and splendor. They stood in awe before it in the warm sunshine, watching as their king raised his hands to pray. Solomon began his prayer by praising God's character and thanking Him for what He had done.

Today, find some concentrated time alone. (Not an easy thing for moms with young children. Maybe for today you'll have to get up early or turn in late or use naptimes.) Before you begin to pray, list the ways God has been faithful to you in the past day, the past week, the past year, the past ten or twenty years. Try to be very specific.

Sit, stand, or kneel—however you're comfortable—when you're ready to pray. Then spread your hands in a gesture of submission and gratitude to God and thank Him for all the faithfulness you recorded. Praise Him for who He is in your life and in the life of your family. Thank Him for His goodness as well as His faithfulness. Then close your time of prayer with quietness, meditating on Him, listening for His voice, enjoying the sense of His presence with you.

God the Father, I thank You for faithfully keeping all Your promises to me. God the Son, I thank You for Your submissive journey to the Cross to gain my forgiveness and salvation. God the Spirit, I thank You for Your presence with me here today. Amen.

Israel's Last Rulers, Last Days

Monday

Reading the Word
1 Kings 12:25–33; 15:25–16:34; 22:29–40;
2 Kings 9–10; 17

THE STORY

Jeroboam walked through the halls of the house he had built for himself. It wasn't as grand as the king's palace in Jerusalem. But it was fine for an upstart king of Israel. He smiled to himself, thinking about the power he now had over ten of the tribes of Israel. They had rejected Rehoboam, Solomon's son, as their king and had crowned him instead.

He knew his power as king was shaky. As long as the people of Israel traveled to Jerusalem to worship in the temple, there was danger of their allegiance reverting to Rehoboam. The more he thought about it, the more he realized he needed to come up with a plan, something to keep the people away from Jerusalem.

With the help of his advisors, Jeroboam came up with a foolproof plan—one that not only kept the people from Jerusalem but also played on their unreliable devotion to God. He presented the people with two golden calf idols, putting one in the northern section of his kingdom and one in the southern. How convenient! No long trips to Jerusalem required. Jeroboam smiled with satisfaction. Mission accomplished!

THE MESSAGE

The story of the Israelite nation and their kings is one of repeated and expanding sin. The stories of all but one of the kings of Israel include some form of denunciation for sin. Jeroboam: 1 Kings 13:34; Nadab: 1 Kings 15:26; Baasha: 1 Kings 15:34; Elah: 1 Kings 16:13; Zimri: 1 Kings 16:18–19; Omri: 1 Kings 16:25; Ahab: 1 Kings 16:30; Ahaziah: 1 Kings 22:52; Jehu: 2 Kings 10:31; Jehoahaz: 2 Kings 13:2; Jehoash: 2 Kings 13:11; Jeroboam II: 2 Kings 14:24; Zechariah: 2 Kings 15:9; Shallum: 2 Kings 15:13–16 (Shallum reigned only one month; his record includes no denunciation, but he assassinated the king to gain the throne and then was assassinated himself); Menahem: 2 Kings 15:18; Pekahiah: 2 Kings 15:24; Pekah: 2 Kings 15:28; Hoshea: 2 Kings 17:2.

THE MAIN POINT

Continued sin has its consequences. The Israelite nation paid for their rejection of God by the loss of their identity as a nation, the loss of their land, and the loss of their homes when they were transported as slaves to other lands. Over and over again, God sent prophets to warn them that continued disobedience would be punished. And they didn't listen. In 2 Peter 3:9 the writer assures you that God is just as patient today. He doesn't relish punishing sin. But He will not wait forever. Eventually sin that hasn't been repented will be punished.

TAKE NOTE

1 Kings 16:31—The god Baal, the most significant god in Canaanite worship, lured the Israelites away from the one true God more than any other idol that was worshiped in that area. People depended on his "power" for fertility of the land and cattle. His influence waxed and waned throughout Israelite history, until both nations went into exile for worshiping him as well as other false gods.

2 Kings 17:6, 24—In a heartless form of ethnic cleansing, Assyria moved conquered nations from one place to another in an effort to keep them subjugated. When the Assyrian army conquered the Northern

Kingdom of Israel, they took the people captive, split them up, and moved them into various other conquered areas. Then, as the Assyrians conquered other nations, they took those peoples into captivity and moved some of them into the vacated Israelite lands. These people, who came to be known as Samaritans, were of mixed ancestry. They combined the worship of their ancestors' gods with the worship of the God of their new land.

Tuesday

Reflecting on the Word
1 Kings 16:29–33

These verses begin the story of King Ahab, known throughout history as the most wicked of the kings of Israel. His reign is covered more thoroughly than any other of the kings of Israel, and these first few verses merely set the stage for twenty-two years of flagrant disobedience of God's laws.

Scripture calls Ahab's father, King Omri, the most wicked of all of Israel's kings thus far. Then, in sin's natural progression, Ahab receives the same denunciation—even more wicked than his father before him, Ahab surpassed Omri and became the most wicked of all the kings of Israel. No other king receives the condemnation that this father-son team receives.

The writer of 1 Kings wings the word *trivial* at his readers to describe Ahab's attitude toward sin. He not only committed the same sins as Jeroboam, first king of Israel, he saw them as trivial, no big deal. And he went on to commit more, marrying Jezebel, whose very name brings images of evil to mind, building a temple for Baal in Samaria (evidently Jeroboam's golden calves in Bethel and Dan were no longer enough), and creating a wooden idol for the people to worship.

The word *trivial* means something that is of no consequence or value, something that's insignificant. An important thing to remember: no sin—no matter how small or innocuous in your eyes—is *trivial* in God's eyes.

All sin, whether you're Ahab or Jezebel or David or *you*, stems from the same place: your fallen nature. It's your natural inclination. Sins—whether big or small, whether intentional or unintentional, whether they affect others or only you—are still sins and call for repentance and confession before God.

Paul faced the same dilemma with sin as Ahab. But his response couldn't have been more different. When faced with sin, Ahab just kept on committing more, until he was measured as the most wicked of Israel's kings. Paul also faced the inclination to sin but went to God for forgiveness and to Jesus Christ for victory (Romans 7:21–25).

Wednesday

Studying the Word
2 Kings 17:7–23

The more you read of the kings of Israel, the more you'll realize that God was faithful to them, but they were blatantly unfaithful to Him. God was patient, but not unjust. His justice eventually demanded punishment. Read the obituary of the kingdom of Israel in 2 Kings 17:7–23 and answer these questions:

1. What was the first sin of Israel recorded in these verses (2 Kings 17:7–8)? What was their second sin (2 Kings 17:9)?
2. How did God respond to their sin (2 Kings 17:13)? What does this show you about God?
3. What means does God use today to warn that repentance is needed?
4. Second Kings 17:14 NKJV begins with the word *nevertheless*. What turning point in the people's relationship with God does this word signify?
5. Compare the denunciation of these verses of 2 Kings with the words of Deuteronomy 28:15–20, 36–37. Why do you think God finally decided to fulfill His promised punishment for disobedience? Why did He wait so long before doing so?

Thursday

Responding to the Word
2 Kings 17:7–23

Like piling one block on top of another until the whole tower comes crashing down, Israel's sins kept piling up one on top of the other until God had no choice but to punish. The words in these verses distressingly describe how deeply sin had invaded the Israelite nation and individual. Like an attorney for the prosecution, the writer of Kings listed all the accusations against Israel, most of them involving the depraved practices of idol worship. Then, after the accusations were finalized, judgment was pronounced. God could no longer allow these people to live in His holy presence in the Promised Land. They would go into exile in Assyria.

This passage in 2 Kings begins with a recollection of God's action on behalf of the Israelites when they were exiled and slaves in Egypt. He saw their misery there and took action through Moses and Aaron to bring them out of Egypt and into the Promised Land. Now, years later, because of their repeated refusal to follow His laws and worship Him alone, they would go back into exile and slavery, this time in Assyria.

God will always forgive sin. Never doubt that. But when sin goes repeated and unrepented, He will punish. Never doubt that.

God isn't necessarily looking for a people who are sinless. But He is looking for a people who are sin sensitive. He's looking for people who, as soon as they become aware of sin in their lives, turn to Him in repentance.

The kings of Israel richly illustrate this truth. Look at Jeroboam, first king of Israel. His sins piled up on each other. God sent prophets to point out his sin to him. He responded with more sin. Eventually, God denounced him (1 Kings 13). Compare David. He was far from perfect. His sins included blatant adultery, then murder. God sent a prophet to point out his sin to him. And David responded with abject sorrow and repentance (2 Samuel 12:1–13; Psalm 51). Jeroboam's epitaph is repeated over and over again in 1 and 2 Kings. The sins of each king of Israel are compared to those of Jeroboam. David's epitaph is one of God's acceptance and compassion and understanding (Acts 13:22).

As you read the stories of the kings, take their examples to heart. Carefully pattern your life after those who followed God faithfully, who repented when they sinned, who worshiped Him alone.

Friday

Praying the Word
2 Kings 10:28–29

A spark of good action gives some hope to the dismal situation in Israel. Jehu seized the throne from the sons of Ahab and one of his first acts as king was to destroy all the priests of Baal and their temple in Samaria. But it just wasn't enough. Although passionate about destroying Baal worship, Jehu continued in the sinful ways of the kings before him and worshiped the golden calves that Jeroboam had set up in Bethel and Dan.

What was true in Israel's time is just as true today in the twenty-first century. God is still looking for those who will follow Him with their whole hearts, who will not let anything get in the way of their love for Him.

Today, examine your heart and your life to discover what might be getting between you and God. What do you think about most? What takes up most of your time? You might find some clues in those areas. Confess to God anything that compromises your commitment to Him and ask Him to give you a heart that is wholly devoted to Him. Use your own words or the words of Jesus in Luke 16:13 to frame your prayer today.

Lord of all, I commit my heart and life wholeheartedly to You today. You taught that I can't serve two masters. I know from experience that this is true. I ask You to help me to remove from my life and my affections anything that supplants You as first. You, and You alone, are my Lord, my Master. Amen.

Judah's Last Rulers, Last Days

Monday

Reading the Word
2 Kings 11–12; 18:1–19:19; 20:1–11; 21–25

THE STORY

Jehosheba's heart pounded in her breast. Her breath came in jagged gasps as her shaking hands picked up little Prince Joash, her nephew, and held him tight against her body. She brought her flowing robes around him, hoping to hide him, to shield him from the horror of the day's events. Just as she rounded the corner to leave, the emissaries of Joash's grandmother Athaliah entered. Jehosheba knew those emissaries' intent: to kill all of the royal family.

Tears started in her eyes as each prince's face appeared in her mind. With only the time and arms to grab one small child, her heart broke with the realization that death awaited those she left behind. A sob caught in her throat as she realized how far into evil the power-hungry Athaliah had traveled. Hurrying toward a darker, less-used part of the palace, Jehosheba put little Joash in a bedroom and left him in the care of his nurse. Then she went to find her husband, the high priest (2 Chronicles 22:11), to tell him what she had done. Unknowingly, in saving little Joash, she saved the family line of David from extinction and, therefore, the family from which Jesus the Messiah would come.

THE MESSAGE

As the events in Judah spiraled down toward the same level of wickedness found in Israel, one person, a woman, stepped in to change the course of history. Her brave action, saving a baby prince from certain death, not only preserved the family line of David but also preserved truth and righteousness in the nation. For six years Athaliah, Joash's grandmother, ruled in Judah, her wicked ways seeping into all levels of society. But when rescued Joash came to the throne at the tender age of seven, he did all he could to reverse her evil effects and to bring the people back into a right relationship with God.

THE MAIN POINT

God loves His people with a desperation that causes Him to wait patiently for them to turn away from their sin and to turn toward Him. Even when affairs are their darkest, He is working, often behind the scenes, nudging events along in a way that will make His people see, if only they will look, that their only hope is in turning to Him.

TAKE NOTE

2 Kings 18:4—The bronze serpent (which is probably what the word *Nehushtan* means) Moses fashioned in order to bring healing to the people when they were being poisoned by snakes in the desert (Numbers 21:4–9) had become an idol to the people of Judah. This object of good became an object of sin when the people began to worship it. The tendency of the people of Judah, the people in the early church, and people today as well, is to turn something that God intends for good into something that replaces or supercedes their love for God. They begin to worship what was created rather than the Creator (Romans 1:25).

2 Kings 18:13—The campaign of Sennacherib (one of Assyria's most powerful kings) against the nation of Judah and its cities is recorded three times in the Bible (2 Kings 18:13–19:17; 2 Chronicles 32:1–22; Isaiah 36:1–37:38). His campaign is also recorded on many clay tablets, uncovered by archaeologists and on display in world museums today. He

conquered a number of Judah's fortified cities. Although he failed to defeat Judah's capital city, his records claim that he shut up Hezekiah in Jerusalem "like a bird in a cage."

Tuesday

Reflecting on the Word
2 Kings 25:21*b*

The words of this verse are some of the saddest in Judah's history: "So Judah went into captivity, away from her land" (NIV).

Throughout the books of the Bible, God promises again and again that the land belongs to His people, Israel and Judah (Psalm 105:8–11). The land was a very specific evidence of God's faithfulness to them, and a very specific evidence of God's blessing when they were faithful to Him. Trouble was, these people had trouble with faithfulness.

The book of 2 Kings outlines in depressing terms the ways that God tried to get the people's attention and repentance, and the deaf ears they turned to Him. In the books of Moses, the primary Bible text of that day, God made very clear that He would heap blessings on His people if they obeyed Him and punishment if they didn't (Deuteronomy 28). In addition to His written Word, God sent prophets to remind the people and urge them to repent. They ignored both written and spoken word.

Finally, God could ignore their disobedience no longer. Eager for their repentance and willing to forgive, He waited long and patiently for them to respond. But His justice finally took over and punishment had to be meted out. The words of Deuteronomy 28:36 came true: "The LORD will bring you and the king whom you set over you to a nation which neither you nor your fathers have known" (NKJV).

The Promised Land was the Israelites' birthright and most precious possession. Now they would forfeit that possession. It was their gift from

God, their evidence of His love for them above all other peoples of the earth. And they tossed it away with their fascination for other gods.

Wednesday

Studying the Word
2 Kings 19:6, 10–19

Hezekiah knew he was in trouble. These weren't just idle words on Sennacherib's part. He had every intention as well as the ability to fulfill them and destroy Hezekiah and Jerusalem. But Hezekiah's outlook on the situation had more to it than physical destruction. Read these verses to find out the king's perspective.

1. What did the letter sent to Hezekiah contain (2 Kings 19:10–13)?
2. What did Sennacherib tell Hezekiah about God (2 Kings 19:10)? What had Isaiah told Hezekiah about God (2 Kings 19:6)?
3. What was Hezekiah's primary concern in this situation (2 Kings 19:16)? What does that tell you about him?
4. What can you discover about people's true beliefs when they're going through good times? When they're going through difficult times?
5. Hezekiah acknowledged that what Sennacherib had said about destroying other gods and nations was true (2 Kings 19:17–18). But what else did he say was true (2 Kings 19:18*b*?)
6. What was Hezekiah's reason for wanting deliverance from the Assyrian threat (2 Kings 19:19)? Why would most people be looking for deliverance? What can you learn about Hezekiah from this verse? What does this say to you about your own priorities as a believer?

Thursday

Responding to the Word
2 Kings 22–23

Josiah's reign of thirty-one years, from the tender age of eight to age thirty-nine when he was killed in battle with the Egyptians, shines as a lonely bright spot in the last centuries of the nation of Judah. His father and grandfather before him (2 Kings 21) as well as his sons after him (2 Kings 23:31–37) did evil in God's sight.

Sandwiched between ancestors and descendants who were wicked and idolatrous, Josiah somehow gained a love for God and a desire to do right that stayed with him throughout his reign. When he had been king eighteen years, the law of God, which had been ignored and lost, was rediscovered. When Josiah heard the words, he was stunned by the truth of his sin and the sin of the people of Judah. He knew they deserved God's anger for their disobedience. Josiah's tender heart responded with humility and repentance before God (2 Kings 22:11, 19).

When you're faced with your sin, what's your first response? Do you think you're being accused unfairly? Do you tend to scoff and go your own way? Do you try to ignore the condemnation you know deep down is deserved?

Or when you're faced with your sin, do you respond as Josiah did—with tears of humility and repentance? The Bible is filled with stories of those who responded both ways. The choice is yours. Please don't pass it off as something you'll deal with later. Or worse, something you don't have to deal with. The stories of Judah and Israel reveal in staggering clarity the danger in ignoring the choice before you. Join with Josiah and his ancestor, Joshua, and "choose for [yourself] this day whom you will serve . . . But as for me and my house, we will serve the LORD" (Joshua 24:15 NKJV).

Friday

Praying the Word
2 Kings 20:1–11

Imagine Hezekiah's surprise when Isaiah returned to his sick room and told him his prayer would be answered. Even when it seemed as if God had to change His mind to answer, answer He did. And wonderfully! You can trust God to do the same thing for you. When your prayer seems like it would be next to impossible to fulfill even for God, He hears and He answers. Not always in the way you would expect, not always in your timing, but He always answers. What is your most outrageous prayer request? What do you want or need God to do in your life that would take a miracle to fulfill? Spend your time in prayer today asking and believing God for its realization. Use your own words to describe your need to God, then use the words of Mark 11:24 and Matthew 6:10 to frame your belief in God's ability to fulfill it and your desire for His perfect will in your life.

Father God, I lay my request before You today. With a humble heart I acknowledge that You alone are God, that You alone can fulfill this request. I believe in You, Lord. But even more, I trust You to decide what is best for me. More than the fulfillment of my request, I want Your will in my life. In Jesus' name, Amen.

Week Seventeen

Elijah and Elisha

Monday

Reading the Word
1 Kings 17–19; 21; 2 Kings 2; 4–7

THE STORY

King Ahab slumped down in his seat under the shade of his canopy. He watched with hooded eyes as the prophets of Baal became more and more frenzied in their attempts to call down fire on their sacrifice. He groaned as God's prophet Elijah began to mock Baal's prophets, then Baal himself. Where was Queen Jezebel when he needed her? She would set this troublemaker Elijah straight in a hurry.

What was he doing now? Ahab watched as Elijah ordered water to be poured over his sacrifice. This was ridiculous. When there was a drought, such a wanton waste of water should be punished. Ahab began to rise from his seat, until he saw Elijah raise his hands toward heaven and begin to pray. Ahab collapsed back on his chair, wondering what would happen next. Would Elijah's simple prayer bring fire down on his altar when the Baal prophets' frantic dancing and shouting and cutting didn't bring any response?

He heard it coming before it hit. A thin whirr then a high pitched shriek pierced Ahab's ears just before he saw the ball of fire explode on Elijah's altar. He shielded his eyes to watch as the flames consumed the sacrifice, the water, the wood, and even the stones. Ahab shook with the knowledge that only a God who was living and active could do such things.

THE MESSAGE

Throughout the history of the Old Testament God used prophets to speak to His people. Elijah and Elisha both ministered to the people of Israel, telling them to turn away from their sin and obey God. In the face of hardship, danger, even the possibility of death, they both faithfully spoke God's message to His people.

THE MAIN POINT

As is true throughout Israel's history, obedience is the main point. That's all God is looking for from His people. Elijah and Elisha reiterated this truth again and again as they talked to Israel. Their instructions on obedience are just as true for you as they were for Israel. God is looking for people who will obey Him.

TAKE NOTE

1 Kings 21:1—In Judah's mountainous regions, growing grain in large fields wasn't always possible. So the people grew viny plants, especially grapes. They used the grapes to make juice and wine, they dried the grapes into raisin cakes, and they used the sugar from the grapes to sweeten food. Because vineyards were such an important part of their agriculture, healthy vines came to represent prosperity and well-being.

2 Kings 5:1—Leprosy, a common disease in early Bible times, manifested itself in gross physical deformity, social banishment, and hopelessness. Because there was no known cure, a miracle was the only hope for those struck by this dreadful disease. Moses' laws included strict instructions on handling the disease in community (Leviticus 13).

Tuesday

Reflecting on the Word
1 Kings 17:1–24

First he ate bird food, and then he ate flour and oil cooked by a woman who wasn't even an Israelite. But Elijah ate when others in Israel were starving.

God gave Elijah the disagreeable task of telling King Ahab that because of the people's continued apostasy no rain or dew would fall in the land for the next few years. In a society dependent on its crops for food, no rain or dew was a death sentence. Elijah and Ahab both recognized that many would starve.

The king and his evil queen had led the people away from the worship of God to the worship of Baal. This false god, whose worship was supposed to bring fertile crops, brought just the opposite: drought, stunted growth in the fields, and disaster. God would no longer look the other way while His people ignored Him. But, while others starved, God provided in a miraculous way for Elijah.

God first sent Elijah to a brook that ran through a ravine east of the Jordan River. He drank the water that ran in the stream and ate the bread and meat brought to him twice daily by ravens sent from God. Ravens are large birds, members of the crow family, who will eat any food they can find. God used them to provide for Elijah.

Eventually, however, with no rain, the stream dried up. And God sent Elijah off to Zarephath, a Philistine city about sixty miles from Elijah's hometown of Tishbe. There, in a foreign land, God provided for Elijah as well as a hospitable woman and her son by keeping a handful of flour and a little oil at a constant level in their jugs. No matter how often the woman used them to put together meager meals for Elijah, her son, and herself, the flour and oil never ran out.

The lure of the story is in its contrasts. While others had little to drink, Elijah drank fresh water from a stream. While others futilely grubbed in the ground for the last of the produce, Elijah ate meat and bread brought to him by ravens and then by a woman who was willing to share what she thought was her last meal. When the cupboards and baskets of others were empty, Elijah always had just enough flour and oil for one more meal. While others ignored God in their efforts to make the land or Baal produce food, God provided for His faithful servant Elijah.

Wednesday

Studying the Word
1 Kings 19:1–8

Sometimes life throws you a curve ball. Sometimes, even when things are going great, you feel like you're totally out of the game. After his phenomenal success on Mount Carmel, roundly defeating the pranks of the prophets of Baal, Elijah sank into a pit of despair. Read through this portion of his story and then answer these questions to discover where and how he found relief. And how you can as well.

1. What had Elijah done to make Queen Jezebel so angry with him (1 Kings 18:16–38; 19:1–2)?

2. Why, after such success, do you think Jezebel's threats made him afraid (1 Kings 19:3)? What did Elijah do in response to her threats?

3. What makes you afraid? What do you do when you're afraid?

4. How deep was Elijah's anguish (1 Kings 19:4)? What words do you use to express yourself when you're feeling down? What actions do you use? What attitudes come out when you're depressed?

5. Compare 1 Kings 18:42, 46 and 19:5. What do these verses tell you contributed to Elijah's feelings?

6. Name the three ways that the angel ministered to Elijah (1 Kings 19:6). How do those three things also minister to you when you are feeling down?

7. After the rest, food, and drink, the angel told Elijah to do something. What was the first word of his instruction to Elijah (1 Kings 19:7)? Why was that word important to Elijah? To you?

Thursday

Responding to the Word
2 Kings 5:1–15

But. That one three-letter word changed everything about Naaman's life. Successful soldier, influential statesman, prominent leader—all the successes of Naaman's life were stripped bare by that one little word. Because in addition to all of his successes, Naaman had leprosy. All of his achievements meant nothing in the face of this disease and its horrid deformities.

A man of influence in Syria, Naaman had little to do with the people of Israel other than to conquer them. At one point in his battles, he took a young girl captive and brought her home to be his wife's slave. Rather than responding with bitterness to her situation, celebrating her master's misfortune, she responded with compassion. Her words revealed not just knowledge of how his disease could be healed but an intense desire for him to be healed.

The only act required of Naaman was to dip himself seven times in the Jordan River. Not much more than a grubby stream in his estimation, Naaman reacted with anger and stomped off. He expected something more thrilling, perhaps? More suited to his position as a leader in Syria? Whatever the reason for his anger, Naaman's servants used simple logic to convince him to take a dip in the Jordan, where he found the healing he so desperately sought.

Each of the people involved in this story of healing—from Naaman to the king to the slave girl to Elisha—had a task to do, a role to fulfill. The obedience required from each serves to emphasize again the primary focus of the history of Israel and Judah. Obedience is paramount.

If someone were to record your history, the story of your life, would obedience be the focus? Would your steady obedience to God be apparent? Or does your story need to be rewritten? Praise God—it can be! How your story reads now is not how it has to conclude. You can begin today to write a life history of loving obedience to God. Think of what

The Women's Devotional Guide to the Bible

you'd like that story of obedience to be about, then ask God for His power in your life to make it come true.

Friday

Praying the Word
1 Kings 19:11–13

How does God speak to His people today? Is it ever anything like He spoke in these verses to Elijah? Check out this scene on the mountain, and you'll pick up a few clues to hearing God's voice in your life.

First, Elijah had to be available. He had to be where God wanted him (1 Kings 19:11). If you're living in a place or in a way that you know isn't pleasing to God, you won't be able to hear His voice.

Second, Elijah had to be quiet (1 Kings 19:12). That's the only way to hear a whisper. You can't hear a whisper if you're already talking. You can only hear the whispers of God when you're silent.

Third, Elijah had to get rid of distraction (1 Kings 19:13). He covered his eyes with his cloak. Do whatever you have to do to remove distractions from your listening. Cover your eyes. Or look at something peaceful and soothing. Turn off the radio and TV. Reduce the clamor of your life in order to induce the sound of the whisper of God.

Fourth, Elijah had to take the time to hear God's voice. The events of these verses didn't happen quickly. Learning to recognize God's voice takes time.

Today, rather than praying with words, pray with silence. Spend your time today in stillness before God. Focus on Him. Let your whole being be filled with an awareness of His presence in your life. Then listen for His voice, for His quiet whisper.

Lord, speak to me. I'm listening . . .

Ezra and Nehemiah Lead the People Home

Monday

Reading the Word
Ezra 1–3; Nehemiah 1–6; 8

THE STORY

Zerubbabel walked slowly around the foundation that had been laid for the temple, inspecting the stones and their shape and placement one last time. As he walked, the priests and people began to gather to celebrate this milestone. They had been back in Jerusalem a little more than a year, and their dream of a rebuilt temple was finally being fulfilled. Coming full circle to the front of the temple, Zerubbabel waited as the Levites took their places with horns and cymbals. Excitement bubbled up in Zerubbabel as he heard the first notes of praise to God: "He is good, for His mercy endures forever!" The hundreds of exiles who had returned to Jerusalem joined in the praise, not just grateful for the new temple, but grateful that God had brought them back to their land.

The smile on Zerubbabel's face, however, slowly turned to confusion. He could hear the laughter and praise coming from the people. But mixed in, and just as loud, Zerubbabel could hear crying and wailing. As he looked around at the people, Zerubbabel recognized immediately what was happening. All those who were praising were young. They had been born in captivity and hadn't seen the magnificence of Solomon's temple. Only those old enough to have seen the former temple were crying. They could see that this new temple wouldn't compare with the one that had been destroyed by the Babylonians. Zerubbabel closed his eyes and simply absorbed the cacophony of sound, knowing that in his heart he too felt like both laughing for the good of what was happening and crying over all they had lost.

THE MESSAGE

Judah hadn't been abandoned by God. He had punished them for their continued sin and their refusal to repent and turn back to Him. But He also had promised, especially through the prophet Jeremiah, that He would bring them back to their homeland after a time (Jeremiah 23:3; 25:8–12). That promise had now been fulfilled when the first groups of exiles were allowed to leave Babylon and return to Judah.

THE MAIN POINT

Abandonment is simply something that God doesn't do. He's promised never to leave or forsake those who love Him (Psalm 9:10; Hebrews 13:5). Though He may punish or discipline, always for your good and growth (Hebrews 12:5–11), He won't desert you.

TAKE NOTE

Ezra 1:5—Those who returned to Judah from exile in Babylon formed a minority of those who were living there at the time. Close to seventy years had passed since the destruction of Jerusalem. Many of those living in Babylon had been born there and had never seen Judah. They had become accustomed to and comfortable with their lives in Babylon and had no wish to uproot and move to what was now a foreign land.

Nehemiah 1:11b—Nehemiah's position as the king's cupbearer required him to taste all food and drink for the king to be sure the food was suitable and had not been poisoned. Because a king's cupbearer played such a significant role in the king's everyday life, he was often in close relationship with the king and had privileges others might not have enjoyed.

Tuesday

Reflecting on the Word
Nehemiah 3

Nehemiah's inspiring example of godly leadership is recorded in detail in this chapter of his book. Nehemiah combined practical activity with a passion for God, an unbeatable combination when facing a task as staggering as this one. He didn't just go ahead and begin the work, trusting in his ability to motivate the people. Nor did he simply stand around, waiting for God to move. He combined his spiritual fervor with action. Nehemiah marshaled all those most affected by the wall and got them individually to work on the portion most important to them, that is, the broken down wall closest to where they lived and worked. No professional wall builders here. No engineers to design a beautiful and strong structure. No specially designed tools. Just one person and his (or her!— see Nehemiah 3:12) neighbors, going to work each day, putting one stone on top of another.

In an area where invading armies were a real and frequent threat, city walls were built as a defense for property and the people who lived in the city and its surrounding villages. Naturally, the higher and stronger the wall, the better the protection it provided. The small city of Mizpah in Judah had a city wall that was thirty-five feet high and fifteen to twenty feet thick. Only the smallest villages didn't have a wall of protection around them.

When Nehemiah was still in Persia, he heard the bad news that the walls of Jerusalem had not been rebuilt and the people who had returned there were discouraged. He immediately recognized that the dangers they faced were not only physical but also emotional and spiritual. The longer they went without defense the more likely they would be assimilated into the peoples around them. Losing their identity as God's special people would be even more tragic than the exile from which they had just returned.

Nehemiah arrived on the scene to save the day. Trusting in God for success (Nehemiah 2:20) and in the people as teammates (Nehemiah 4:6), they began to rebuild. The undertaking was monumental in size, the people got tired and worried, the detractors offered only discouragement, but Nehemiah never gave up. Offering encouragement and protection, trumpet signals and long hours, they rebuilt Jerusalem's walls in just fifty-two days (Nehemiah 6:15). Everyone involved, Nehemiah included, realized that this great work had been accomplished only because God had given His help and blessing (Nehemiah 6:16).

Wednesday

Studying the Word
Nehemiah 8:1–9

The people—men, women, and probably older children—stood for about five hours as Ezra read God's Word aloud to them. The service they held that day, and for seven more days (Nehemiah 8:18), celebrated their release from captivity and their renewed commitment to following God.

1. What books of the Bible make up the "Law of Moses" (Nehemiah 8:1)? How long do you guess it would take to read all five of these books out loud?

2. Why would the people specifically ask Ezra to read (Nehemiah 8:1) and be especially attentive (Nehemiah 8:3) at this time?

3. How long do you think you could *stand* (Nehemiah 8:5, 7) and listen to a reading of God's Word? How much do you think you would actually hear and digest? How much would you be thinking about your aching feet?

4. What did the congregation of people do as well as listen (Nehemiah 8:6)?

5. What did the Levites do for the people (Nehemiah 8:8)? Why do you think this was necessary? How might this compare with the sermons pastors preach today?

6. How did the people respond when they understood what was being read (Nehemiah 8:9)? Why do you think they responded in this way? How was this different from the people's response before they went into captivity? What does that tell you about the discipline that God sometimes metes out?

7. How often does the knowledge of your sinfulness before God (and, as Scripture reminds, *everyone* [Romans 3:23] is sinful) reduce you to sincere sorrow? What can you do about it (2 Corinthians 7:9–10)?

Thursday

Responding to the Word
Nehemiah 8:10

Throw a party! Bring out the band. Bake a cake. Today is a day for joy.

Sure you've got sorrow and sadness in your life because of your sin. Sure you're repentant before God for the wrong things you've done. But your strength is not in your sorrow. Your strength is in your joy.

And that's truly good news.

The writer of Ecclesiastes reminds you that there is "a time to weep, and a time to laugh; a time to mourn, and a time to dance" (Ecclesiastes 3:4 NKJV). Nehemiah wanted God's people not to get caught up in grief and misery over how they hadn't measured up to His law. Instead, they needed to be joyful, to celebrate the goodness of a God who was ready and eager to forgive.

Hundreds of years later, Paul reminded his readers of the same thing. He was happy because their sorrow led them to repent. Sorrow that brings a person down, wallowing in despair and discouragement, accomplishes little. However, sorrow that causes a person to repent is a cause for joy—and brings strength with it.

Christ offers abundant life to all who follow Him (John 10:10). He didn't come to bring a spirit of doom or gloom. He didn't offer His life so that your life would be filled with the burden of somehow paying Him back for His sacrifice. He came so that you could find enjoyment, peace, and a strong sense of purpose in following Him.

Today, offer to God whatever may be drawing you down into pain or misery or remorse. Replace those negative emotions with His Spirit of joy and gladness. Instead of your sin and your failings, focus your eyes on Jesus and the joyful strength He offers.

Friday

Praying the Word
Nehemiah 2:4

Nehemiah stood in the presence of the king—probably surrounded by advisors, guests, and others—and prayed to God. No quiet room. No kneeling. No closed eyes or folded hands. No word spoken out loud. Just a quick prayer for help sent up to God. And He answered Nehemiah immediately.

You can pray wherever, whenever you need immediate help, support, or comfort from God. Whether you're in a boardroom, a classroom, a home, or a car—pray. If it's three in the morning or five in the evening—pray. Whether you're alone, with a few family members or friends, or in a crowd—pray.

Be sure to note that Nehemiah's prayer life was made up of more than these quickie prayers, however. Most of the first chapter of Nehemiah is devoted to one of Nehemiah's concentrated times of fasting and prayer, this one lasting "many days" (Nehemiah 1:4 NKJV).

As you go through this week, pray at times when you wouldn't ordinarily pray. When a person enters your mind or when a need springs up, pray about it. Immediately! Do it deliberately, asking God to meet some immediate need. And trust Him to respond.

Omnipresent God, wherever I am, I know You're there. I also know Your ears are always waiting to hear from me. Nudge me to pray at times when I wouldn't usually pray, keeping the lines of communication with You open. Thank You for listening and answering my prayers, even those shot up to You in quick and immediate need. Amen.

Week Nineteen

Esther Saves Her People

Monday

Reading the Word
Esther 1–10

THE STORY

Esther laid her head back and tried to relax as one young servant girl worked fragrant oil through her hair and another massaged her feet. But as relaxed as her body may have appeared, Esther's mind was in turmoil. She had just gotten news from her uncle Mordecai about a sinister plot to destroy all the Jews in Persia. Mordecai seemed to think Esther was their only hope. As queen of Persia, Esther had many privileges. But running to the king with every problem wasn't one of them. If the king wasn't pleased to see her, he could simply decide to have her killed.

Esther thought about the former queen, Vashti, and knew her position wasn't as secure as some might think. Had God actually put her here just so that she could save her people? Did He actually work that way? And did He expect her to take such a risk? Esther rubbed her aching head. There was just so much at stake here. The back of her neck prickled with fear when she thought of going to see the king without being invited. But deep down, Esther's decision had already been made. She would go to the king, invitation or no. She would reveal the plot to destroy all the Jews in the land. And when he asked why she cared, she would reveal her full identity—that she, Esther, was actually Hadassah, a Jew.

THE MESSAGE

Esther was beautiful. But she didn't become queen because of that. Esther was gracious. But she didn't become queen because of that. Esther pleased King Ahasuerus, but she didn't even become queen because of that. She became queen because God needed her in that position, where she could act to save her people, the Jews. All throughout her childhood with Mordecai and her preparations to go from the harem to be with the king, God was preparing Esther for her moment of destiny.

THE MAIN POINT

God uses His people to bring about His purposes. In this case, God used Esther to save His people from annihilation. She was put into her position as queen "for such a time as this" (Esther 4:14 NKJV). God has a special purpose for you as well. You may not be a queen who steps in to save her people, but you're the exact mother God chose for your children, you're the exact woman for the job in your workplace or church, you're the one God wants to use.

TAKE NOTE

Esther 1–10—Esther is the only book of the Bible where the name of God does not appear. That omission has caused some to question its place in the Bible. However, the fact that God's name doesn't appear in Esther in no way diminishes its importance or place. The events of the book reveal a God who is at work, involved in the lives of His people and concerned for their protection.

Tuesday

Reflecting on the Word
Esther 2:8–9

How about twelve months of beauty treatments for you? Add seven maids ready to do your bidding. Include oils and perfumes and cosmetics prepared just for you. Then add long, warm baths, good food, and no responsibility except to make yourself look beautiful. Sound good?

That was life in a harem. But harems in ancient times weren't always the happiest or most relaxing places. Those in harems were often young girls, abducted from their homes and brought to the harem simply for the pleasure of the king. And since the women outnumbered the king hundreds to one, the competition for his attention caused jealousy and hostility.

In a sea of beautiful faces and bodies in the harem in Shushan, Esther blended in with all the others. She didn't remain that way, however. First, she gained the attention and favor of the head of the harem. He moved her to the best part of the harem, where she would be insulated from the contention that was almost certainly part of everyday life there. As others got to know Esther, she gained favor and special treatment from them as well. Then, of course, there was the king. He was so enamored with her that of all the women in his harem, he chose her to be his queen.

Was all this success due purely to Esther's beauty? Highly unlikely. A beautiful woman in a harem is about as likely to stand out as one apple in a bushel of apples. Something other than her good looks made Esther stand out from the others and gain the favor of those around her. Was it a gracious demeanor? A keen mind? A compassionate nature? A ready smile? A contented countenance? Scripture doesn't tell us. One thing is certain, however. Esther made the most of her situation. She obeyed Mordecai, her uncle. She pleased the leaders of the harem and the king. And she willingly put her life on the line for her people.

You have more in common with Esther than you might think. Seriously! You do! You may not have seven maids to do your bidding, you may not have a queen's crown to wear, and you may not have a king for a husband. But you do have a special place in the kingdom of God and a special usefulness to Him in His plan. You are *where* you are and you are *who* you are for just "such a time as this."

Wednesday

Studying the Word
Esther 4:1–14

Esther was relatively secure in her royal position when Mordecai asked her to put herself at risk by going to see the king without an invitation. She struggled with his request, then realized his words (in Esther 4:14) were true. She willingly put herself in danger in order to save her people. Read her story and discover how you can follow her example and allow God to use you in your own particular situation.

1. Why was Mordecai so distraught (Esther 4:1)? Why were the Jews in Persia troubled as well (Esther 4:3)?
2. Why do you think Esther knew nothing about what was going on (Esther 4:4–5)? As the queen, wouldn't she be informed of such edicts?
3. Why do you think Esther had to have the edict explained to her (Esther 4:8*a*)? How much schooling do you think she might have had? Do you think she would have even known how to read? Why or why not?
4. What did Mordecai want Esther to do (Esther 4:8*b*)?
5. What was Esther's response to this news (Esther 4:9–11)? How dangerous do you think going into the king's presence uninvited actually was?

6. How do you think you might have responded to a similar request? What sorts of things are you afraid to do that you think God might want you to do anyway?

7. Mordecai's response in Esther 4:14 has gone down in history as a great lesson in being willing to be used by God. How do you think God might want to use you in the position you now hold, whatever that might be?

8. Do you think God actually works this way? Review all the events that had to take place before Esther was even put into her position as queen. What events in your life might be preparation for the work God has for you to do?

Thursday

Responding to the Word
Esther 10:3

Mordecai often takes a back seat to Esther in this great story of redemption for the Jews. Esther stands out as the star, Mordecai as the supporting actor. Esther was, of course, the one who put her life on the line. But Mordecai was no slouch. The final words of the book of Esther are a tribute to his character as well as his accomplishments.

As second only to the king in Persia, Mordecai didn't use his position of power to gain wealth or status for himself. He didn't forget his heritage as a Jew. And he didn't overlook his fellow Jews. Although he was part of a nation of dispossessed people, captives in the land of Persia and far from their homeland in Israel, Mordecai used his position to do good for his people.

What's the lesson here for you? Whatever your position, use it to do good for those around you rather than to gain anything for yourself. Nothing shows the character of a leader more quickly than when he or she has power and authority and uses it to help others rather than gain anything for self.

A more contemporary, but similar individual, is George Washington. He won the Revolutionary War in the United States without adequately trained, fed, or clothed troops. After the war he was elected president of the new country. The people offered to make him their king. He refused. They offered to make him president-for-life. He refused. His sole goal and purpose was to bring good to the people of this fledgling country, not to gain power or wealth for himself.

You may not be a Mordecai or a George; your position may not have nearly the authority theirs had. But you do have the power to do good to those around you. Whether it is in your family, your workplace, or your neighborhood, seek opportunities to do good. Follow the ultimate example of One who had amazing authority and power, yet gave it up in order to help those around Him: "Jesus . . . went about doing good" (Acts 10:38 NKJV).

Friday

When Esther faced a difficult situation, a possibly deadly one, she asked Mordecai and the Jews in Shushan to pray and also to fast for three days and nights. Esther and her maids fasted also. Their goal was to prepare themselves for Esther's interview with the king. The New Testament recommends fasting also, as when the church in Antioch prepared to send out Paul and Barnabas as missionaries (Acts 13:2–3). Today, consider fasting in order to clear your mind and body of all hungers except for your hunger for God, or fasting in order to present a special request to God. Whether you fast now or sometime later, it's a spiritual discipline that will deepen your communion with God.

Dear Savior, as You fasted in the desert before You began Your ministry, I offer my fast to You as a picture of my desire to be more like You, to live in closer communion with You. Help me to clear my mind and body of all that gets in the way of my desire for You. Amen.

Week Twenty

The Story of Job

Monday

Reading the Word
Job 1–3; 10:1–7; 16:1–5; 19:23–27; 38:1–15; 42

THE STORY

Tears spilled from Job's eyes, the salty liquid stinging the open sores on his face. He picked up a piece of broken pottery and used its sharp edge to scratch the sores on his arms and legs. He hurt everywhere, but even worse than the pain from the sores was the agony in his heart from losing all of his children in a great windstorm. His wealth was gone, as was his health. But neither of those hurt like losing his children. A ragged moan came from deep within Job as he struggled to understand all that had happened. What had he done to deserve such an outpouring of trouble? Job collapsed on the ground, his body seeming to shrink into the dust with his despair.

THE MESSAGE

Throughout the story of Job and the pain he suffered from the events outlined in the first two chapters as well as from friends who came to accuse rather than comfort, God was behind the scenes, watching all. Contrary to what we'd like to have happen in Job's life and in our own, God didn't step in to fix it and make it all better. But He did eventually speak. And though He left most questions unanswered, He did reassure Job of His love and His belief in Job's blamelessness. God's words humbled Job and helped him recognize that God was bigger than all his questions, answered and unanswered (Job 42:1–6).

THE MAIN POINT

Take God at His word. When He says He'll work "all things . . . together for good to those who love God" (Romans 8:28 NKJV), He means it. In the middle of all the difficulties and sorrows and pain that life can throw your way, you are not alone. God is with you. Even more, He's willing, if you'll allow it, to use those troubles to make something good, to create something bigger with your life and character than all the good times could ever produce. As much as you might hate the pain and want to get rid of the sorrow and want to go back to life as you knew it before trouble came your way, watch Job and follow his example.

TAKE NOTE

Job 1:1—The land of Uz was probably a region east of Canaan, a fertile land, judging by Job's wealth in cattle. When the story of Job took place is uncertain, but historical references cause many scholars to place it around the time of Abraham. It may have been a story that was passed down orally for many generations and only written down long after it took place.

Job 41:1—The leviathan referred to here was probably a crocodile or some other large and fierce creature. The exact species isn't certain. What is sure, however, is that it was a creature that only God could tame and use for His purposes.

Tuesday

Reflecting on the Word
Job 2:11–13

Job's three friends heard of all that had happened to him and came to mourn with him and to comfort him. Their first act was their best act—total silence. When they later opened their mouths and disgorged all their combined lack of wisdom on the reasons for Job's sufferings, they quickly obliterated this first positive action.

When Job's three friends arrived, they barely recognized him. The grief and illness he suffered had taken their toll on his appearance. They immediately began to show the customary signs of extreme grief: tearing their clothes, crying out loud, and tossing dust or ashes on their heads. Collapsing next to Job, they shared his grief. And they were blessedly silent.

Jeremiah's book of Lamentations, a book of mourning, also talks about silence in the face of extreme distress. The elders of Jerusalem sat silent in the face of the city's destruction and suffering before Judah went into captivity. Like Job's friends, they also sprinkled dust on their heads (Lamentations 2:10). Such an act might seem a bit foolish to you. Whatever do particles of dust have to do with mourning? You also might be uncomfortable with the loud weeping with which mourners in eastern lands still express themselves. And tearing clothes? Well, that may seem like carrying things just a bit too far.

However, silence is something everyone from every culture can appreciate. Often silence is the best comforter. Words only serve to diminish the trouble of the one who suffers, as the speechifying of Job's friends later revealed. Compassionate quiet usually offers more solace than words. When you visit a friend who is mourning or who is going through a difficult time, remember to use words sparingly, if at all.

Wednesday

Studying the Word
Job 1

The book of Job's torment creates a transition between the books recording Israel's history and the books of poetry and prophecy. Its tough lessons are the same as those faced by thousands of individuals. What is a proper response to God when life doesn't make sense? Read the first chapter of Job and then answer the following questions. You may not find the answer to life's hardest situations (Job never did), but you will discover from Job how an upright person faces those situations.

1. Was Job a perfect man or just a good one (Job 1:1)?
2. Why is Job's wealth at the beginning of the story important (Job 1:2–3)?
3. How seriously did Job take his duties as a father (Job 1:4–5)? What lessons as a parent can you learn from these verses about Job?
4. How did God view Job (Job 1:8)? Why would God point Job's righteousness out to Satan?
5. How did Satan respond (Job 1:9–10)? What part did Job's wealth play in his righteousness?
6. What did Satan think would cause Job to turn his back on God (Job 1:11–19)?
7. How did Job respond (Job 1:20–22)? Place yourself in Job's situation. What would be the hardest part of all that happened? Realistically and honestly, how do you think you would respond if faced with similar events? What would you say to God?
8. While comfort during terrifying and terrible events may be hard to find, what do Psalm 34:18 and Lamentations 3:21–24 tell you? What could you gain from remembering these verses when suffering comes your way?

9. Review Romans 8:28. How does God use the negative events of life to bring about your good? Is that good always easy to find? What sort of suffering might make this verse difficult even when you know it to be true?

Thursday

Responding to the Word
Job 38:1–15

After pages and pages of discussion by Job and his friends, God spoke. Finally. He came to Job and his friends in a storm, somehow communicating so they could hear and clearly understand. Rather than answering all the questions they had raised, however, God asked a few questions of His own, using His queries to point out His ultimate authority and power and sovereignty—and their lack of it.

Job's friends' mistake was their assumption of Job's sin. They assumed that good things happen to good people and bad things happen to bad people. But their simple equation wasn't accurate at all. God reprimanded Job's friends for their lack of compassion and understanding.

Job's only mistake was in his ignorance of God's ways. He knew he was innocent, that he didn't deserve the punishment he had suffered in the form of all his losses. He assumed God was angry with him. Unlike the readers of the book, Job had no knowledge of Satan's audience with God, recorded in chapters 1 and 2.

The questions God asks throughout Job 38–41 served only to put Job and his friends in their proper places, and God in His. God's power was greater than their power. God's knowledge superceded their own. God's understanding of life's events eclipsed any reasoning they might have produced.

Job never really received a reason for his suffering. God didn't share with Job the role of Satan in those sufferings. Nor did Job ever discover that all of this had happened because God was *proud* of Job. Yes! Read Job 1:8 again to discover how God felt about Job.

In the face of your own troubles and trials and suffering, are answers what you truly want? Or do you want to know that God is still in control when the events of your life seem like they're spinning out of control? Do you want to know that God loves you when the events of your life seem to demonstrate the opposite? Do you want reasons? Or do you want God? Job didn't get answers, but he did get the reality and pleasure and comfort of God's presence. And it was enough (Job 42:5).

Friday

Praying the Word
Job 19:23–27

No matter that his world was falling apart around him, Job found relief and comfort in the knowledge of a future that included a living Redeemer. When all was said and done, his Redeemer would bring comfort and vindication. In the end—all the traumas of his life past—Job would see God. God! Himself! In the best of times, but especially in the worst of times, that goal was something his heart yearned for.

Does your heart yearn like Job's? Do the things of this life—good and bad—pale in comparison to knowing and seeing your Redeemer? Spend time in prayer today thanking Him for the eternal perspective God can give to your life.

My Lord and my God, You are my living Redeemer, my Savior. I praise You for giving me the promise of eternity, that all the events of earth are but a preparation for forever with You. I give You my days filled with peace and contentment and my days filled with trouble and heartache. I love You, Lord. Amen.

David's Poetry

Monday

Reading the Word
Psalms 8–9; 13–25; 27–28; 37;
51–52; 57; 86; 103; 139

THE STORY

David sat with his back against the tree, its shade offering cool relief from the heat of the sun. He sighed when he looked around him and realized that he was finally alone. The work of a king was never done. The advisors and pleaders and hangers-on were forever crowding him, forming a cacophony of noise and busyness that drained his mind and heart. He needed solitude. Serenity. Only then could his mind function and his heart fill with a sense of God's presence. A longing pierced David's chest with a pain that was physical, a longing for the days of quiet in the fields with his father's sheep. Just as had happened often then, words and images began to float through David's mind, expressions of all that he was feeling and experiencing. A soft smile creased his weathered face. David recognized the words and images as another poem forming in his mind, working its way out of his heart.

THE MESSAGE

David wrote seventy-three of the psalms, the songs and poetry of the people of Israel. Spilling all of his feelings—anger, joy, fear, remorse—with a looseness of tongue that at times is almost discomforting, David exposed his true inner self in his poetry. He stood before his readers and God with all his best and worst characteristics bared.

THE MAIN POINT

In the psalms, David modeled the freedom of expression that God allows His people. You can be as free as David with God, expressing all that you're feeling and experiencing and thinking, without reservation, knowing that God filters it all through His eyes of love. Your God is a big God. He can handle your worst as well as your best. He already knows you more intimately than you know yourself. With God, you are free to strip away all the falsity, the pretense that all is well when it isn't, the facades you so easily wear for others. You never need to be afraid to bare your true self before God, as David did.

TAKE NOTE

Psalm 3:1 subtitle—"A psalm of David." The poems of the Hebrew people are called *psalms*, from the Greek word *psalmoi*, meaning "twangings, as of stringed instruments." The Hebrew name for the book of Psalms is *Tehillim*, meaning praises. Much of the book of Psalms is made up of writings that praise God for His strength, His goodness, His watchful care.

Tuesday

Reflecting on the Word
Psalm 18:1–3

How often when you think of a safe place do you think of a fortress or a huge rock where you can take shelter? Probably not too often. You're more likely to think of your home, perhaps with the doors locked, the dog ready to bark at the slightest noise, the alarm system set. Or perhaps you think of your basement in a storm.

David thought in very different terms. When he was running from King Saul, he often took refuge in places that were fortified—cities and towns with high, strong walls and towers from which to see and fight the enemy (1 Samuel 23:14, 29). When such a place was not available, he took refuge among the huge rocks of the desert, where guerrilla fighting gave him the advantage over his enemies (1 Samuel 23:25).

David's writings resonated with the truth of his situation—before and after he became king. He knew where his true safety resided, and it wasn't in a pile of rocks.

David wrote Psalm 18 after God had provided exceptional protection from Saul. King Saul looked at David as an upstart, a rebel, a threat to his throne and authority. David ran, Saul pursued. Recognizing that his escape from Saul and other enemies came from the hand of God, David wrote the words of this psalm, calling God his fortress and rock.

Martin Luther, the fifteenth-century reformer, acknowledged the same truth when he wrote the words of one of the greatest hymns of all time:

A mighty fortress is our God, a bulwark never failing;
Our helper He, amid the flood of mortal ills prevailing:
For still our ancient foe doth seek to work us woe;
His craft and power are great, and, armed with cruel hate,
On earth is not his equal.
Did we in our own strength confide, our striving would be losing;

Were not the right Man on our side, the Man of God's own
   choosing:
Dost ask who that may be? Christ Jesus, it is He!

Wednesday

Studying the Word
Psalm 103

David's song of praise to God records the confidence and knowledge
of God that is evident in much of his writings. Read through this exceptional psalm of praise, and then answer the following questions to discover deeper meanings in it for your life today.

1. Where did David's praise for God originate (Psalm 103:1)? What
    does this mean? Why would David express himself this way?
2. What five things does God do for those who believe in Him (Psalm
    103:2–5)? Put each of these five things in personal terms: What
    has God done for *you*?
3. If God were to treat you as your sins deserved, what would He do
    to you (Psalm 103:10)? Why do you think He *doesn't* treat you as
    your sins deserve?
4. How much does God love you (Psalm 103:11)? How does that
    make you feel?
5. Where has He put your sins (Psalm 103:12)? How does that
    change how you might feel about your sins?
6. How long does the human life last according to Psalm 103:15–16?
    Does life seem that fleeting to you? Why or why not?
7. How long does God's mercy and love last (Psalm 103:17–18)?
8. Of those who bless the Lord in Psalm 103:20–22, where do you fit
    in? What does it mean for you to bless the Lord?
9. Being very specific, how will you bless God today?

Thursday

Probably recited more often than any other passage of Scripture, Psalm 23 NKJV has provided comfort to millions going through the troubles and tragedies of life. Carefully crafted by poet David, each line of his psalm pictures God's presence and involvement in the lives of His people.

David began by calling God his shepherd, a very personal guide and protector, who provided daily nourishment ("green pastures" and "still waters") and rest ("lie down"), filling his emotional ("He restores my soul") and spiritual ("paths of righteousness") needs. When David went through troubles so severe he called them "the valley of the shadow of death," he didn't travel that road alone. The shepherd went with him, offering comfort, protecting him with His rod and guiding him with His staff. Even when enemies closed in, David could commune with God in safety and security. David closed by exclaiming that God's goodness and mercy were with him all throughout his life—not that he would never face adversity, not that suffering would never come into his life, but that he would never have to handle them alone.

Few people escape the painful suffering that life in a broken world produces. When all you used to be sure of eludes you in the middle of tough times, when tragedy enters your life, when the specter of death visits your family, you can walk with David through this psalm and know that the Shepherd goes with you. The shadowy valley, with its unexpected twists and turns, with its darkness that makes knowing the way difficult, is a valley that you walk with God—not alone.

If you've never memorized this psalm, begin to do so today. Then, when your darkest night arrives, as it most certainly will, the words and truth of David's poem will rise in your mind and heart and speak God's peace and comfort.

Friday

Praying the Word
Psalm 86

David was clear about who he was. He knew his faults and failings as well as his needs and his devotion to God. Many people today spend hours and days and weeks getting to know themselves, a worthy task. But then they miss the other side of the equation. They don't bother to get to know the One who created them, the One who knows them better than any other, the One who loves them. Don't make the same mistake! As David did, learn to know yourself *and* the God who created you. Use the words of David's prayer in Psalm 86 to talk to God about who you are and to praise Him for who He is. Spend some time putting this prayer psalm into your own words, carefully and very personally fitting it to who you are and who you know God to be.

Hear me, O Lord, and be sure to answer me. I'm a needy person in so many ways; I need You most of all. And I'm devoted to You, Lord, fully devoted to following and obeying You all my life. I trust You and ask You to be kind to me and to bring joy to my life. I lift my heart and soul to You, O Lord, for You are forgiving and good. Amen.

Week Twenty-Two

The Other Psalmists

Monday

Reading the Word
Psalms 42; 46–50; 72; 75; 89–90;
100; 121; 149–150

THE STORY

Throughout the time of the Bible, writers other than David used Hebrew poetry to record their praises to God. Solomon and Moses wrote several. Asaph wrote twelve. He led the music of worship in the temple during the time of David and Solomon (1 Chronicles 16:4–6). The sons of Korah were also responsible for quite a few psalms. These men of the tribe of Levi were musicians and doorkeepers in the temple (1 Chronicles 6:22). The book of Psalms forms a collection of Hebrew poetry gathered as well as written over hundreds of years, giving a glimpse into the heart of Israelite praise and worship at different times in their history.

THE MESSAGE

Sound the trumpet! Clang the cymbals! Dance with abandon! Shout out loud! God deserves praise. The psalmists wrote with unrestrained enthusiasm and abandon, praising God for all He was to them and all He had done for them. They offered praises that resounded with superlatives and fully expressed the love of a people for their God.

| 153

THE MAIN POINT

God deserves your praise. As you review your life, both past and present, you'll begin to appreciate all the workings of God in and through events and people and circumstances. As you review, stop along the way to praise God for what He did and what He does. Also, allow the past and present to reveal to you all that God is, thanking Him for being a strong or loving or vigilant or gentle God. Make it a point to spend time each day praising God, following the lead of the psalmists of old.

TAKE NOTE

Psalm 150:3–5—This last psalm mentions several musical instruments common in worship and praise in Old Testament times. The trumpet called the people to worship. It was commonly made of a ram's horn and was called the "shofar." The harp had twelve strings and was played with the fingers. The lute or lyre had ten strings and was played with a pick. Both formed the stringed instrument component of any worship orchestra in the temple. The timbrel, which today is known as a tambourine, provided the rhythm for other instruments or dancing. It was made of a small wooden ring with animal skin stretched across. They didn't have the metal jingles common on tambourines today. The flute or pipe was a common wooden pipe, often used by shepherds to entertain themselves in the fields. The "loud cymbals" in this verse refer to large instruments, one held in each hand. The "clashing cymbals" were probably much smaller, one attached to the thumb and one to the middle finger. Both provided beat and rhythm for temple worship.

Tuesday

Reflecting on the Word
Psalm 48

"Ten measures of beauty descended to the world; nine were taken by Jerusalem and one by the rest of the world" (from the Babylonian Talmud).

The rabbis, who argued and discussed every point of Hebrew law and recorded those discussions in the Talmud, agreed on one thing without reservation: Jerusalem was the most beautiful city in the world.

The "city of our God" (Psalm 48:1 NKJV), Jerusalem, is indisputably the most important city in the history of the world. Located on three hills in central Israel, the northern hill—God's "holy mountain" (Psalm 48:1 NKJV)—was the site of Solomon's famed temple. The first reference to Jerusalem in Scripture occurred when Abraham met the priest Melchizedek, king of Salem (Genesis 14:18). When the Israelites returned to the Promised Land under Joshua's leadership, they were unable to overthrow Jerusalem, and it remained a Jebusite rather than Israelite stronghold until King David and his army defeated it. The Babylonians destroyed the city and Solomon's temple in 597 BC and took many of its people captive. The returning exiles rebuilt the city a century later. It became again the center of Israelite law, culture, and religious activity although usually ruled by a people more powerful than the Jews.

Jesus ministered there during His time on earth and was tried, convicted, and crucified there as well. In 70 AD the city was again destroyed, this time by the Romans. Since that time the city has been ruled by one group of people after another, the Persians, Egyptians, Turks, Crusaders, and British. Still today its safety is fragile with both Jews and Palestinians claiming ownership.

The poet who wrote Psalm 48 praised this city of God and its fortifications. More than the city, however, the psalmist praised her primary resident—God. Although she may have been strong and well fortified, her true strength and beauty came directly from God.

Wednesday

Studying the Word
Psalm 121

Psalm 121 was written to be sung or recited as people approached their favorite city, Jerusalem. They ascended up to it since it sat on three hills and viewed its beauty as they approached. This particular "song of ascent" praised God for being a Helper and Protector of the pilgrims on their way to Jerusalem. Read through it, and then answer the following questions to discover how God is your Helper and Protector.

1. What hills might the psalmist have been referring to in Psalm 121:1–2? Why would he refer to his help coming from these hills? Who lived in the city on these hills?

2. Where do you see your help coming from? How quickly do you recognize the source of your help? Immediately? Or only when trouble gets too great to handle yourself? Why?

3. What sort of protection is offered by a God who doesn't "allow your foot to be moved"—that is, to slip (Psalm 121:3 NKJV)?

4. What comfort can you gain from the fact that the One who watches over you doesn't slumber or sleep (Psalm 121:4)?

5. What sort of protection do you think is meant by the Lord being "your shade at your right hand" (Psalm 121:5 NKJV)?

6. What "evil" has God protected you or your family from (Psalm 121:7)?

7. How has He "preserve[d] your soul" (Psalm 121:7 NKJV)?

Thursday

Food, water, air. These are the most important components of life for animals on earth. When one is missing, everything else fades to the background as the animal fights for food or water or air. The psalmist compares his thirst for God to a deer's thirst for water. When a deer has difficulty finding water, it will spend all its time in the search, focusing only on that one thing, satisfying its thirst.

The psalmist who wrote Psalm 42 was apparently living far from Israel, perhaps in exile, and was denied the most important part of serving and worshiping God, the temple in Jerusalem. His thirst for God grew greater the longer he was away. He recalled the wonderful times of going to Jerusalem and the temple for special religious feasts, enjoying the crowds who were there for the same purpose. He remembered the beautiful hills and valleys of his homeland. And those who ridiculed him because his God seemed absent made his life miserable.

The longer this situation went on, the more intense the psalmist's thirst for God grew. His yearning for God must be fulfilled. Nothing mattered more. Twice, the psalmist gives a glimpse of quenched thirst. He asks himself why he's so troubled. He has total confidence in God, knowing he will eventually fully praise Him and have every longing satisfied.

Be honest with yourself for a moment. How often does your thirst for God equal that of the psalmist? How close does your thirst for God come to the thirst of a deer that has gone for a prolonged time without water? Most believers in today's culture have a certain level of hunger for God, one that drives them to worship and to their Bibles and prayer. But few actually thirst so much for Him that all else—the distractions and attractions of life in today's culture—fades into the background. Ask God to give you a profound hunger and thirst for Him, something that can only be satisfied with well-balanced meals made up of communion with Him.

Friday

Praying the Word
Psalm 100

Whoever wrote this psalm had a particularly good handle on the art of living thankfully and joyfully. Psalm 100 paints a picture of a life filled with delight because God's hand protects and guides His people. Try to spend all of your time in prayer today thanking God, offering Him your gratitude for how He has been your Shepherd in particular ways in your life and how His goodness and love have been shown throughout generations of your family. This particular psalm also easily lends itself to grateful prayer; use the poet's words to express your own heart of gratitude.

Lord of lords, I shout my joy and praise so that even heaven hears. You are my ever-watchful Shepherd, the One I trust with the hearts and lives of all generations of my family. I come to You with a thankful heart and a song of joy. Hallelujah and Amen!

Solomon's Wisdom

Monday

Reading the Word
Proverbs 1–4; 12; 15; 17; 19; 22; 31;
Ecclesiastes 1–3; 12; Song of Solomon 1; 8

THE STORY

Solomon walked slowly through the halls of his palace. The day's heat had gradually dissolved to cool dampness, and the stone floors felt refreshing under his bare feet. Solomon often took these nighttime walks when everyone else was settled and sleeping but sleep eluded him. Restlessness took him from his bed to walk the halls and gardens of his palace. He had everything money could buy and his heart could ever want. His riches surpassed anything anyone had ever known; he had opportunities to read and study; peace reigned in his kingdom for the first time in centuries; he had more beautiful wives and children than he ever expected to have. And still he was restless. Unhappy even. Solomon raised his bowed head, realizing that his meandering had taken him back to his bedroom. He went inside, but rather than climbing into his bed, he walked to his table, picked up his pen, and began to write.

THE MESSAGE

No amount of money or experiences or learning or admiration could take the place of a relationship with God. Solomon, with all he had, found that to be true. If anyone in life could claim success and wealth and a great job and beautiful wives and honor and prestige, that person was Solomon. The same man who penned the desperate words, "Meaningless! Meaningless! . . . Utterly meaningless! Everything is meaningless" (Ecclesiastes 1:2 NIV).

THE MAIN POINT

Without God, all the dollars, the education, the great job, the family mean nothing and offer little fulfillment. With God, a life of poverty and failure and anonymous living can be filled with great satisfaction and meaning. God has a way of turning all this world offers into hollow effort, unless He's at the center of it. But if He has the central position, the efforts, whether successful or not, the money or lack of it, the admiration of others or not, all of it, good or bad, takes on a deep significance and value. That's the abundant life (John 10:10) He offers for the taking!

TAKE NOTE

Proverbs 1:1—A proverb is a short statement of general truth, put into words that will be easier for the reader to recall. When reading these bits and pieces of Solomon's wisdom, remember that proverbs are not promises that you should expect to come true. Instead, proverbs describe in a broad way how life works in most cases, but not always; what results from most actions, but not every time.

Tuesday

Reflecting on the Word
Proverbs 1:1–7

An older grandmother climbs to the top of a stepladder, determined to reach the last fly speck on her window. She teeters and falls.

A mother struggles with her temper-tantrum-throwing daughter, in the middle of the grocery store, of course, and she wonders what to do.

A young woman responds to the advances of the handsome married executive in her office.

All of these women need something called wisdom. Wisdom to know when to climb and when to stay on the ground, when and how to discipline, how to handle sexual advances.

According to Solomon, all these situations in life, as well as many others, require wisdom, which he defined in these first verses of the book of Proverbs. All of the words that accompany wisdom in these verses give insight into exactly what it is. It involves instruction and understanding (Proverbs 1:2), justice and judgment and fairness (Proverbs 1:3), discretion (Proverbs 1:4), and a listening ear (Proverbs 1:5). True wisdom includes a competence for living and decision-making, an ability and desire to follow God's course for life. Of course, all that's often easier said than done. How often have you wished you had the wisdom you needed to handle a particular situation with your child, your husband, a friend or neighbor, a coworker?

Solomon was uniquely qualified to pen this poetic discourse on wisdom. Early in his reign over Israel, Solomon had asked God for wisdom (1 Kings 3:1–15), and God answered his prayer unstintingly, making him the wisest of the wise (1 Kings 4:29–32). He used that wisdom in ruling Israel, in instructing others, and in authoring this book.

No piece of knowledge, no experience, no learning, no occupation, no *thing* is of greater value and will produce wisdom more adequately and fully than fearing God, than honoring and obeying and following

Him. In Him you'll find the foundation of wisdom. In Him you'll discover the skill to unravel life's complexities, to make right decisions, and to live well.

Wednesday

Studying the Word
Proverbs 31:10–31

For many women the words of this proverb seem designed to make them feel inadequate. That is not the intent, of course. Rather than looking at Mrs. Far-Above-Rubies (Proverbs 31:10) as someone to make you feel guilty, look at her as a symbol of a wise woman, an example to follow in the areas where you are gifted. Read these verses carefully and then answer the following questions in order to discover how you're like her—and how you're not.

1. In general terms, how does a "virtuous wife" bring her husband good (Proverbs 31:10, 12, 23 NKJV)? In specific terms, how can you, whether married or not, bring good to the people in your life?

2. This woman had specific gifts in weaving and sewing, using them to decorate her home, to clothe her family, and to sell to others (Proverbs 31:13, 19, 21–22, 24). You may not be an accomplished seamstress, but how can you be wise in how you provide for your home and clothe your family?

3. Mrs. Far-Above-Rubies bought, grew, and provided food for her family and servants (Proverbs 31:14–15). OK, so you probably don't have any servants that you need to feed, but you likely do have a hungry family. As a woman in today's society, how do you go about providing the food your family needs daily? How could you be more wise or creative in preparing that food?

4. This virtuous woman had a good head for business (Proverbs 31:16, 18, 24). If you do also, how do you use that business sense to bless your family? If you don't, hey, that's OK. What gifts *do* you have that you use to bless your family?

5. Moving outside her home, this wise woman generously helped those in need (Proverbs 31:20). What can you do to help those who have less than you? Move beyond those who have less materially to those who have less in other ways.

6. Why could this woman "rejoice in time to come," that is, "laugh at the days to come" (Proverbs 31:25 NKJV, NIV)?

7. The pinnacle of all the virtues of this woman appears in verse 30. Read this verse carefully, and then spend a few moments assessing where you focus your attention and where you need adjustment.

Thursday

Responding to the Word
Song of Solomon 8:6–7

Song of Solomon might surprise you with its sensual beauty and its delicate but explicit picture of sexual love between a man and a woman. Using poetry, which expresses feelings and emotions better than prose, Solomon wrote of the love between the lover, the male, and the beloved, the female. If you wonder why God would include such a book in the Scripture, remember that God is the Creator of human love and sexual intimacy. He inspired the author of this book to write of this aspect of human existence, just as He inspired the authors of Psalms to express worship and the author of Proverbs to express wisdom.

The book of Song of Solomon reaches its pinnacle in the final chapter. The passionate expressions in verses 6 and 7 give today's reader an image of the love between a man and a woman as God designed it to be. The seal the bride wanted to put on her husband marked him as belonging to her and to no other. The seal on his heart demonstrated the emotional love they shared. The seal on his arm demonstrated to others that the groom belonged to her. Comparing love to the strength of death and the cruel and unyielding nature of the grave demonstrated the lifelong commitment that God intended for love and marriage. The writer then used fire and its flames to demonstrate the passion that emotional and physical love in marriage can produce.

Solomon's song of the beauty of love has little that compares to it in all of literature, both ancient and contemporary. You can read it to kindle or even rekindle the kind of love for your husband that God desires. Or you can read it to measure the love you have for a potential husband to be sure it is worthy of marriage.

God knows that you long to love and be loved. As you read Solomon's book, let it reveal to you the depth of loving that God has put in place for husbands and wives, for families, for all to experience.

The Women's Devotional Guide to the Bible

Friday

Praying the Word
Ecclesiastes 3:1–8

Besides Psalm 23, the words of Solomon's discourse on time are some of the most often recited words of Scripture. Carefully meditate today on these verses, remembering that not only is there a time for everything, but also that God lovingly carries all of time in His hands. As you read, perhaps you'd like to write your own thoughts on time, designed to describe the season of your life. You can use the words of these verses or your own text in your prayer time today.

Lord and God, Creator of time and seasons and me, I give You all the minutes and hours and days and years of my life. I know that You are fully aware of the seasons of my life, of the times of ease and times of difficulty, times of joy and times of sorrow, times of growth and times of decline. Give me Your grace, Lord, for the times of my life. I love You and trust You. Amen.

Isaiah Prophesies

Monday

Reading the Word
Isaiah 6; 9–12; 35; 40; 43:1–13; 53; 55

THE STORY

Smoke swirled around Isaiah's feet and wafted up around his face. He breathed deeply but tasted only fresh air. He looked around and could see nothing of his surroundings, only the holy smoke of God and eerie winged creatures hovering above him. Their unearthly voices rang through the temple, echoing and ringing as they offered their praises to God: "Holy, holy, holy is the LORD of hosts; The whole earth is full of His glory!" (Isaiah 6:3 NKJV).

Isaiah collapsed to the floor, his heart pounding with the awful awareness of his unworthiness before such a God. Tears ran between the fingers of his hands as they covered his face. "I'm ruined. I'm undone. I have seen the Lord! Unclean! My lips are unclean, and I live with people whose lips are unclean." As the last words rushed out of his mouth, he felt a burning sensation on his lips. He opened his eyes to see one of the creatures before him, touching Isaiah's lips with a fiery coal and saying, "Your sins are gone" (Isaiah 6:5–7, author's paraphrase). A flush of pleasure and well-being raced through Isaiah's body. He was forgiven! All of his sins had been taken away! He was clean and no longer unworthy!

Almost before the creature had finished asking the question, *Who will go?* Isaiah raced to his feet and answered like an eager schoolboy who raises his hand and shouts, *Pick me! Pick me!* With eagerness but also humility, Isaiah answered, "Here am I! Send me"(Isaiah 6:8 NKJV).

THE MESSAGE

This temple experience, whether it was an actual event or a vision, colored all of Isaiah's future, giving him the confidence and courage he needed for the task of pronouncing judgment on Judah and the surrounding nations. God provided exactly the kind of experience Isaiah required to prepare him for the mission ahead.

THE MAIN POINT

Perhaps better than anyone else in Scripture, Isaiah understood the great chasm that exists between God's holiness and humanity's unworthiness. Isaiah also understood the freedom of having that chasm bridged and being made clean and worthy before God. Scripture teaches that you can't gain that worth on your own. The creature that touched a burning coal to Isaiah's lips brought him forgiveness of sins. Like Isaiah, you have Someone who has bridged the chasm between you and God: Christ Jesus. With His death on the cross and your acceptance of His sacrifice, you can be worthy and righteous in God's eyes.

TAKE NOTE

Isaiah 6:2—The seraphim mentioned in this passage appear nowhere else in the Bible. The word means "burning ones" and is also used in describing the snakes that attacked the Israelites in the desert (Numbers 21:6). That connection causes some to think that the creatures viewed by Isaiah were snakelike in form with wings, faces, and feet.

Isaiah 11:1, 10—The "stem" or "Root" of Jesse in these verses refers to the Messiah. Jesus was born into the royal line of King David, whose father was Jesse. The family ancestry of Jesus can be studied in Matthew 1:1–16, with Jesse appearing in verses 5 and 6.

The Women's Devotional Guide to the Bible

Tuesday

Reflecting on the Word
Isaiah 9:1–7; 53

The funeral dirge of the previous chapters, where Isaiah revealed the upcoming destruction of Judah and Jerusalem, makes a total about-face in chapter 9. With one splendid word, *Nevertheless,* Isaiah shifted the focus from gloom and distress to joy and freedom. All the sorrows of the past were eclipsed by the wonderful news that the Messiah was coming.

Isaiah's description of the Messiah in 9:6–7 NKJV revealed a King who has a wonderful plan to fulfill ("Wonderful, Counselor"), who is divine ("Mighty God"), whose reign will last forever and will be one of compassion ("Everlasting Father"), and who will bring peace and justice ("Prince of Peace").

Isaiah continued his description of the Messiah in another famous prophecy found in Isaiah 53 NKJV, adding even more information about Him. He would be "wounded for our transgressions." (Compare Isaiah 53:5 and John 19:18, 34; 20:25.) He would be "bruised for our iniquities." (Compare Isaiah 53:5 and Mark 15:34.) Your peace was purchased with His punishment and suffering. (Compare Isaiah 53:5 and Luke 23:32–43.) His stripes, that is, His beating, brought your healing. (Compare Isaiah 53:5 and John 19:1–3.)

The prophetic climax to all these injuries comes in Isaiah 53:6: The Messiah suffered all of these injuries and then death so that you would be free. As a wayward sheep, a sinful human being, all of your "iniquities," your sins, have been laid on Jesus. The fulfillment of Isaiah's prophecies took place more than seven hundred years after he spoke them. The astounding accuracy of his description of the Messiah, the One you call Jesus, is just one more evidence that not only is the God you serve all-knowing, He keeps His promises (2 Peter 3:9).

Wednesday

Studying the Word
Isaiah 40

With creative imagery and poetic flair, Isaiah presents a God who has compassion on His people when they're hurting and who will give them strength when they're worn down. Read this beautiful chapter and discover where you can find the power to survive demanding times.

1. Why did the people of Isaiah's day need comforting (Isaiah 40:1–2)? How does God comfort His people today? (See also 2 Corinthians 1:3–5.) Describe a specific situation or event where you experienced comfort from God.
2. To whom does Isaiah 40:3–6 refer? (Compare John 1:19–23 NKJV.)
3. How are people "like grass" (Isaiah 40:6–7 NKJV)? How is God different (Isaiah 40:8)? How does that comparison make you feel about yourself? About God?
4. The "arm" of God is used to describe two different characteristics in Isaiah 40:10, 11 NKJV. What are those characteristics? How have those characteristics been apparent in your life's circumstances?
5. What do you discover about God by reading Isaiah 40:12–14, 22–26? Does this give you fear or confidence? Explain your answer.
6. What does it mean to "wait" or "hope" in the Lord (Isaiah 40:31 NKJV, NIV)?
7. How is the help God provides when you're faced with life's weary difficulties similar to flying like an eagle or running (Isaiah 40:31)?
8. Where can those who hope in the Lord find their strength (Isaiah 40:28–29)?

Thursday

Responding to the Word
Isaiah 55

Have you ever been really and truly thirsty? Perhaps you had surgery and couldn't drink for a period of time. Or perhaps some other circumstance caused you to go without water until your mouth and even your body yearned for just one drip of life-giving H_2O. Have you ever been really and truly thirsty for God? Has your heart and even your spirit yearned for just one moment of life-giving intimacy with God?

Human beings will try anything and everything to satisfy the thirst that only God can quench. Isaiah gave God's invitation to the thirsty of all ages: "Everyone who thirsts, Come to the waters . . . Incline your ear, and come to Me. Hear, and your soul shall live" (Isaiah 55:1, 3 NKJV).

His offer to you is free—no dollars, no checking account or credit card required. So, why would you spend your hard-earned money trying to satisfy your longings with things that never would and never could satisfy your longings (Isaiah 55:2)? Rather foolish, isn't it? Yet people still go running from one thing to another—from work to spending to sports to social or business successes to houses to cars to entertainment to sex—in order to find fulfillment. And they walk away parched, unfulfilled, and looking for more.

Jesus also offered a remedy for your thirst: living water (John 4:10–14; 7:37), water so satisfying that you never will be thirsty again. And He offered it freely also, no cost involved. He already paid the price and paid it in full. He purchased living water for you by His death on the cross.

When you're thirsty, yearning for fulfillment, looking for something more out of life, carefully consider your options. You can drink the dryness of the pleasures of earth. Or you can drink the life-giving, all-satisfying, forever-gratifying water that Isaiah, then Jesus, offered.

Friday

Praying the Word
Isaiah 43:1

God knows your name! John, Beth, Herm, Louise, Adam, Cecilia—whatever your name, common or not, God knows it well. And He's calling to you, using that very personal thing about you, the word that identifies you and separates you from all others, your name. Thank Him today for the very personal relationship He's calling you to share with Him. Or if you know the meaning of your name, use it to form the topic of your prayers today.

Lord who created me, Lord who formed me and knows me better than anyone else, I will trust wholly in You and not be afraid because I know You are with me. I know You have saved me. Thank You, Lord, for calling me by my name. I'm Yours, Lord. Everything I am, everything I have, everything I do—it's all Yours. In my Savior Jesus' name, Amen.

Jeremiah Prophesies

Monday

Reading the Word

Jeremiah 1; 13; 16; 18:1–19:6; 32–33; 36:1–38:13;
39:1–40:6; 52; Lamentations 1

THE STORY

Jeremiah's hands shook as he tried to put the rags under his arms. He hadn't had anything to eat in days. The deep, wet mud of the dungeon had ground deep into his skin. He looked up toward the men at the top of the dungeon. The sun shone brightly behind them, a sun Jeremiah had only had small glimpses of from the deep hole where he was imprisoned. These men had come to rescue him, dropping rags down on ropes to cushion his arms then telling him to put the ropes under his arms so they could raise him up.

Jeremiah did as they told him then groaned when the ropes cut into the swollen flesh beneath each arm. Wet mud dripped from his feet as he was raised higher and higher. Jeremiah closed his eyes and grimaced again as he held to the ropes that would bring him to safety. As he moved through the dungeon's opening, Jeremiah felt the warmth of the sun on his head and closed his unaccustomed eyes to its brightness. Weakened from his ordeal, he collapsed on the ground as soon as the men removed the ropes. But his voice remained surprisingly strong as he spoke, thanking these men for saving him.

THE MESSAGE

Jeremiah served God in difficult times. The Israelites hated him for the message of truth he preached. He continually warned them that God's judgment for their waywardness was coming. He watched as Jerusalem was destroyed, as the people were taken captive, and as the people ignored God instead of turning to Him in repentance. Rather than taking Jeremiah's message seriously, the people took offense and tried to imprison and kill him. But even when faced with death, Jeremiah obeyed God and followed the course set for him.

THE MAIN POINT

Life isn't always easy, even for those who follow God faithfully. Like Jeremiah, difficult circumstances and difficult people can make life miserable. Like Jeremiah, you have God's promise that you will never face those difficult situations alone. He promises that He will be "with you" and will "deliver you" (Jeremiah 1:19 NKJV). That's no glib offer made when the sun is shining but weak when suffering brings dark days. God's offer of His presence is one you can trust. Absolutely.

TAKE NOTE

Jeremiah 38:6—The dungeon where Jeremiah was imprisoned for a time was most likely a cistern. Rainwater and springwater were stored in cisterns for future use. Large holes in rock, either natural or manmade, served as excellent storage tanks for water. Dry summers and little rain in Israel made the storing of water essential. What rain did fall was directed by a system of pipes and channels down into the cisterns. Most walled cities had cisterns that provided water for inhabitants during a siege. The temple area in Jerusalem had as many as thirty-seven cisterns, one of them large enough to hold between two and three million gallons of water. That's one big bucket of water!

Jeremiah 13:1–11—Jeremiah's linen sash may not have much meaning for you, but it was a metaphor the people of his day readily understood. The priests wore linen robes, so the belt was a reminder to the people of the priests and of sincere worship of their God. Jeremiah didn't let the belt get wet. Linen will rot very quickly if it gets wet and stays that way. Staying fresh and clean reminded the people of their calling as God's special people, His "special treasure" (Exodus 19:5 NKJV). God later told Jeremiah to stash the belt in some rocks. When Jeremiah dug up the sash some time afterward, he found a dirty and rotted piece of linen, a reminder to the people of what sin was doing to them and their nation.

Tuesday

God's command that Jeremiah not marry doesn't seem all that unusual or troublesome today, but in Jeremiah's day the conditions and expectations were very different.

Singleness was very rare in Jeremiah's culture and seemed unnatural to them. The expectation was for everyone to be married, for several reasons. First, the Israelites viewed their family lines as something of great significance. Each person had the responsibility and desire to carry on their family's name, to make sure that name continued indefinitely. Second, a family was something of a retirement plan. Having a family was the best means of support when one grew too old or feeble to support oneself. Adult children were expected to support and care for their elderly parents.

Jeremiah had been doing a bit of complaining to God about his lack of companions. Those he did know didn't think much of him (Jeremiah 15:10), and he rarely had good times with others; he was most often alone and probably lonely (Jeremiah 15:17).

Then God arrived with His command that Jeremiah was not to marry or have children. What a surprise! And a disappointment too. Jeremiah would never experience the joys or social acceptance that marriage and children provided. His work for God would consume him, leaving no time or energy for a family. Jeremiah's single status offered the Israelites a picture-perfect view not only of his dedication to his calling but also of the difficulties and pain that faced those with families. The future held only sorrow for a people who had turned their backs on God.

Wednesday

Studying the Word
Jeremiah 32:17–23

In a surprising shift from predictions of coming destruction and misery to praise for all God had done in the past, Jeremiah reminded the people of God's goodness. Read his words of praise and then answer these questions in order to remember the good things God has done for you.

1. Look around you at all God has made, not just in nature but also in you and your family (Jeremiah 32:17). What can you praise Him for specifically? What has God done in your life that would have been difficult or even impossible for you to do?

2. How do children today bear the consequences of their parents' actions and sins (Jeremiah 32:18)?

3. Examine your life, your plans, and your future to discover if they line up with God's "counsel," His perfect purposes (Jeremiah 32:19). If they don't, what can you do to bring yourself into alignment with Him?

4. What miraculous signs do you see in your world today that only God could perform (Jeremiah 32:20)? How have you given Him credit, or praise, for those works?

5. Just as God brought the Israelites out of slavery in Egypt, He has brought you to the place you are today. How has He worked in order to bring you where you are today, spiritually? Physically? Emotionally?

6. God did all these things for the Israelites, yet they ignored and disobeyed Him. How's your obedience quotient? Perhaps *quotient* is the wrong word. God isn't looking for a portion or a percentage of your obedience. He wants your *complete* obedience. Remember that as you examine your obedience or lack of it.

Thursday

Responding to the Word
Jeremiah 18:1–12

Have you ever watched a potter at work? Spinning the potter's wheel with the push of a foot, working a lump of clay up into a pot or bowl or dish with deft hands? If you've watched for any length of time, you've probably seen not only beautiful pots form but also pots that don't turn out well. Sometimes, a defect in the clay becomes apparent only when a pot is being formed. While the clay is still pliable, the potter will squish and smash it in order to start over again or at times may have to discard that mass of clay.

God sent Jeremiah down to the potter's house in order to teach him a lesson that would form the foundation of a message to the Israelites. Just as the potter had complete control over the clay, so God had complete control over the nations, Judah in particular. He could build up or destroy according to His desire and the condition of the people. He could take a flawed nation or people and begin again to form and build them. Or He might destroy them altogether if their imperfections are irreparable, if they see His work but stubbornly refuse to listen to Him (Jeremiah 19:12).

Today God deals more with individuals than with whole nations, blessing or disciplining or punishing as individual hearts deserve. And that's where the potter and the clay imagery breaks down. You are not a mere lump of passive clay. You are a person with feelings and choices and desires. You have the choice to listen to or ignore God, just as those in Israel did. You can obey and gain His favor and blessing. Or you can disobey and finally earn His punishment.

Sound harsh? Like God can just willy-nilly smack nations and people around? If it does, remember that God is above all a God of love and mercy. As a potter works and reworks clay, so He'll work and rework you. He sent His Son and allowed Him to be ridiculed and murdered on the cross in order to pay for your sinfulness and make you righteous before

Him (Romans 3:23–26). In return, He asks for your heart, a heart He is willing to shape, like a potter shapes a pot, into something beautiful and useful and treasured.

Friday

Praying the Word
Jeremiah 1:5

Who knows you best? A friend? Mate? Child? How well does that person know you? Not completely, that's for certain. No one on earth can fully know another. There are always the hidden, the unknown, the secret places of a person that are never revealed to another. And even if they are revealed, they are not fully understood.

But praise God, there *is* Someone who fully knows and understands you. He formed you in your mother's womb, He planned your life, He even knows how many hairs you have on your head this very moment (Matthew 10:30). Spend time praising God that you are fully known and loved by Him.

Greatest Friend of all, I thank You that You have known and understood and loved me since before I was born. What a comfort that is to me when I'm feeling misunderstood and unloved. You are the great God and You love me. What more could I ask in life? I praise You! Amen.

Week Twenty-Six

Ezekiel Prophesies

Monday

Reading the Word
Ezekiel 1–5; 11:16–24; 22; 24:15–27; 33; 37; 40:1–43:12

THE STORY

Ezekiel's head was spinning just like the wheels in his visions. Colors and motions and creatures and fire and lightning combined to form fantastic sights that assaulted his senses. He shook with the certainty that this vision was from God and had to be communicated to God's people. But how? Ezekiel knew that putting what he saw into words—to speak it or, worse, to try to write it down—would prove almost impossible. What exactly was he seeing? Who was this God, this "appearance of the likeness of the glory of the LORD" (Ezekiel 1:28 NKJV)? The wheels gave Ezekiel the impression that this God, their God even while they were captives in Babylon, was moving and active and ready to come to their aid. There was judgment, Ezekiel was sure, but there was also hope.

THE MESSAGE

All of the bizarre images of Ezekiel's visions can be unpacked to reveal one overriding message: God is awesome and glorious. Through these visions God revealed to His prophet Ezekiel that He loved His people, the Israelites, that He wanted to bless them, that He would bring judgment on them for their sins, but that He would rather forgive them if they would just repent.

THE MAIN POINT

Fifty-seven times throughout the book Ezekiel recorded God saying, "I am the LORD." God wants all of His people to remember who He is, the Lord of all of life—past, present, and future. His touch is seen throughout history, His presence can be sensed in your life this very day, and His hand can be trusted to guide your future.

TAKE NOTE

Ezekiel 2:1; 3:1; 4:1; 5:1—Around ninety times throughout his book, Ezekiel is called "son of man." Every time he received a message, the phrase reminded Ezekiel that he was a frail human being, under God's authority.

Ezekiel 24:15–17—God asked Ezekiel to do all sorts of strange things in order to get His message across to the Israelites. However, this had to be the hardest. His wife would die, and he wasn't to mourn, at least not in the customary way. In Ezekiel's day loud crying, tearing of clothes, and sprinkling ashes or dirt on one's head all signified grief and honored the one who had died. Ezekiel's lack of proper mourning would be immediately obvious to his fellow Israelites. When they asked "Why?" Ezekiel could share God's message of the coming destruction of Jerusalem and their inability to properly mourn that loss.

Tuesday

Reflecting on the Word
Ezekiel 40

The temple in Jerusalem served as Israel's place of worship and sacrifice throughout the time of the kings. The third king, Solomon, built
the first temple in 950 BC. Its descriptions in 1 Kings 6 present a magnificent structure of carved wood and gold. The invading Babylonians
destroyed Solomon's temple in 587 BC. They burned that structure as
well as much of the city, taking the gold and silver temple articles back
to Babylon with them.

When the captives were allowed to return to Israel, they built another
temple on the same site in 515 BC under the direction of Zerubbabel.
This new temple was so little like Solomon's original that those who had
seen Solomon's temple cried when they saw this new one (Ezra 3:13).
Although the exiles took back many of the temple articles stolen when
Jerusalem was destroyed, the Ark of the Covenant was not among them.
Therefore, the Holy of Holies stood empty in this new temple.

It seems likely that the Jews enlarged and beautified this temple over
the centuries, although no historical documents make mention of it. In
168 BC the Syrian king, Antiochus Epiphanes, robbed the temple and
sacrificed a pig on its altar, totally desecrating it according to Hebrew
law. Three years later the Jews recaptured the temple and cleansed and
rededicated it for worship and sacrifice.

In 63 BC the Romans conquered Jerusalem and took the temple.
Although they didn't destroy the structure itself, they did plunder all of
its gold. Forty years later, under the Roman rule of Herod the Great, a
beautification and enlargement of the temple began. Typical of Herod,
that untiring builder of cities and temples, the project was complex and
long-term. In order to maintain full temple service and sacrifice during
the project, the new temple was built piece by piece around the old. The
temple itself was completed in around eighteen months; however, the

structures and court around the temple took many years, forty-six according to the Jews in Jesus' time (John 2:20). Herod's temple rivaled Solomon's in its beauty with walls of marble and gates of gold.

Only a few years after Herod's temple was complete, it was destroyed by the armies of Rome in 70 AD. The destruction ended the Hebrew religious system of sacrifices and temple worship. The mount where the temple stood in Jerusalem is now occupied by the Muslim Dome of the Rock.

Where Ezekiel's vision of a future temple fits into this scheme is something about which Bible scholars disagree. Some say he was seeing Solomon's temple. Others say he saw the temple the exiles would build when they returned to their land. Still others interpret this passage as a picture of the temple to be built in a future age, when Christ returns and sets up His kingdom on earth.

Wednesday

Studying the Word
Ezekiel 1

It might seem like a huge and impossible task to tackle, but for today give it a try. Read Ezekiel's vision and then answer the following questions to discover some major meanings.

1. Where was Ezekiel when he saw these visions (Ezekiel 1:1–3)? How had he ended up there (2 Kings 25:8–12)?
2. What clues do Ezekiel 1:4–5 give you that Ezekiel had a hard time describing what he saw?
3. What parts of creation might each of the four faces of Ezekiel 1:10 represent? The man? The lion? The ox? The eagle?
4. If each of these faces is the greatest of that part of creation, what does that tell you about God's relationship to them? Where do they fit in relationship to God?
5. How fast were the creatures moving (Ezekiel 1:14)?
6. What might the wheels of Ezekiel 1:15–17 tell you about God?
7. What might the eyes of Ezekiel 1:18 tell you about God?
8. What directed the movement of these creatures and their wheels (Ezekiel 1:20)?
9. Who is Ezekiel describing in verses 26–28? Why do you think he is careful to only say that this was "a likeness with the appearance of a man"?
10. What sort of impression of God do you think Ezekiel got from these visions (Ezekiel 1:28)? What impression of God do these visions give you?
11. How did Ezekiel respond? What does that tell you about how you might respond?

Thursday

Responding to the Word
Ezekiel 22:30

Sheep run back and forth and around in circles inside their pen. The walls of stone and brush keep them gathered for the night. The door of the pen is a simple opening, guarded by the shepherd, who will sleep in that opening in order to protect his sheep during the night hours.

Through Ezekiel, God called for Someone like that shepherd, Someone to stand in the gap, the opening, for His people, in order to protect them from His judgment. The picture was one the Jews would readily understand since they were a sheep-herding culture and since several stories in their history spoke of One who stood in the gap for them or for others.

Many years before, the patriarch of the Israelite nation, Abraham, stood in the gap for the sinful people of Sodom and Gomorrah (Genesis 18:16–33). God had decided to destroy both cities for their wickedness. When He revealed His plan to Abraham, that generous man stood before God and pleaded with Him to save the cities for fifty, forty-five, forty, thirty, twenty, even just ten righteous people. God listened to Abraham and promised not to destroy it if ten righteous people could be found. How pitiful that not even ten were found and the cities were destroyed in a horrific firestorm.

The story of Moses standing in the gap for a rebellious Israelite nation is one of staggering self-sacrifice. He was willing to lose his own life, his own place in God's kingdom, in order to save the people he led. He stood between an angry God and a people who had sinned, protecting the people from God's judgment, from certain annihilation (Exodus 32:30–32; Numbers 14:11–23). God listened to Moses and relented from destroying His people. In Ezekiel's day, God was looking again for such a leader, one who would stand before God to protect the rebellious people from His coming wrath.

The Women's Devotional Guide to the Bible

Sadly, it appears that no one could be found. God's judgment was certain to come.

For whom could you be a Moses or an Abraham? For whom could you "stand in the gap"? Is there a child, a grown son or daughter, a family member or church member who needs you as a shepherd? An intercessor to stand before God and plead for his/her repentance? God is still looking for faithful people who will willingly give their time and effort and prayer so that others will turn to Him. Are you that person? If so, press on! If not, ask God to fill your heart with as much love for the rebellious around you as Moses had for those around him.

Friday

In this verse Ezekiel recorded what has become the heart cry of many of God's people over the centuries. More than anything else, they want a heart that is tender, pliable, made of flesh rather than stone, a heart that loves and serves only God. What's your heart like today? Is it divided in its loyalties, serving God but at times also serving self? Is your heart tender? Or is it hard, not easily moved? In your prayer time today, examine your heart for anything that keeps it from undivided love and loyalty to God. Ask God to make you soft and tender, easily stirred to change by the hand of His Spirit.

As I examine my heart today, Lord, reveal to me anything that gets in the way of being wholly devoted to You. It truly is my heart's desire to give You my undivided love and loyalty. But my own desires and wishes and the sins of my life often get in the way. O Lord, just as the Israelites couldn't change without a touch from You, I cannot become what I wish to be without Your divine help. I'm open and willing, Lord. Do whatever it takes—and I don't pray that lightly—to make my heart a heart of flesh rather than stone. In the name of my King, Jesus, Amen.

Daniel Prophesies

Monday

Reading the Word
Daniel 1–9

THE STORY

Daniel raised his arm and wiped the sweat from his face with his sleeve. The king had asked his wise men, Daniel included, not only to interpret his dream but also to tell him what his dream had been. The wise men complained to Nebuchadnezzar. It would be like getting inside the king's mind, something no one on earth could do. Nebuchadnezzar stood stubbornly on his request, however, threatening to kill all the wise men in his kingdom if they didn't reveal his dream and its meaning.

Daniel worshiped a God who knew the whole of the king's dream. He and his friends in Babylon prayed that God would reveal that dream and its interpretation. Otherwise, death was a certainty.

Sitting on his bed in the dark, late into the night, Daniel closed his eyes, asking God to simply fill his mind with the dream of the king. He sat there, hour by hour, focusing on God and waiting. Waiting. His legs ached and his back throbbed from sitting in the same position, but he refused to move. Just waiting, waiting. He took a deep breath and realized the room around him was beginning to lighten in the hours before dawn. And still he waited.

Just before dawn, with a disturbing clarity, Daniel saw in his mind exactly the dream that Nebuchadnezzar had dreamed. He saw the huge image with feet part clay and part iron and its body of various other metals. As the image grew larger in his mind, Daniel also understood what the dream meant, and knew, finally, the ominous news he had to tell the king.

THE MESSAGE

Daniel understood that the dreams and visions and events of his time had meaning for the future. God revealed through him the work that He would do in Judah and the world for decades and centuries to come. God's revelation of future happenings gave Daniel and his fellow captives confidence in God's ability to control not only their present circumstances but also their future.

THE MAIN POINT

Today's events have implications for the future. Your choices impact your future for good or evil. Just as Daniel saw the future God revealed to him and gained trust in God, you can know that your future is as much in God's control and your life is as valuable to Him. God manages with infinite care all your todays and tomorrows.

TAKE NOTE

Daniel 1:8, 12—Daniel and his friends in captivity wouldn't eat foods prepared by foreign hands with little or no understanding of Hebrew religious law. Meats had to be prepared in certain ways and some meats were unclean, something no self-respecting Israelite would eat. Vegetables and fruits, however, were all acceptable and posed little problem.

Daniel 9:27—The abominations that Daniel described here came to fulfillment several centuries later when a ruler named Antiochus Epiphanes defiled the rebuilt temple in Jerusalem by placing a pagan altar in it. A future interpretation is also possible of a revolutionary who will rebel against God and cause horrible trials for God's people in the end times. Jesus referred back to Daniel and called this person the "abomination of desolation" (Matthew 24:15 NKJV). You've probably heard him called the *Antichrist*.

Tuesday

Reflecting on the Word
Daniel 2:24–49

Have you ever had a dream that seemed—maybe even just in retro-spect—to have a future meaning? God used dreams with frequency in Old Testament times to reveal the future to His people. He still uses them, but with far less frequency, since believers today have His written Word, something those in ancient times lacked.

Daniel clearly saw the dream that God had given to Nebuchadnezzar and recognized its interpretation just as clearly. The image in the king's dream had five parts: feet of clay, legs of iron, belly and thighs of bronze, chest and arms of silver, and a head of gold. Each part grew successively weaker as the image grew from head to feet. Daniel himself had several other visions with the same interpretation as Nebuchadnezzar's dream (Daniel 7–8).

Most Bible scholars see the dream as having an understanding of the near future and a separate interpretation of the far future. The head of gold represented the present kingdom of Babylon. The chest and arms of silver symbolized the conquerors of Babylon, the Medes and Persians. The belly and thighs of bronze corresponded to the coming Greek king-dom and rule. And the legs of iron represented the rule of Rome. The feet of clay symbolized the weak federation of rulers that followed Rome.

Some scholars see this last federation of nations as something arising in the future, a bloc of nations that will defy God and will eventually be thoroughly destroyed by the "rock" of Daniel 2:34 NIV. Jesus is that Rock, the One who will destroy evil and establish a final, everlasting kingdom under His rule. No matter how you think these verses should be interpreted, their main point remains the same: all of the world's events are under the control and supervision of a God of love, a God who will triumph over sin and death and who will reign forever in a kingdom where His people live in peace and victory.

Wednesday

Studying the Word
Daniel 6

The much loved and often repeated story of Daniel in the den of lions is more than just a Bible hero's adventure. More even than the rescue of that hero. This story is an account of the faithfulness of God when all seems hopeless. Read this exciting narrative and then answer the following questions to discover where you can find courage when you face desperate situations.

1. Why did the king promote Daniel above all the other administrators (Daniel 6:1–3)? How did his peers respond (Daniel 6:4–5)? Why do you think they responded this way? Share how you or someone you know experienced a similar situation in the workplace.

2. What snare did Daniel's peers devise to trip him up (Daniel 6:6–9)? Why would King Darius agree to such a thing?

3. How did Daniel respond (Daniel 6:10)? What does this tell you about him? How does this confirm the assessment of Daniel 6:3–4? Where do you think Daniel found the courage for such a response (Daniel 2:23; 5:17)?

4. What do Daniel 6:14, 16, 18–20 tell you about what the king thought of Daniel?

5. To whom does Daniel give credit for his rescue (Daniel 6:21–22)? Why do you think God saved Daniel in this situation (and his three friends in chapter 3), yet others have been martyred through the years for their faith? Is God more faithful in one situation than the other? Explain your answer.

6. What happened to Daniel's peers (Daniel 6:24)? What do you think about this punishment?

7. What was King Darius's response to Daniel's rescue (Daniel 6:25–27)? When have you been rescued miraculously by God from

some dire or not so dire situation? How do you think God might be rescuing you on a daily basis from evil and danger?

Thursday

Responding to the Word
Daniel 3

Looking at a story like this one from the perspective of past events will often dim the reality of those events, making them seem less momentous than they actually were. For today, try to look at this event as though it is the present and future, rather than something of the past. You know the final outcome, but the three men had no idea what the result of their defiance would be.

Nebuchadnezzar had a huge image or idol made, one that rose about ninety feet into the air. He then proclaimed that everyone—all of his subjects of whatever nationality or religion—had to bow down to his idol when the musical signal came. No problem for most people in that day, when most cultures worshiped multiple gods. But for the Israelites, a big, big problem. Huge. As big as the idol itself.

Long ago, when God declared Himself to Moses, He commanded that the people not worship any other god but Him. It was the first of the commandments (Exodus 20:3–4), and the bedrock on which all Israelite culture stood. Shadrach, Meshach, and Abed-Nego knew the commandment well.

Put yourself in their place, standing before an angry king whose power is supreme, with the heat of a flaming furnace burning your face. There seems to be little hesitation in their actions or words, no wavering or uncertainty. They know full well that if they disobey, they die a horrible, fiery death. With fierce determination to obey God, they defy the king: "Your edict means nothing to us. Our God is more powerful than you and can save us from your fiery furnace. But, even if He doesn't, we still won't worship you or your idol. Never!" (Daniel 3:16–18, author's paraphrase).

You know the end of the story, that God did miraculously save Shadrach, Meshach, and Abed-Nego. But when they declared their defiance of Nebuchadnezzar, they had no idea what the outcome would be. Most likely, they assumed death would be their fate. All the more reason to admire and emulate men like these, men of courage and conviction even in the face of certain death.

Martyrs throughout the centuries have declared their faith and obedience to Christ when confronted with horrific persecution and death. Would your convictions and your love for your Savior be enough to make you stand strong in the middle of such events? It's a heavy question, one that can probably only find its full answer in the heat of the trial, when God's grace proves sufficient (2 Corinthians 12:9).

Friday

Praying the Word
Daniel 5:27

Scary thought, isn't it? To be weighed on God's "balances," God's scales, and found wanting? Short? Too lightweight? If you belong to Jesus, however, you don't have to fear. Your weight, your righteousness, your rightness with God is never measured on its own. You have Jesus with you on your side of the scale, so you can be confident you will never be found wanting. In your prayer time today, consider your former state, when you would have been found wanting if you had been weighed on God's scales. And then thank God for your present state: secure and safe because of Jesus' blood and righteousness.

I trust in You alone, O God, for my salvation. I know that through Jesus' blood and His work for me on the cross, I will never be weighed in the balances and be found wanting. I give You the most solemn praises of my heart, my Father and my Savior, for lovingly saving me. Amen.

Hosea, Joel, Amos, and Obadiah Prophesy

Monday

Reading the Word
Hosea 1; 3; 13–14; Joel 1–2; Amos 4–5; Obadiah

THE STORY

With the sounds of crying children (Hosea 1:3, 6, 8), with swarms of locusts (Joel 1:3–4), with earthquakes and the roar of God (Amos 1:1–2), with the noise of battle (Obadiah 1), these four prophets of God spoke His words to the peoples of their time. These four men followed Moses' job description for prophets, given in Deuteronomy 18:18, and spoke to the people all that God commanded them.

THE MESSAGE

Although these four prophets ministered at different times and in different places, their messages have a common link: God's heart was broken because of the sinful ways of His people and their lack of love for Him and others. He would wait patiently for them to repent, but if they didn't, He would eventually punish them for their sins. Yet even after punishment would come restoration and renewal.

THE MAIN POINT

Sin still breaks God's heart, and He still longs for His people to come to Him in repentance. Not much has really changed since these prophets wrote to Israel and Judah. People still ignore God, look out for their own interests without concern for others, and disregard the poor and home-less. Messengers from God still teach the truth and call for people to turn away from their sin. Some still respond and others still don't—"second verse, same as the first."

TAKE NOTE

Joel 1:4—Joel began his prophecy with a description of the devasta-tion brought by a huge "army" (Joel 2:2 NCV) of locusts. The insect—more commonly called a grasshopper today—could then, and still some-times does, cause wholesale loss of crops. Swarms of the insect soar over the land like a dark cloud, landing where they please and stripping the land of everything green and edible. Joel proclaimed that such devasta-tion from locusts was a form of judgment from God.

Tuesday

Reflecting on the Word
Amos 4:1–3

God abhors the way you take advantage of the poor, Amos told the Israelites throughout his book. In these first verses of chapter 4, he directed that message specifically to the women of Israel, calling them "cows of Bashan" (Amos 4:1 NKJV). Not a very pleasing image to contemplate, especially if you're a woman!

The area of Bashan encompassed flat land east of the Sea of Galilee. The land was originally assigned to the half-tribe of Manasseh (Deuteronomy 3:13). With its rich, fertile soil and lush, broad fields, it quickly became known as the best place to raise sheep and cattle. The cows raised in Bashan were like the cows Carnation milk used to advertise— "contented cows." Amos went one step further and suggested that they were also spoiled cows. Their only concern was themselves, filling their own bellies, chewing their own contented cuds, oblivious to anything around them.

And he compared these spoiled animals to the women of his nation, spoiled creatures who were only concerned with their next meal, their next drink (ordering their husbands to bring those confections), oblivious to the needs of the people around them. And worse, uncaring.

Nothing is intrinsically wrong with a good meal or a good glass of liquid, but when oblivion led to heartless treatment of those with less or callous disregard for the needs of those nearby, Amos flashed in with censure and condemnation. These coldhearted women would bear God's judgment, being led into captivity by "fishhooks" (Amos 4:2 NKJV).

The image proved to be frighteningly accurate. Assyrian pictures depict men and women captives being led single file by long ropes with hooks. The hooks went through their noses or lips, sensitive areas that quickly discouraged escape attempts.

Most of those taken captive by the Assyrians were the rich and royal, the upper class of Israel. And those were the women most likely to have the attitudes Amos expressed. Their lives were filled with rich foods, wine, and prosperity. And their hearts were filled with selfish ambitions and little concern for the poor.

Throughout Scripture God has called His people to a loving concern for the poor. It was one of His main concerns when He gave the laws of the nation to Moses (Exodus 23:6, 11; Leviticus 19:10; 23:22; 25:6, 35–41; Deuteronomy 15:7–8, 11; 24:14–15). Jesus also took the part of the poor, instructing His followers to take care of them (Matthew 19:21; 25:34–36). God still looks on with dismay when His people are so concerned with their own comforts and their own luxuries that the needy fade into life's background. So, if you don't want to be called a cow (and what woman does?), use every opportunity to give to those less fortunate than you, whether you give money, usable clothing, garden produce, your time, or your attention.

Wednesday

Studying the Word
Hosea 14

Hosea's prophecy to the people of the northern tribe of Israel called them to repentance and gave them certainty of God's love and forgiveness. Read this last chapter of the book to discover how God will forgive and heal not only His people, the Israelites, but also His people today.

1. What did Hosea call the people to do (Hosea 14:1–2)?
2. What did He tell them to promise God (Hosea 14:3)?
3. What did God promise in return (Hosea 14:4)? What do you think is meant by "heal their backsliding"? What confidence for your own walk with God can you gain from reading this promise?
4. Hosea 14:5–7 pictures growth and maturity. How is this picture played out in a believer's everyday life?
5. Who is Hosea talking to in Hosea 14:9 NKJV? How would you go about being "wise" or "prudent"? (Compare Proverbs 1:7; 2:1–10.)

Thursday

Responding to the Word
Joel 2:12–13

I sat low in my hard camp chair, watching as the old man stumbled forward to the altar. The message of the evening had been a call to sincere repentance and many had responded. But if I thought anyone didn't need to respond, it was this old gentleman. His life had been one of giving and service, one of commitment to the Lord and His work. Yet there he was, collapsed, crushed, weeping with his need to repent and find forgiveness.

You may not have experienced such events in your church's culture. This was a first for me, and I was distinctly uncomfortable with the outpouring of emotion. However, I was also humbled. What drove this gentle, spiritually mature man to his knees? And why wasn't my sinfulness as obvious to me? Wait, wrong question. Why didn't my sinfulness— because I certainly knew I was sinful—reduce me to the miserable sorrow I saw before me?

Then I read Joel. His words of warning and judgment revealed a passionate God, One who looked for His people to respond to Him in kind. The repentance Joel called for didn't involve simply spoken prayers or meager actions. Joel called for *heartrending* repentance, the kind of sorrow for sin that breaks the sinner's heart. And Joel promised that God would then respond with wholehearted forgiveness and overwhelming blessing.

Is your sorrow for sin even remotely what Joel called for in these verses? Are you aware of how your sin breaks God's heart? And does your sin break your heart when you stand before Him? Ask God today to reveal to you the depth of your sin and along with it His wonderful, healing forgiveness.

Friday

Praying the Word
Obadiah 15

Obadiah predicted a coming "day of the LORD" (NKJV), a time when retribution and punishment would come to the nation of Edom for her ridicule of Israel when those people went through their trials. Many also see a future fulfillment of this "day," when Jesus will return and establish His forever kingdom, when His rule will be absolute, when judgment and reward will be meted out. Today, pray for yourself as well as your nation as you meditate on the coming "day of the LORD."

Holy Father, Ruler of all, I know that You will soon come to judge the nations and all people in Your righteousness. I thank You for the saving righteousness I have through Jesus' blood. And I ask You to help me be aware of the need of those around me for Jesus' saving righteousness. Great and coming King, I praise You! You are worthy of all of my honor and worship! Amen.

Jonah, Micah, Nahum, and Habakkuk Prophesy

Monday

Reading the Word
Jonah 1–4; Micah 4–6; Nahum 1; Habakkuk 3

THE STORY

Jonah, Micah, Nahum, and Habakkuk all grappled with the Assyrian threat to their nation and how God could and would use this powerhouse to punish His people for their repeated offenses. Jonah actually visited the Assyrian capital of Nineveh—after a brief detour in a fish—and called the people there to repentance. Micah watched from Judah as the Northern Kingdom was destroyed by the Assyrians, warning his people that their punishment would be similar if they continued to ignore God. Nahum came on the scene later and warned the people of Assyria that judgment would be coming their way. Next, Habakkuk arrived with his questions of why God allowed such evil and hardship to exist in Assyria and Babylon as well as his own nation of Judah.

THE MESSAGE

All of these prophets struggled with the conflict between God's goodness and mercy and His judgment and punishment. The hardships of their times made God's goodness difficult to process. Was God really in control? Could He truly be trusted?

THE MAIN POINT

These same hard questions have confronted believers throughout the ages. Why, if God is loving and in control, do people suffer? Why are terrorists allowed to do their cruel work, causing thousands to die? Why do mammoth storms cause wholesale destruction and death and suffering? Why do babies die and parents suffer? Why do wicked people prosper, while God's own people go hungry and hurting? The questions could go on and on. You can write your own. Unfortunately, you won't find too many solid answers to these questions in these four little books. But fortunately, you will find solid evidence of God's control and love, and you will find Someone to trust in life's worst times.

TAKE NOTE

Jonah 1:2—If you look at the extenuating circumstances, you'll probably have a bit more sympathy for Jonah's hesitancy to go to Nineveh. The city was the capital of the Assyrian Empire, the people who were terrorizing both Israel and Judah, the archenemy of Jonah's people. Around fifty years later, the Assyrians would conquer the nation of Israel and take its people into captivity.

Jonah 2:1—Many kids grow up with the notion that Jonah was swallowed by a whale. And he could have been. The Hebrew word used here for *fish* can mean any large fish, including a whale. All that is known for sure is that the fish was big enough to swallow Jonah whole and then hold the prophet in his belly for three days and nights. (That had to be one big—and from Jonah's perspective—scary fish!)

Tuesday

Reflecting on the Word
Micah 5:2

Micah is the lone prophet who announced where the Messiah, Jesus, would be born. He called Bethlehem by its name as well as its region, "Bethlehem Ephrathah" (Genesis 35:19). Bethlehem was a small town about five miles west and south of Jerusalem. Its name means "house of bread," appropriate since the region of Ephrathah means "fruitful."

Jacob's wife, Rachel, was buried there when she died giving birth to her son Benjamin (Genesis 35:19). Ruth and Boaz lived and raised their family in Bethlehem. Their great-grandson, David, took care of his father's sheep there. After being anointed by the prophet Samuel, he left his little hometown to become king of Israel (1 Samuel 16). During David's reign over Israel, the town became known as the city of David (Luke 2:4).

Micah prophesied that a ruler would come out of this little town of Bethlehem, one whose origins were from times long past (John 8:58) and whose reign and kingdom would last forever. The religious rulers at the time of Jesus' birth recognized this passage in Micah as a prophecy of where the Messiah would be born (Matthew 2:4–6). Centuries after Micah, a descendant of David was born in a stable in Bethlehem, the baby destined to grow up to be the Savior of the world.

Only the person of Jesus Christ fits the fulfillment of Micah's prophecy.

Wednesday

Studying the Word
Micah 6:6–8

Micah wanted his worship of God to come from somewhere deeper than the usual outward signs of praise. And he wanted you to know that the same is important for you. Read this passage and then answer these questions to discover where you are as a worshiper and where you might need to take action.

1. Why did Micah assume that the worshiper must bring something in order to come before God (Micah 6:6 NKJV)? What does God's "High," or exalted, status have to do with this?

2. What importance did "burnt offerings" and "year old" (Micah 6:6 NKJV) calves have (Leviticus 1:3–4)?

3. Micah used hyperbole in 6:7 NKJV. He exaggerated in order to make his point. What point was he trying to make with his "thousands of rams" and "ten thousand rivers of oil" and "firstborn"?

4. What sort of actions might people today be tempted to use in order to "prove" their love and devotion to God?

5. Read through the four questions in Micah 6:6–7 again. What is the obvious answer to each of the questions?

6. Micah 6:8 moves on to state the truth, to make the obvious point. What is God looking for, if not all the things listed in the previous two verses?

7. How will you as a believer today do things "justly" (NKJV)? What does that mean for your everyday life?

8. How can you "love mercy" (NKJV)?

9. How can you "walk humbly" (NKJV) with God? What does that look like in common terms?

10. How are the three things listed in verse 8 a better expression of your devotion to God than those listed in verses 6 and 7?

Thursday

Life is hard. There's just no getting around it. At some point every person faces disappointment, tragedy, sorrow, trials. Perhaps years go by with little trouble. But seldom does anyone get through his or her whole life unscathed by suffering of one sort or another.

As a prophet, Habakkuk's life was doubly hard. He saw what was coming. He knew the troubles that were on the way before they got there. He knew that famine and destruction and wholesale catastrophe awaited the people of Judah. And Habakkuk determined, before calamity slammed into his life and that of his nation's, that he wouldn't let those troubles shake his faith and trust in God.

Today, write your own statement of determination to trust in God. If you're in the rough seas of suffering right now, use your declaration as a lifeline to God. If your life is going well right now, use it as preparation for the days ahead that might bring challenging circumstances or agonizing affliction. Begin by recording the troubles that life has thrown or could throw your way: death, sickness, job loss, rebellion of family members, financial ruin, whatever. Then, starting with Habakkuk's sweeping "Yet" (Habakkuk 3:18 NKJV), tell God that you will trust Him even when life is hard, that you will find joy in Him when life brings anything but joy, that you will count on Him to bring you peace even when you're in the middle of distress.

Friday

Praying the Word
Nahum 1:15

After months of defeat and bad news, Nahum wrote about the messenger who would bring the good news that Judah's enemy, Nineveh, was destroyed and no longer a threat. Peace was a definite possibility. Nahum's good news could also be applied to the Messiah, who would defeat sin and bring reconciliation and peace with God. What sort of messenger are you? One who brings good news? Or do you carry a cloud of gloom with you wherever you go, swathing all those who enter your vicinity in darkness and doom? Nahum's messenger proclaimed the good news of victory over enemies and of Jesus, the One who would bring peace and joy to a world in darkness. Pray today that you would be known as one of God's messengers, one who brings the good news of salvation to those around you who are lost.

Jesus, may my words and my very lifestyle bless those around me with good news, the good news of salvation in You, the good news of abundant living to be had in You, the blessing of a life lived for You. Amen, Lord!

Zephaniah, Haggai, Zechariah, and Malachi Prophesy

Monday

Reading the Word
Zephaniah 3; Haggai 1–2; Zechariah 1–2; 7; 13–14;
Malachi 1–4

THE STORY

All four of these prophets preached to the nation of Judah. One, Zephaniah, spoke to Judah before she was taken into captivity. The other three, Haggai, Zechariah, and Malachi, spoke to the people after they returned from captivity and reestablished their lives and worship in Judah. These prophets confronted issues of their day that are just as relevant for you today, issues of justice, spiritual smugness, discouragement and encouragement, and God's place in your life.

THE MESSAGE

The four prophets called Judah to continued or renewed faith in God, a faith that was evidenced by their actions. Malachi looked for eager giving to God (Malachi 3); Zechariah looked for acts of mercy and justice (Zechariah 7); Haggai called the people to care for God's house before their own homes (Haggai 1); and Zephaniah preached a repentance that went beyond ritual to the heart (Zephaniah 3:9).

THE MAIN POINT

The same call still goes out today for believers who show their faith by their actions. The apostle James put it in the starkest terms possible: "Faith without works is dead" (James 2:26 NKJV). The Old Testament prophets and the New Testament teachers all called for the same thing, an inner faith in God that expressed itself in the lifestyle of the believer.

TAKE NOTE

Zephaniah 3:14—The Bible uses the phrase "daughter(s) of Zion" (NKJV) thirty-two times. It usually refers to the city of Jerusalem, Zion being one of the hills on which Jerusalem stood. Cities are often referred to as female in ancient literature. The term reflects God's affection for the city where He lived among His people.

Zephaniah 1:14—The phrase "day of the LORD" (NKJV) is used throughout the Bible to refer to a time when God would win a decisive battle against His enemies. It can refer to a specific battle, as when the Israelites defeated their enemies with God's help. It ultimately refers to a future time when all of God's enemies throughout history will be defeated and punished and when grace will be extended to all those who belong to God.

Tuesday

Reflecting on the Word
Zechariah 1:7–2:13

In both the Old and the New Testaments of the Bible, God used dreams and visions to speak truth to His chosen people. He often used them to communicate the messages His prophets were to preach to the people. Zechariah certainly had his share of visions, some of rather ordinary events, some of extraordinary incidents. Daniel had his own visions (Daniel 7–8) and interpreted the dreams or visions of his king (Daniel 2). Peter had a vision of a sheet with food to eat (Acts 10). Paul had a vision of Jesus on the road to Damascus (Acts 9:1–19) and while in Corinth (Acts 18:9–11). The apostle John had a series of visions that eventually became the book of Revelation.

Zechariah's visions were designed to communicate God's encouragement and blessing to the people of Judah. They had returned from captivity in Babylon, but life in resettled Judah was difficult, daunting. Zechariah's message gave them the support and motivation they needed in order to rebuild the land and trust God for their future. God promised that He would make them prosperous again (Zechariah 1:17), their enemies would be destroyed (Zechariah 1:21), God would live among them (Zechariah 2:10), and they would know rest and contentment (Zechariah 3:10). Each of these messages came through a vision given to the prophet Zechariah.

Does God still use visions and dreams to communicate? Perhaps. But certainly not as often as in biblical times when the entire written Word of God was still being formed. You now have God's whole message to His people in the Bible, therefore, visions and dreams, while not entirely out of the realm of possibility, are no longer God's chosen method for delivering His truths.

As you read Zechariah's message, remember that many of his messages have application not only to the ancient nation of Judah, but to your life as well. God is just as eager to bless you as He was them. He is just as eager to live among His people today as He was then.

Wednesday

Studying the Word
Malachi 3:6–18

In these verses the prophet Malachi accused the Israelites of robbing God, of withholding their resources as well as themselves from Him. Use these verses, as you study them, to examine your own giving habits.

1. What did God begin by saying about Himself (Malachi 3:6)? Why was this an important place to begin?
2. What did He say about the Israelites' past history (Malachi 3:7)? What did He want from them?
3. How did God say their unfaithfulness in following Him revealed itself (Malachi 3:8)?
4. What did God want from them? What is a tithe? What is an offering (Malachi 3:8)? How are they different?
5. What is the result of not giving to God (Malachi 3:9)?
6. What did God promise if they gave generously (Malachi 3:10)? Is this promise still good for believers today (2 Corinthians 9:6, 11)? How have you experienced God's blessing when you give generously?
7. Does this verse make it sound like you should give more in order to get more? What is it actually telling you about your giving and about God's generosity?

Thursday

Responding to the Word
Haggai 1

The little book of Haggai is all about priorities, about what comes first for God's people. Or more accurately, what *should* come first.

The people of Judah had returned to their homeland after seventy years in captivity in Babylon. Life in their homeland was nothing short of chaotic. They tried to reestablish themselves as a nation, only to have their efforts hampered by enemies, by an unstable political situation in Babylon, by drought and famine. It seemed like whatever they decided to do failed, and failed miserably. Their dreams of a new life in their native land were turning out to be more like nightmares.

Haggai knew exactly where the problem resided, and he came out of obscurity to preach the message God had given him. In three short words, he offered the solution to all their problems: build the temple (Haggai 1:8).

The returning captives had neglected what was most important, what should have taken precedence over anything else. After an enthusiastic start (see the book of Ezra), they quickly turned away from rebuilding the temple to building their homes and rebuilding their lives.

And things just didn't seem to be working out as planned. As Haggai put it, "You looked for much, but indeed it came to little; and when you brought it home, I blew it away" (Haggai 1:9 NKJV). He also said all their efforts were like putting their hard-earned wages into a bag with holes in it (Haggai 1:6 NKJV). God promised the people, through Haggai, that if they got their priorities straight, if they built His temple, He would bless them.

For once, rather than ignoring a prophet, the people responded and rebuilt the temple. Perhaps the painful lessons of captivity in Babylon had been well learned? Haggai recorded a response that was stark in its simplicity but breathtaking in its import: "all the remnant of the people, obeyed" (Haggai 1:12 NKJV).

Take a close look today at your spiritual priorities. Who or what comes first in your life? How can you tell? Assessing where your mind spends most of its time will give you a good indication. If you recognize that there are adjustments that need to be made, follow the lead of the remnant of Israel and do one, simple thing—obey.

Friday

Do your spirits need lifting today? Are you feeling a bit down in the dumps? Whenever you're experiencing the blues, you can use the praise of these verses in Zephaniah for a spiritual lift. Let the beautiful message of God's love and care seep into your soul and give you reason to rejoice.

Lord, my God, how wonderful You are! Thank You for turning away my punishment with the blood of Jesus. Thank You for conquering all my enemies. And thank You most of all for delighting in me. In me! Quiet my spirit with Your love, Lord. Let me hear Your voice singing words of rejoicing to me. Amen.

John the Baptist Leads the Way

Monday

Reading the Word

Matthew 3:1–12; 14:1–12; Mark 1:1–8; 6:14–29; Luke 1:1–25, 39–45, 57–66; 7:18–35; John 1:19–27; 3:22–36

THE STORY

John loosened his leather belt and dragged his coat of camel hair back into its more comfortable position. As he tightened his belt, he scowled. He enjoyed his calling as a preacher when those who heard him responded to his appeal for repentance. In the Jordan River, he had baptized thousands who had recognized their need of forgiveness. His scowl today was for those who came to listen, then shrugged their well-dressed shoulders with arrogance, thinking not only that they didn't need forgiveness but that they were just a bit, actually more than just a bit, better than those around them. John's voice carried across the river water as the frown on his face produced harsh words of denunciation: *Snakes! Vipers! You think you know the way, that your birthright in Abraham gains you entrance to God. But I tell you, repentance is the only way, and One is coming who will separate the forgiven from the unforgiven. Be careful.*

THE MESSAGE

As the forerunner of the Messiah, John prepared the way for Jesus' ministry. He called the people to repentance, to a change of heart that would enable them to recognize Jesus as the Messiah and make them ready to hear Jesus' messages and to respond to His works. John's job was one of preparation, clearing the path for Jesus to step in and take over.

THE MAIN POINT

Repentance is key. John the Baptist wasn't the first to call the people of Israel to repentance, and he wasn't the last. Many before him—Isaiah (Isaiah 59:20), Jeremiah (Jeremiah 15:19), Ezekiel (Ezekiel 14:6), Hosea (Hosea 11:5)—joined ranks with contemporary preachers today who call God's people to seek forgiveness and the righteousness that can only be found in Jesus Christ.

TAKE NOTE

Matthew 3:4—John the Baptist's diet of "locusts and wild honey" might seem unappetizing today but in his day was considered if not normal at least not extraordinary. Leviticus 11:20–23 specifically mentions the acceptability of locusts and grasshoppers and crickets as food. Those with little means to purchase food or those who lived where other foods were not as accessible used these wild insects, which were often abundant in number, as a part of their diet.

Tuesday

Reflecting on the Word
Matthew 14:1–12

With a young girl's sensual dance, John the Baptist joined the hall of fame of those martyred for their allegiance to God. While the circumstances and names of many martyrs are long forgotten, the death of John the Baptist and the disgraceful details of the story surrounding it are worth remembering and studying.

With the complicity of a young dancer, the repulsive proposal of her mother, and the willingness of a king to do as his subjects asked, John's fate was sealed. He had faithfully run his course, preparing the way for his cousin, Jesus, the Messiah. He suffered not only the horror of beheading but the after-death indignity of his head being paraded before a banquet crowd.

Throughout history, the devoted have been called at various times to prove their faithfulness with their lives. The prophet Elijah thought death was imminent at the hand of his archenemy, Jezebel (1 Kings 19:1–3). If not for his friends' work, the prophet Jeremiah would have died in a dungeon (Jeremiah 38:6–13). Daniel and his three friends were all called to remain true to their God in the face of death (Daniel 3:8–30). The first Christian martyr, Stephen, testified to the faithfulness of God even as he died (Acts 7:54–60). Paul boasted of the many and varied ways he had suffered for Christ (2 Corinthians 11:16–29). The writer of Hebrews regaled his readers with the great courage of those who suffered various fates rather than denounce their faith (Hebrews 11:32–40).

Of Jesus' twelve disciples, ten were martyred for their faith, most following their Savior, dying by crucifixion. Only John died a natural death. And Judas Iscariot, of course, committed suicide after betraying Jesus (Matthew 27:5).

Early church believers by the thousands suffered martyrdom rather than renounce their Savior. Most famous are probably those who were killed in the coliseum in Rome, used as sport for the entertainment of Rome's citizens.

And the story continues even today, when dictators and terrorists and renegade governments control the lives of those who would rather die than abandon their faith. While you may never be called to circumstances as radical as these, you are called in many ways daily to stand up for your faith rather than renounce it. Be watching. Be ready, as were Peter and John, when they said: "You want us to obey you, but we cannot. We will obey God and only Him" (Acts 4:19–20, author's paraphrase).

Wednesday

Studying the Word
Luke 1:5–25

Today study the story of John the Baptist's parents. As you study, begin to discover principles for living that you can apply to your own life.

1. How did Luke describe Zacharias and Elizabeth (Luke 1:7)? Put into your own words what you think they were like.

2. What does Luke 1:7 say about Elizabeth? How did her condition affect her (Luke 1:25)? What other biblical women can you recall who also had children when they had been barren for many years?

3. Why do you think God used such women to bear these children? What can be learned under such heart-wrenching conditions that can't be learned any other way?

4. How did Zacharias respond when he saw the angel (Luke 1:12)? Why do you think he responded this way? How do you think you might have responded?

5. What did the angel tell Zacharias about the child he would have (Luke 1:14–17)?

6. How did Zacharias respond (Luke 1:18)?

7. What did the angel have to say about Zacharias's lack of faith (Luke 1:19–20)? Others had responded with little faith to such pronouncements before (Sarah in Genesis 18:9–15). Why do you think Zacharias's punishment was so harsh?

8. What do you think you would have said to the angel at such news?

Thursday

Responding to the Word
Matthew 3:2, 8–9

John the Baptist's message of repentance and change is just as pertinent today as it was when he preached it on the shores of the Jordan River before Jesus began His earthly ministry. John called the people of his day to examine themselves, to repent of their sins, and then to live lives that revealed their faith. He wanted to be sure they knew they couldn't escape judgment simply because they were physical descendants of Abraham.

People still hang on today to the same weak impressions—if they live good enough lives, if they look right and talk right, if they have parents who are believers—they'll make it to heaven just fine. While the truth is, there is no sure way to get to heaven except one way, through Jesus, personally, individually—no coattails or apron strings allowed.

Spend some time today examining yourself. Where does sin have a foothold in your life? Or if there's no foothold, where do you flirt with sin, getting close to the line but not quite crossing over it? You're the only one who knows your heart and your condition. Well, you and God, of course. Don't think that if you're fooling others you're fooling Him. He knows the true condition of your heart. And He's waiting. Not to pounce on you with judgment and punishment, but rather to offer you absolution, forgiveness, righteousness. What an offer! One you can't possibly refuse!

Friday

Praying the Word
Luke 1:14

Do you pray often for your children? Do you pray specifically for them, bringing their particular needs, problems, and challenges before God? Do you pray for God's help in knowing the best ways to raise and love them? Use the news of the angel to Zacharias to frame your prayers for your children today. If you don't have children, use the words to frame a prayer for the children of family members or friends.

Father of all, including my children, I thank You for them, for the delight they are to me. I know I often concentrate more on the problems they cause, rather than on the joy they bring. Help me to remember that You chose these children for me, I am the mother You wanted for them. You trusted me with them; now I ask You to instill me with all I need to bring them up to make many people glad. I love You, Lord. Amen.

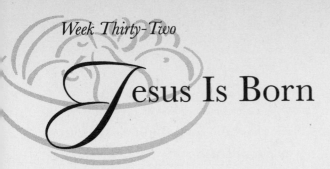

Jesus Is Born

Monday

Reading the Word
Matthew 1–2; Luke 1:26–56; 2:1–52

THE STORY

Mary stirred on her cushion of robes and straw, stretching legs that ached with the efforts of hours ago. Her hands moved to feel a belly now soft and flat, no longer stretched taut to hold her infant. A soft smile played on her young face as she recalled the miracle of birthing, the wonder of holding her firstborn child. She got to her knees and peeked into the manger where she had carefully placed Jesus to rest only minutes before. A pang of love that was almost pain streaked through her as she watched His small face, His eyes closed, His tiny mouth moving, making sucking motions even as He slept. Resisting only for a moment, she reached in and picked Him up, holding Him close to her breast, putting her face to His and breathing in His baby scent.

Mary looked up to see Joseph enter the stable, letting in a puff of cold, fresh air. He lowered himself on the straw next to her, reaching over to pull her robe closer around her for warmth. Their eyes connected, then separated, looking at this baby, this fulfillment of the angel's announcement to them both. They wondered to themselves what the future held, what this baby, this Messiah that they and their people had been anticipating for centuries, would mean to them and the nation. In the warmth of the stable, with farm animals looking on, the threesome sat close together, Mary and Joseph quietly celebrating the birth of their Savior.

THE MESSAGE

This is not just good news. It's the best news ever pronounced, ever written, ever broadcast. "A Savior has been born, Christ the Lord! Come, meet Him!" (Luke 2:10–11, author's paraphrase).

THE MAIN POINT

Matthew and Luke didn't record only historical fact in this story of Jesus' birth. They recorded the beginning of a chain of events that would revolutionize religion. No longer would God be a God far off. He was now a God who took on humanity, who lived and then died and then, most wonderful, rose again to life. So significant is the historical birth of Jesus that all of time is marked and charted by this one event.

TAKE NOTE

Matthew 2:1—The wise men from the East, also called Magi, were probably men from Arabia who studied the stars to discover the future. How many were there? The Bible doesn't say. The legend that there were three can be traced back to medieval times, possibly based on the fact that they brought three gifts to Jesus—gold, frankincense, and myrrh (Matthew 2:11).

Tuesday

Reflecting on the Word
Matthew 1:1–17

Interest in genealogies has been gaining momentum over the last few years, especially with the advent of the Internet and easier accessibility of information on ancestors. Not that interest in genealogies is anything new. The Israelite people put great emphasis on knowing and memorizing their ancestry, proving they were descendants of Abraham, the father and founder of their nation.

Matthew's genealogy of Jesus is unique in that it includes four women. Even more extraordinary, all four have some sort of stain on their character or ancestry. Tamar (Matthew 1:3) seduced her father-in-law by playing a prostitute (Genesis 38:6–26). Rahab (Matthew 1:5), a Canaanite, worked as a prostitute in Jericho before it was conquered by Joshua and his armies (Joshua 2:1–2). Ruth (Matthew 1:5), while an honorable and principled young woman, was not a Hebrew, but came from the nation of Moab (Ruth 1:3–4). Bathsheba, whom Matthew named as "the wife of Uriah" (Matthew 1:6), was King David's partner in adultery (2 Samuel 11:1–5).

If you were writing a list of ancestors for the Savior of the world, wouldn't you be likely to keep the not-so-noble relatives in a closet? Locked away so no one knew what was in His background? But that is not and never will be God's way. He's in the business of using the not-so-noble as well as the noble, the infamous as well as the famous, the sinner as well as the righteous.

That is incredibly good news. If He could and would use a Tamar in Jesus' family line, don't you think He can use a Susan, a Kristen, a Beth, a put-your-name-here? God isn't looking for perfect people. He's looking for willing people. He will use you to accomplish His purposes in your world if you'll let Him—even if your character and ancestry leave a bit to be desired.

Wednesday

Studying the Word
Luke 2:8–20

The shepherds were the first to hear the news that a Savior had been born in Israel. Study their actions and reactions for information on how you could act and react to the same news in your life.

1. Try to put the usual serene Christmas scenes out of your mind and picture what the night and shepherds and their sheep might have been like (Luke 2:8).

2. How did they react when the angel suddenly appeared (Luke 2:9)? Why do you think they reacted this way? What caused this fear besides the angel itself (Luke 2:9)? What do you think this "glory" might have been like? How do you think you would have reacted in the same situation?

3. What news did the angel have for them (Luke 2:10–11)? How were the shepherds told they would be able to recognize that the baby they found was actually the Savior (Luke 2:12)?

4. What is the significance of this simple sign that the King of kings had been born?

5. Put yourself in the field that night as the angels sang a glory song to God (Luke 2:13–14). How would your understanding and plans for Christmas change if you had actually been there?

6. How did the shepherds respond to the news the angels brought to them (Luke 2:15–16)? What one word from these verses describes their reaction best?

7. After they saw the baby Jesus, what did the shepherds do (Luke 2:17, 20)?

8. How did the people who heard the news respond (Luke 2:18)?

9. What reaction did Mary have to all the events of those early days in Bethlehem (Luke 2:19)?

10. How have you responded to the news that a Savior was born in Bethlehem more than two thousand years ago? How do you celebrate that birth? What might change about your celebrations if you responded as the people in Luke 2:18 did or as Mary, Jesus' mother, did?

Thursday

Responding to the Word
Matthew 1:18–25; Luke 1:26–38

Angel announcements bring to Mary and Joseph the news that Jesus would be born. They had been chosen to parent this baby, this One that would be the Savior of the world. When you read these two parts of the story, one of an angel's pronouncement to Mary and the other of an angel's intervention in Joseph's plans, a major theme quickly reveals itself.

These two people, unmarried, still young, engaged, with plans and dreams and desires, were *right*. Right with God (Matthew 1:19, 24; Luke 1:28, 38), right and still pure with each other (Matthew 1:18; Luke 1:34), and willing to be obedient to God's plans for their lives, even if those plans were not what they had in mind.

Obviously, a pregnancy before marriage would not be what Mary had planned. Or Joseph for that matter. They well knew the censure and disgrace they and their families would experience in their village. Perhaps that is why Mary went to visit her cousin Elizabeth, to get away from the troubles her unwed pregnancy had caused (Luke 1:39–40). Or did God somehow protect them from this turmoil? Scripture gives no indication.

What Scripture does, however, is give a clear picture of two righteous people, willing to do as God asked, individually and as a couple. With little fanfare and an obvious desire to remain low-key and in the background (Matthew 1:19), they began a journey that would lead to the work of the Messiah. They shared in His work by nurturing and caring for Him as an infant, a toddler, a child, a teen.

What's the role you play as a believer, a woman, a mom? Do you have any idea of God's specific design for your life? Or do you just "go with the flow"? Whatever your mode of operation, give priority to discovering how God would use you in your particular roles. Has He called you to some particular difficulty or suffering? Has He called you to serve your husband and children in a time of quiet, in separation? Does He want to use you to bring about some particular change in your home? Your church? Your culture? Whatever your call as a believer, follow it willingly and wholeheartedly. Like Mary. Like Joseph.

Friday

For the second week in a row, use this day to pray for your children. Luke 2:52 is a verse any mother can use to form a prayer for her children. It speaks of the growth of Jesus from a child to a man. He grew up emotionally, intellectually, spiritually, and physically. More than that, all He was becoming made Him a favorite with other people and with God. All of the ways Jesus grew are ways you can pray for your children, that God would work in them and through you so they grow in "wisdom and stature, and in favor with God and men" (NKJV).

Dear Father God, my children need You. So do I. I wish for them to grow up well, to be spiritually and emotionally and intellectually fit for Your kingdom. I wish for them to be accepted by others for who they are. Help me to be the mother to them that will produce such splendid growth. Keep their hearts tender toward You and toward others. In the name of Jesus I pray, Amen.

Jesus' Baptism, Temptation, Disciples

Monday

Reading the Word
Matthew 3:13–4:22; Mark 1:9–20; 2:13–17; 3:13–19;
Luke 4:1–13; 6:12–16; John 1:35–51

THE STORY

The muscles on Peter's rough, strong arms bulged as he threw the largest of their fishing nets across the water. He and his brother Andrew spent every day fishing, fishing, fishing. Not that it wasn't an honorable and even, most of the time, profitable occupation. But Peter felt like there should be more to life, something else he could do. Peter picked up one side of another net and waited for Andrew to pick up the other side. In tandem, with the grace of years of practice, they tossed the net over the water. Peter used the edge of his robe to wipe the sweat from his forehead. The morning sun was hot, the day ahead long.

Just as Peter opened his mouth to complain to Andrew, a stranger approached. Peter stared. A young man—looked like He was used to physical labor, maybe a farmer or carpenter. An unusual man. Peter continued to stare, wondering why he had even thought that. But there was just something about the man, something he had never seen before, something indefinable. Just as Peter turned to look at Andrew, the stranger spoke.

"Come, follow Me, and I'll make you fishers of men." Andrew's eyes held the same excitement and anticipation that Peter felt. Without a word, they dropped their net, turned from their equipment, and followed (Mathew 4:18–20, author's paraphrase).

THE MESSAGE

Jesus' ministry on earth involved people. Lots of them, from crowds of thousands (Matthew 14:21) to close friendships with individuals (John 11:1–44). But most important in Jesus' life and ministry were the twelve individuals known as His disciples (Luke 6:12–16). Each was called individually to leave his life and work and to follow Him, learning from Him, seeing His works, and being prepared for a larger role in the church that would be established after Jesus' death and resurrection.

THE MAIN POINT

Jesus is still looking for disciples, those who will leave behind, put in second place, all those things that make up everyday life, and follow Him first, wholeheartedly, without reserve. He wants more than just a part of your life, He wants it all. While that may sound like He asks a lot, more perhaps than you want to give, what He offers in return will more than make up for whatever it is you must give up. He promises (John 10:10).

TAKE NOTE

Luke 6:12–16—One of Jesus' first acts in ministry was to call twelve men to follow Him. Those men were His apostles or disciples. John the Baptist had his disciples (Matthew 9:14), as did the Pharisees (Matthew 22:16). Simply put, disciples are those who are willing to be led, to learn and put into practice the teachings of their leader.

Tuesday

Reflecting on the Word
Matthew 3:13–17

Water played an important role in religious ceremony throughout Israelite history. Aaron used water to purify the priests before they participated in a tabernacle ceremony (Exodus 29:4). Water was used for ceremonial cleansing after being infected with a skin disease (Leviticus 14:8–9) as well as after a woman's monthly period (Leviticus 15:19–23; 2 Samuel 11:2–5).

When John the Baptist arrived on the scene, he stepped into the Jordan River and continued the tradition of using water for spiritual and ceremonial cleansing. But he instilled additional significance to the act, calling his listeners to repent and to be baptized, using the river's water to immerse those who responded. No longer a simple religious ceremony, baptism now had implications for an individual's moral and daily life.

One day, as John stood again in the river, preaching and baptizing, Jesus joined him in the water and asked to be baptized. Not that Jesus needed to repent or change anything about His lifestyle. His baptism pictured for His followers what was to come—His death and resurrection. And Jesus' baptism offered more than mere water. Jesus came to baptize with the Holy Spirit as well (Mark 1:8), giving His followers the power to live the changed life baptism signified.

On the day of Pentecost, when Peter preached his first sermon, he called his audience to repentance and baptism, and three thousand responded (Acts 2:38–41). Paul continued that teaching, helping believers to understand that the act of baptism signified their new life in Christ (Romans 6:3–4). Today, baptism continues to be a crucial sacrament of church life, indicating a person's participation in the death and resurrection of Christ.

Wednesday

Studying the Word
Luke 4:1–13

Here's a model for you to follow. When you're tempted by Satan, use the story of Jesus' temptation in the wilderness to discover how you can resist. Satan, that one of calculating and conniving evil, will flee if you follow Jesus' example.

1. What event had just happened that caused Jesus to be filled with the Spirit (Luke 4:1)? Where did that Spirit lead Him? Why do you think the Spirit led Jesus to such a place?
2. What weakness did the devil first use to try to tempt Jesus (Luke 4:2–3)? Why would it be wrong for Jesus to do this?
3. What tool did Jesus use to resist the devil?
4. What did the devil offer Jesus in His second temptation (Luke 4:5–7 NKJV)? Didn't Jesus already have this "glory" and "power"? Or was there something He needed to do in order to gain it (Revelation 5:12)?
5. What tool did Jesus use to resist the devil?
6. What craziness did the devil want Jesus to do next (Luke 4:9–11)? How does the devil try to use Jesus' own tool against Him?
7. What tool did Jesus use to resist this temptation?
8. What tool do you have at your disposal to resist temptation? What could you do to have that tool more readily available to you?
9. What does Luke 4:13 tell you about temptation in Jesus' future? What tool do you think He will use to resist?
10. What promise does 1 Corinthians 10:13 make to you? What temptations have you faced lately? How does this verse give you confidence when you face those temptations?

Thursday

Responding to the Word
Matthew 4:18–22

Just a minute. Hold on a sec. Wait. Hold it!

How often have you heard those words from your children or family or friends? A quick response isn't often crucial, so a few extra minutes of waiting might be more a nuisance than a true problem. But the quickness and eagerness of a response when someone is asked to do something can be an indication of their willingness, their love for the asker, their depth of character.

When Jesus called the first four men to follow Him and become His disciples, their response to Him is noteworthy. Peter and Andrew's response was to follow "straightway" (Matthew 4:20 KJV). James and John followed "immediately" (Matthew 4:22 NKJV). Both left things behind—tools, occupations, family. This Jesus called, and they followed. No questions asked. No just-a-minutes spoken.

How quick are you to obey? Take a far-from-scientific test:

When my husband wants something done, I . . .
When my teens need something, I . . .
When my young children call, I . . .
When my infant cries, I . . .
When my boss calls, I . . .
When a friend is in need, I . . .
When Jesus calls, I . . .

Do you often wait a bit to respond to such requests? Why? Is it simply to be the one in power? To make the one who needs your help play the waiting game? Isn't that foolish? What sort of power is that? Or do you have legitimate reasons for making someone wait?

How will you respond when Jesus calls? He calls disciples today just as He called the twelve when He was on earth. Will you wobble and waver and decide not to decide? Or will you follow in the speedy footsteps of those disciples of old and answer straightway or immediately?

Friday

Praying the Word
Mark 1:11

At Jesus' baptism God spoke words of assurance and love, and spoke them aloud so that all those present heard. "You are my Son, I love You, I'm pleased with You." Who wouldn't want to hear such words from a parent or other loved one? Today, talk to God as your Father, your *Abba*, Daddy (Romans 8:15). Tell Him what's in your heart. Thank Him for His love for you. Then ask Him how you can be pleasing to Him.

Father God, I come to You as a needy youngster comes to his or her daddy. I need You. I'm so grateful that You call me Your child and that You love me. What would I do without Your love? Teach me of Yourself, Father, what You want me to become, how You want me to serve You, how I can please You. In Your Son Jesus' holy name, Amen.

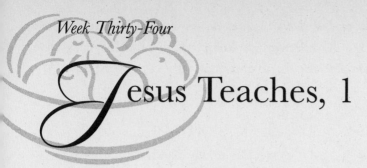

Jesus Teaches, 1

Monday

Reading the Word
Matthew 5:1–7:23; Luke 6:17–45

THE STORY

John sat down on grass that was still a bit damp with the morning dew. His robe folded under him for protection, he settled himself into a comfortable position. Jesus had begun to talk, to teach, and John wanted to be able to listen without distraction. John had been following Jesus as His disciple for only a short time, and already Jesus' teachings had turned most of what John thought upside-down. The hungry would be filled, the poor, rich, the sad, comforted. A lot of what Jesus taught was the opposite of the teachings of John's culture and religion. But strangely, it made more sense to John than all the rules and regulations he had followed since birth. Those had produced nothing in the way of peace or satisfaction, only guilt. What Jesus taught filled a yearning within John that had long gone unsatisfied. He eagerly turned his eyes, his ears, and his heart to hear what Jesus had to teach today.

THE MESSAGE

Expect the unexpected. If you think the teachings of Jesus are conventional or will mesh easily with the teachings of the world around you, you're about to be surprised. Jesus taught much that went against the wisdom of His age. His teachings continue to go against people's natural inclinations, against the ways of culture, sometimes even against the teachings of the church. Listen carefully. What you learn just might change your life!

THE MAIN POINT

Jesus didn't change anything about the Old Testament. He simply fulfilled it. What had been a set of rules and regulations, impossible to keep perfectly, He kept. What had been a matter of lifestyle became a matter of the heart. What people couldn't accomplish in themselves, He accomplished for them.

TAKE NOTE

Matthew 5:1; Luke 6:17—Matthew and Luke recorded what appears to be the same incident—Jesus' teaching these particular lessons—but seem to contradict each other about the location. Matthew placed this event on a "mountain," while Luke placed it on a "level place." Perhaps they are the same location, a level plateau on a mountain. Or perhaps Jesus taught these same things on separate occasions in different locations. Either way, what appears to be a contradiction really isn't.

Matthew 5:3–11; Luke 6:20–22—These teachings of Jesus are often called the *beatitudes,* a word that doesn't appear in the English Scripture. The English word *beatitude* is derived from a Latin word that means "a statement of blessing."

Tuesday

Reflecting on the Word
Matthew 5:21, 27, 31, 33, 38, 43

This "sermon on the mount," as it is commonly called, probably took place early in Jesus' ministry. Jesus stood before the crowd gathered to hear Him and immediately began to refute the usual teachings of the day. A common thread in the verses listed above is His statement, "You have heard that it was said to those of old." Then He probably shocked His audience with His audacious and revolutionary, "But I tell you" (Matthew 5:21a, 22, 26, 28, 32, 34, 39, 44 NKJV).

Jesus wanted to be crystal clear, right from the beginning, that His message was new, different. Following the letter of the law wasn't good enough. The heart had to become involved in the process. Therefore, the letter of the law that commanded no murder turned into no hate when the heart became involved. The letter of the law that commanded no adultery turned into no lust when the heart became involved. The letter of the law that said to love your neighbor, said to love your enemy when the heart became involved. Jesus was looking for those willing to obey the spirit of the law, not just practice legalism.

The religious leaders of Jesus' day were first-class legalists. From laws describing what could and couldn't be done on the Sabbath to laws about clothing and behavior, the leaders upheld a minutiae of rules that no one could keep perfectly. Most prescribed outward behavior rather than heart obedience. In this sermon, Jesus clearly opposed those legalists, going to the heart of the law with His "You have heard it said . . . but I tell you."

Legalism is rampant in many circles yet today. What is it about humans that we would rather follow a list of rules than turn our hearts to the Savior? We try and try to follow the rules, fail, and try again. The solution before us is not to try harder, but to give our hearts over to the One who kept the rules perfectly—Jesus.

Wednesday

Studying the Word
Matthew 6:9–13

When Jesus' disciples wanted to be taught how to pray (Luke 11:1), He taught them what is commonly called "The Lord's Prayer," a model for believers' prayers. Read through it, study it by answering these questions, and then *pray* it.

1. How did Jesus address God (Matthew 6:9)? Do you think this was a common way to address Him at that time? Why or why not?

2. When you think of God as Father, what sorts of characteristics come to mind?

3. What does it mean to *hallow* God's name (Matthew 6:9 NKJV)? What more common word would you substitute?

4. Why would you ask for God's will to be done on earth? How is God's will done or not done in your life? In your church? In your culture?

5. Why do you think this prayer asks for only daily bread? Why not for longer periods of nourishment?

6. What does the word *debts* refer to in Matthew 6:12? What other word could you use? Why do you think God's forgiveness of your sins is tied to your forgiveness of others? (See also Matthew 6:14–15.) How does your forgiveness of others, or lack of it, influence the effectiveness of your prayers?

7. Does God actually lead you into temptation (Matthew 6:13)? If not, what does this phrase mean?

8. How does God deliver from the "evil one" (1 Corinthians 10:12–13; Galatians 6:1; Hebrews 2:18; 4:15; James 1:13–15)?

9. How does Jesus teach believers to end their prayers (Matthew 6:13*b*)?

The Women's Devotional Guide to the Bible

Thursday

Responding to the Word
Matthew 6:25–34

"Don't worry. Be happy."

The words of an older popular song seem trite and condescending when compared with Jesus' loving call in this passage to leave your worries behind and trust in God. He's not giving another hard-to-keep law to live by so much as He's giving you an invitation to trust.

After rehearsing the things people generally worry about—daily needs like food and clothing—Jesus asked His listeners a rhetorical question, one with an obvious answer. Can you add one hour to your life by worrying? Can you bring about *anything* purely by worrying? The obvious answer is, nope, not a thing. In fact, if you think about it, you can actually remove hours from your life by worrying, with the emotional and physical damage worry can cause when it goes unchecked.

What is at the root of most worry? Jesus answered that question clearly, forthrightly, with little diplomacy or care for the feelings of those listening. At the root of worry is a lack of faith in God's ability to provide. Ouch.

In the last two verses of this passage, Jesus made a shift from worry itself to the lifestyle differences the worrier and the truster evidence. Those who trust in God reveal it by their concentration on the significant rather than passing things of life. Rather than focusing their lives on the temporary, which is what the "Gentiles" (NKJV), the "pagans" (NIV), do (another ouch!), they focus their lives on the things that last, God's kingdom and the righteousness to be gained through faith in Jesus.

Without a doubt you've had times when you've worried about something. Maybe you've even had lots of times, times when worry has taken the place of trust and belief in God's power to provide what you need. Perhaps you're in one of those times right now. Maybe you simply need to adjust the level of your trust in God by spending more time with Him.

Or perhaps you're in the midst of a time of suffering or extreme difficulty, when God seems distant, unable or unwilling to meet some need. Those times are tough. There are no ready answers. But one thing is sure: God is just as present in those times as when you feel Him near. All the worry in the world won't change a thing. But trusting God? With that you can change the world!

Friday

Praying the Word
Matthew 6:9–13

Spend some time today putting the Lord's Prayer into your own words, using the language you would use every day. Go through the prayer carefully, using what you learned in Wednesday's study to decipher the meaning of each phrase. Use your written words to begin your time of prayer today.

Father, I know that when I pray to You I release Your power and Your purposes in my life. I thank You that Jesus has taught me clearly what and how I should pray. Help me to faithfully present my praises and my needs before You. I love You, Lord. Amen.

Week Thirty-Five

Jesus Teaches, 2

Monday

Reading the Word

Matthew 9:35–38; 11:25–30; 22:34–36; Mark 7:1–23; 9:33–37;
Luke 14:25–35; 18:18–30; 21:5–38; John 3:1–21; 4:1–42;
6:25–59; 14:5–16:33

THE STORY

Jesus felt the burning heat of the road through the leather soles of His sandals. He and His disciples had traveled far, were weary and hungry. When they came to the well outside the town of Sychar, Jesus lowered Himself to a nearby wall with a sigh. This would be a good place to rest. His disciples looked at Him in amazement. Most Jews didn't travel through Samaria, this neighboring area of unclean, low-class citizens. Now Jesus was actually stopping to rest in one of their towns. But the disciples had come to expect the unexpected from this Jesus they followed. So, when He asked them to go into the town for food, they complied.

Jesus rested back on His elbows, lifting His feet from the cool dust. His parched throat could use a drink of the cool well water, but He had nothing to draw the water. A young woman came to the well. With one measured look, Jesus knew all about her—her husbands, her loose lifestyle. He looked with love and compassion on this woman, this one who searched in all the wrong places for love and satisfaction and contentment. With a goal of more than quenching His own thirst in mind, Jesus asked her a simple question: "Will you give me a drink?"

| 247

THE MESSAGE

Nothing in life satisfies. People will try anything for a sense of peace and well-being: success, money, respect, sex, excitement, anything. At some point, most come to a dead end, realizing that all their efforts have produced nothing, no longings fulfilled, no satisfaction. The woman at the well was at just such a point when Jesus stopped her and offered her living water.

THE MAIN POINT

Living water is available to all who are thirsty, which is pretty much everyone on earth. The only thing that will ever fully satisfy the yearning of the human heart is Jesus. He is living water. Drink, and you'll never be thirsty again.

TAKE NOTE

John 4:9—When the Assyrians conquered the Northern Kingdom of Israel, and its capital, Samaria, they deported many of its citizens and resettled the land with other conquered peoples. Those peoples inter-married with the Israelites who still lived in the land. The resulting Samaritans were of mixed race and mixed the worship of the gods they had brought with them from their countries with worship of the God of the land of Israel. The Jews of Jesus' time considered Samaritans to be second-class citizens, people with whom they desired to have little contact. Which makes Jesus' conversation with the Samaritan woman all the more striking. He brought a message of freedom that fulfilled every longing, and He revealed through this incident that His message was intended for more than just His own Jewish race.

John 3:2—The Jews called the teachers of the law "rabbi," which was a label of respect. In general, the word can mean "master" or "teacher." Jesus' followers often called Him "rabbi," especially when they were asking Him to answer a question about the law.

Tuesday

Reflecting on the Word
John 3:1–21

One simple visit from a fearful Pharisee, one who came sneaking in to see Jesus at night, produced the most concise, most often repeated salvation verse in the Bible. Nicodemus had a reputation to protect, after all. He was a respected member of the ruling class of the Jews, a man others looked up to, a man hungry to know the truth. His peers were offended by this upstart Jesus, who turned all their careful teachings and rules and lifestyles into something to be disregarded rather than imitated. Nicodemus knew exactly what his friends would think if they knew he went to talk to Jesus. So, rather than visiting openly, he tiptoed in the dark of night to find Jesus.

And he discovered that what his friends thought was true. This Jesus taught things that went against the grain. And yet Nicodemus knew Jesus' teachings had the ring of truth. He knew from watching and listening that Jesus was no ordinary human being—that He was "from God" (John 3:2 NKJV).

Jesus' teaching on being born again appears only in the book of John. No other gospel writer recorded the story. Understandably, Nicodemus was confused by Jesus' statement. He could only think in physical terms of being born again. An impossibility. But Jesus saw beyond the physical and was helping His followers see beyond it as well. With careful words and compassion for Nicodemus, Jesus taught that being born again meant to be changed, to be *re*born.

The Holy Spirit comes and brings new life to those who are dead in sin (Romans 6:11). You deserve only death. But through Jesus' faithful work on earth, His ministry, His death, and His resurrection, you can be reborn into new life in Him. Your physical life continues, and your new, living spiritual life begins when you turn to Jesus and receive His offer of rebirth. You are no longer the old you. You are a new, fresh, living you—a spiritual being with potential and mission. Your old life in sin is now dead; you are a new creation in Christ (2 Corinthians 5:17). Although you didn't deserve it at all, you now have friendship with God. You are now a child of God!

The apostle John, who was most likely present when Nicodemus had his conversation with Jesus, taught what that new life produces in those who have been born again. It can all be summed up with one word: *love* (1 John 4:7–21).

Wednesday

Studying the Word
Mark 9:33–37

Jesus taught His disciples the paradoxical ways of the kingdom. First is last, big is small, great is ordinary. Study His teachings in these verses and consider your position as a child of God and your service to the children of God.

1. What had the disciples been arguing about (Mark 9:33*b*)? Why were they hesitant to tell Jesus?
2. In common, everyday terms, what does it mean for a believer to be last (Mark 9:35)? Think in terms of specific parts of life: as a wife, as a parent, as a friend, as an employee, as the boss, as a church member.
3. What does being a servant of all look like today (Mark 9:35)? How did it look to Jesus (John 13:3–17)?
4. How can/could you be a servant in your everyday life? Why do you think this role is hard for most people?
5. What was Jesus trying to show the disciples by using a child as an example (Mark 9:36; Matthew 18:2–4)? What characteristics of a child do you think Jesus wants to see in believers? How does that look in your everyday life?

6. When Jesus said you should accept little children, what sorts of people was He referring to (Mark 9:37 NKJV)? What people in your life are like these "little children"?
7. How important is this teaching (Matthew 18:6)?

Thursday

Responding to the Word
Luke 21:5–38

Read these predictions of Jesus and you just might get pretty uncomfortable. Scared even. Wars. Famine. Death. Destruction. Signs in the heavens. Weapons. Every bad thing you can think of is described in these words.

Jesus was responding to His disciples' admiration of the temple and its beauty. He warned them that not one stone would be left on another (Luke 21:6), something they found hard to imagine. They asked for a sign so they would know when this was about to happen. And they got a whipping with words, a scenario set to frighten the most daring. In their generation (Luke 21:32) the destruction of the magnificent temple and all of Jerusalem would take place. And it did. The Romans came in with their strength of men and weapons and destroyed Jerusalem in AD 70.

But Jesus had in mind here more than just the first century destruction of the temple and Jerusalem. His words are also a warning of events still in the future. The prophetic words of Jesus can be compared to the prophetic words of John in the book of Revelation. The time near the end of the world will be filled with signs, terrible events designed to get people's attention, to make them aware that the time is short before judgment. Catastrophe has the capability to grab people complacent with living in the present, making them think about the future, the end of the world, and their relationship with the God in charge of the events.

Without dissecting all the possible ways the last days could happen, what is your reaction to thoughts of Jesus' return? Does it make you fearful? Excited? Worried? All of the above? Whatever your reaction, remember what Jesus said in Luke 21:28. If you don't know Jesus, get to know Him. If you do know Him, lift your head and raise your eyes and look for His approach. He's your redemption! He's coming to bring you home!

Friday

Praying the Word
Matthew 11:28–30

If you're like most people today, you feel overworked, harassed, over-scheduled, under-appreciated, tense, stressed, worn out—the list could go on and on. Today's culture requires a huge investment from its people in time and energy and gives little in return. No wonder so many, Christians included, feel like they're at the end of their ropes. Today, take comfort from Jesus' offer of rest and relief. Pray His promise back to Him in your prayer time today.

Dear Jesus, I thank You that You realized, even thousands of years ago, how weary I would get with life. I thank You for Your offer of rest. I lay my many burdens at Your feet, and ask that You will help me to leave them there. I lay myself at Your feet, Lord, and ask for the relief that only You can give from the burdens of life. I trust You, Lord, for life-restoring rest. Amen.

Jesus Tells Stories in Matthew and Mark

Monday

Reading the Word
Matthew 7:24–27; 13; 25:1–13, 31–46;
Mark 4:21–22; 12:1–11; 13:33–37

THE STORY

Jesus sat on the bench outside of the house of a friend. He rested His back against the warmth of the wall. The sun was gone, but its stored warmth could still be felt. He looked at the disciples gathered around Him, some sitting on stools, some on the ground. Each one formed such an integral part of the whole of their little band. He loved each one, even those that weren't so easy to love. He had so much to tell them, so much they needed to learn. With love obvious in His voice and on His face, He began to tell them a story.

THE MESSAGE

Jesus spoke His message to the people in story form, in what are commonly called parables. His stories could be easily understood and their meanings quickly deduced by those who were seeking truth. Those not so inclined tended to doubt or misunderstand their meanings or didn't dig deep enough to find them. Which was exactly Jesus' goal. He wanted to make the truth available to those who were ready to listen but keep it from those who would use it for evil (Matthew 13:11–13).

THE MAIN POINT

How are your ears? Are you tuned in to the truth? Are you eager to search for the deeper meanings that can be found in Jesus' teachings? The parables that Jesus taught are like mines that can be entered. You might find a bit of riches at the opening to the mine. But if you're willing to go a bit deeper, willing to dig, you'll find great riches.

TAKE NOTE

Matthew 13:3—In a country where agriculture formed the primary occupation, the people would instantly understand the parable Jesus told about the sower and his soils. Without the equipment common to sowing seed today, a farmer went out to his fields with a bag of seed slung over his shoulder. He would grab a handful of grain with his hand and then fling it out across the soil. Sowers became so adept at this chore that seeds were sown with surprising consistency across the entire field.

Tuesday

Reflecting on the Word
Matthew 7:24–27

Houses can look pretty similar from the outside: well built, strong, attractive. Windows are properly placed, doors open without too much effort, walls are well structured and painted. The builder has done the job well, making sure the house has all that's needed for those who live within it. Except for what the casual observer can't see—the foundation.

Jesus told the story of two houses, both adequate, but with very different foundations. The house built on rock withstood the inevitable storm. The one built on sand, however, wasn't so fortunate. When the storm came, the foundation slipped and the house fell.

Most of Jesus' listeners would immediately identify with these houses and their foundations. They knew the dangers of building in certain areas. Those areas appeared dry and safe in good weather, but when the rains came, the water collected and rushed through violently, carrying down soil and sand—and houses.

Jesus' intent is fairly easy to decipher. Wise builders build their faith well, preparing for the possibility of storms. They listen closely to the teachings of Jesus; they put what they've learned into practice. Foolish builders build their faith only for show. They know all the right practices, they know all the right words, but little of it makes it to their hearts or forms any sort of foundation for their lives.

Then the storms come, as they inevitably, unavoidably, devastatingly, will. The one whose house is built on the solid rock of the rich teachings of Jesus will withstand those storms. The winds of suffering can blow, the waves of tragedy can strike, and that house of faith, though sometimes shaken, stands firm.

Wednesday

Studying the Word
Matthew 25:31–46

The parable of the sheep and the goats holds some secrets about the judgment all humans will someday face. Study these verses, answer these questions, and discover for yourself what that day will be like for you.

1. Close your eyes and picture the scene described in Matthew 25:31–34. Describe it. What will it look like? Sound like? Feel like? Which side of the throne will you be on? On what does Jesus base His separation of the goats from the sheep (Matthew 7:23; 1 John 5:12)?

2. What is your inheritance in heaven based on (Matthew 25:35–36)? (Note: this doesn't say your *entrance* into heaven but your *inheritance* in heaven.)

3. How do the righteous respond (Matthew 25:37–39)? Why do you think they respond this way? What does that tell you about the works of the righteous?

4. To whom did the righteous do these deeds? For whom (Matthew 25:40)?

5. What is the punishment of the unrighteous based on (Matthew 25:41–43)?

6. How do they respond to their punishment (Matthew 25:44)? What's the difference between their actions and those of the righteous (Matthew 25:45)?

7. What sorts of deeds, in everyday life, do you think Jesus is looking for you to do? Be specific, concrete.

8. What sort of attitude should accompany your actions?

9. How does this parable harmonize with the teachings in James 1:27; 2:17?

Thursday

Responding to the Word
Matthew 13:44–46

Jesus' parables of a hidden treasure and of a pearl are stories of passion. The man who found treasure in a field sold all he had to buy the field. The man who found an exquisite pearl sold all he had to buy that pearl. Nothing they already owned held as much value for them as getting that treasure, that pearl. They were passionate about gaining what they had seen.

Jesus said those treasures were like the kingdom of heaven. Nothing is as important as gaining a place in that kingdom. A believer's greatest passion in life should be about the kingdom.

So many things easily pull a person's eyes away from what's truly important. The everyday events and requirements of living in the twenty-first century bring along with them the need to focus on them, the need to make a way through the morass of living life in a confused and confusing world. All those needs pull and push and shove focus away from Jesus and the kingdom.

And they shouldn't. Really! They shouldn't. You need to live in this world. No getting away from that. But your true life is "hidden with Christ in God" (Colossians 3:3 NKJV). And that's something to get passionate about. It's something worth seeking after with all your heart, with intensity, with passion.

Be real today. What's first in your life? Do you seek Jesus and His kingdom first and foremost? Or do other things draw your attention away from Him? Remember, it's not so much those things that draw your attention that are the problem; it's those things that draw your attention *away* from Jesus. Examine those things and begin to put them into proper place in your heart and life. You'll never be sorry. What you'll get is a treasure worth giving up all you own to gain.

Friday

Praying the Word
Mark 13:32–27

You're in the dark as far as the date of Jesus' return. Not too surprising, really, since knowing the date, knowing anything about the future, would hamper your faith more than help it. Today, thank God that He has promised to return, to bring glory with Him, to take you home with Him. That day will come suddenly, He said, and believers need to be prepared. In praying today, ask Him how you can prepare and what He wants you to do with your time on earth.

Dear Jesus, I thank You for the life You lived on earth so long ago. And I thank You for the promise that You will return. Make me aware daily that this life is temporary. Teach me what I am to do with this life of mine here, how I prepare myself and others for Your return. Maranatha, Lord Jesus! Come quickly!

Week Thirty-Seven

Jesus Tells Stories in Luke

Monday

Reading the Word

Luke 10:30–37; 12:16–21; 15:3–32; 16:19–31; 18:1–8; 19:11–27

THE STORY

Jesus only needed one look to see that the person asking the questions wasn't sincere. He was trying to trap Jesus, to test Him. This lawyer, who knew the laws of Israel front to back and side to side and top to bottom, wasn't looking for truth as much as trouble. Getting Jesus into hot water with His cohorts was his sole purpose in questioning the man he called *Teacher*. With love in His eyes and a bit of a smile on His face, Jesus told a story. Jesus made the hero of the story a Samaritan, someone the lawyer would be sure to despise. But also someone that made the point of the story unmistakable. Jesus watched as the lawyer walked away, certain the man had understood the truth, but not certain if he would follow Jesus' suggestion to "Go and do likewise" (Luke 10:37*b*).

THE MESSAGE

Most of the parables told in Luke have obvious meanings. Jesus told them in story form to capture His audience's attention and to make the truth He was teaching stimulating and acceptable. Even those who have difficulty listening to a long discourse are drawn into a good story with a good point. And that's one thing Jesus' stories always had: a good lesson.

| 259

THE MAIN POINT

Heads up! Listen and learn! More good stories, parables, on the way for those seeking truth. Luke recorded more of Jesus' parables than either Matthew or Mark.

TAKE NOTE

Luke 15:8—The coin mentioned in this parable was a drachma. A single drachma was worth a day's wages in Jesus' time. The ten coins were probably the woman's entire savings, or possibly her dowry. She would need a light to search her home because houses in those days had few windows and low doors that admitted little light. Sweeping would help because of the sound a coin would make when moved along by the broom. Jesus' parables often used objects and actions common to the day, easily grasped by those of His listeners who were seeking truth.

Tuesday

Reflecting on the Word
Luke 15:3–32

Jesus included three potential helpers in His story of the Good Samaritan. The first is a priest, one of the religious elite in Israel. Priests were of the tribe of Levi and the family of Aaron in the tribe. Only those who could prove their lineage from Aaron were allowed to serve in the tabernacle and then in the temple. The laws for who could serve as priests came to Moses early in the desert after the people had been freed from slavery in Egypt (Exodus 28:1–4; 29:9; 1 Chronicles 6:48). The first person to pass the beaten man on the road to Jericho? A priest, one who spent his life serving God. Certainly he would stop and help. No, he just drew his priestly robes aside and walked on, leaving the poor man for dead.

The tribe of Levi came from the family of Levi, one of the sons of Jacob. God specifically designated this tribe as the one that would serve in the temple as helpers to the priests (Numbers 1:50–53; 31:30; 1 Chronicles 6:48). They washed and carried and repaired and generally took care of the tabernacle and then the temple. Their service was given for part of each year, rotating from one family of the tribe to another. One of these privileged Levites also passed the man who had been beaten and left for dead. He saw him but couldn't be bothered and went on his way.

Then came a Samaritan, impure by any Jewish religious standards, a racial and religious outcast. Not worth considering or taking any note of as a man. He, too, saw the injured man on the side of the road. No one would expect him to stop. He wouldn't have the moral or religious motivation to stop and help anyone. What's this? He stopped! Not only did he care for the man's immediate needs, he paid for future needs as well.

The first lesson in this parable is to expect the unexpected. The ones you would think would help didn't. The one you would expect to walk on by stopped to give aid. Another lesson? Faith and obedience are heart matters. The religious priest and Levite apparently had it all together religiously, but their hearts weren't engaged in the process. If their hearts had been involved, they would have responded with love and compassion. While the Samaritan probably didn't have it all together religiously, he certainly had the love of God resident in his heart. And that love caused him to reach out to help a fellow human being. In His story, Jesus repeated what Israelite prophets had been telling the people for years. Check out Amos 6:6–8 for proof.

Wednesday

Studying the Word
Luke 15:1–32

Jesus told three stories in a row about lost items in response to some mutterings by the Pharisees. Read these three "lost" stories and discover what is important to Jesus and should, perhaps, be important to you.

1. What were the Pharisees complaining about (Luke 15:2)? Why would Jesus tell three stories about lost items in response to their complaints?

2. In the first parable, a shepherd lost a sheep (Luke 15:4–7). Why would a shepherd worry more about a lost sheep than ninety-nine "found" sheep? What does this parable tell you about the shepherd? About Jesus?

3. The second parable is about a lost coin (Luke 15:8–10). Why would the woman be so concerned about one measly coin? What does verse nine tell you about the importance of the coin to her and to her neighbors?

4. The third parable is perhaps one of Jesus' most famous, the story of the lost son (Luke 15:11–32). What did the younger son want (Luke 15:12)? Why? (Luke 15:13a) What does this tell you about his relationship with his father?

5. What did the son do with his inheritance (Luke 15:13*b*–14)?

6. When his wealth was gone, what was he reduced to doing, to eating (Luke 15:14–16)? Why would this have been especially contemptible to Jesus' listeners (Leviticus 11:4–7)?

7. Describe in your own words how you think the younger son "came to himself" (Luke 15:17 NKJV).

8. What sort of reception did the son anticipate (Luke 15:18–19)? What sort of reception did he receive (Luke 15:20, 22–24)? What does this tell you about the father? About God?

9. Now on to the older son, who had stayed with the father and worked faithfully for him. What was his reaction to his younger brother's return (Luke 15:28*a*, 29–30)? Why do you think he responded this way? What does his response tell you about him?

10. What did the father do when he heard about his older son's refusal to join the party (Luke 15:28*b*)? What additional information does this give you about the father?

11. Consider both sons. Which one(s) was lost (Luke 15:24, 28; Isaiah 29:13)?

12. What do these three parables tell you about lost people? About God and His love for the lost? About what your love for lost people should look like?

Thursday

Responding to the Word
Luke 12:13–21

How big are your barns?

Don't have any barns, you say? Think again.

Jesus told the parable of a rich man who had so much his barns couldn't hold it all. So he tore them down, built bigger and better barns, then sat back to enjoy his riches. He had great plans to take it easy, to "eat, drink, and be merry" (Luke 12:19 NKJV). But God had other plans. No eating. No drinking. No merriment. Only death. And leaving behind those beautiful, new, full barns.

It doesn't take a brain surgeon to figure out Jesus' meaning. Greed was as insidious a problem in the first century as it is in the twenty-first. *Greed*, that ugly vice, is another word for craving more. And more. And *more*. What you have is never quite enough. It's an easy spiral to get whirled into, and it only leads to bigger and bigger spirals where God holds less and less a place of importance. Paul, when he wrote to the church at Colosse, called greed a form of idolatry (Colossians 3:5 NIV). The love of *stuff* lures people away from dependence on God alone more quickly than almost anything else.

In this parable God looked down on the rich man and called him a fool. Strong words, but true. All this man's riches, all his gloriously full and beautiful barns, wouldn't help him one iota when faced with the high and holy God.

What's in your barns? What dreams, desires, and goals do you have that will fill your barns but not your soul? God calls His people today not to work for riches, but to make themselves "rich toward God" (Luke 12:21 NKJV). Think about it for a minute. What do you do or have in your life that will make you rich toward God? What do you do or have in your life that draws you away from the riches of a relationship with God? Assess what a life of riches in God will bring that a life of wealth and good things won't (John 10:10; Romans 2:4; 11:33–36; Ephesians 3:16–21). A full barn just doesn't compare!

Friday

Praying the Word
Luke 18:1–8

Jesus told a parable about a widow who kept going to an uncaring and unjust judge to get justice for a wrong done to her. She refused to give up whenever the judge ignored her or answered no. Instead she kept going to him until finally he gave in, tired of her constant badgering. The lesson here is not that you should badger God until you get what you want. He is loving and far from unjust and is eager to answer your prayers. When you go to Him consistently and persistently, He will answer. Jesus' lesson here is: don't give up!

What have you been praying about for weeks, months, years? Follow the example of the woman in Jesus' parable and don't give up!

Father God, I come to You. Again. I bring the same request I've been bringing to You for weeks/months/years. I trust that You hear me, Lord, and I know You love me. I know that what I'm asking is within Your will and power. Fulfill my request, Lord. Or, if for some reason You must say no, give me the grace and understanding to accept it. Whatever Your answer, I love You, Lord, and will continue to trust in Your faithfulness to me. Amen.

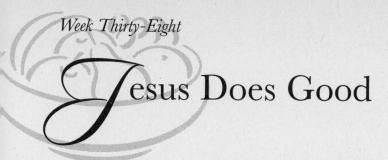

Jesus Does Good

Monday

Reading the Word

Matthew 21:12–17; Mark 1:35–39; 10:13–16;
Luke 19:1–10; John 13:1–17; 14:1–4; 17

THE STORY

Jesus reached out His arms to pick up the little girl toddling toward Him, tripping over her robe in her hurry to reach Him. He added her to the other kids already on His lap, holding her close. He smoothed the hair of one, held the hand of another, and kissed the cheek of one more. As He sat, parents brought more and more children to Him, wanting Him to touch and bless their child too. Jesus smiled in satisfaction, the love and touch of the children bringing as much joy to Him as He brought to them and their parents.

His disciples had other thoughts, however. Jesus just had too many demands on His time for this foolishness with little kids. They began to turn parents away, telling them not to bother busy Jesus.

Jesus shook His head at His disciples' thickheadedness. Did they still not understand the importance of trust and humility and teachability—childlike traits that Jesus wanted from His followers? Holding the children even more closely, Jesus told His disciples, "Cut it out! Let those little children come to me!" Looking again at the children and their parents, Jesus put His arms around as many as He could and gave each a personal blessing (Mark 10:14–16, author's paraphrase).

THE MESSAGE

Every action of Jesus had a point, a lesson involved. Whether He was going away on His own to pray, holding and blessing little children, or clearing out the temple, each act revealed something about Jesus and His character and, even more important, His mission.

THE MAIN POINT

What do your actions reveal to others? Do you think that strangers might be able to tell what you're all about by watching you? Do your actions illustrate that you're a child of the King? If so, keep on keeping on! If you're not sure, examine your actions and reactions and ask God to help you to discover how you can help others see Him by how you act.

TAKE NOTE

Mark 10:13—Children formed an important part of Israelite society, both in the Old and the New Testaments. People viewed children as a sign of God's favor (Psalm 127:3; 128:3). Children, especially sons, were necessary to preserve the family line and also to help in supporting the family.

Tuesday

Reflecting on the Word
Matthew 21:12–17

Money rolling, animals bleating, tables breaking, people running, benches falling, doves airborne—chaos—all a result of Jesus' angry response to the corruption He found in the temple. What had been built as a house for worship had become a strip mall, with dishonest merchants offering their flawed wares at inflated prices. No wonder Jesus flew at them with indignation for His Father's house and honor.

The temple at the time of Passover filled with people from all over Israel, there for the festivities and the ceremonies. Rather than carry or drive the animals necessary for their sacrifices from their hometowns, many brought money and purchased the sacrificial animals when they arrived in Jerusalem.

Also, different temple taxes had to be paid in the form of a shekel. Since many forms of money circulated in Israel during this time, worshipers would bring their form of money and exchange it for shekels when arriving in Jerusalem. The temple shekel had a pot of manna (Exodus 16:31) on one side and Aaron's budding rod (Numbers 17:8) on the other with the words "Jerusalem the Holy."

The temple itself was surrounded by several courtyards, each one more exclusive than the one preceding it. The largest court was the Court of the Gentiles, where those of non-Jewish ancestry could come to worship. A large wall separated that court from the inner courts and the temple itself, with warnings on the wall that any non-Jew who entered would be put to death. The inner courts consisted of the Women's Court, where both men and women were allowed. Next was the Court of Israel, where only Jewish men had access. The Court of the Priests surrounded the temple itself, and only those of the tribe of Levi with ceremonial duties were allowed entrance.

Jesus' anger at those who were buying and selling wasn't because of the activity so much as because of the location. The mercenary activity was taking place in the Court of the Gentiles, the largest of the courts. The activity would have been legitimate and would have caused little problem, if it had been done honestly and if it had taken place outside the temple courts. As it was, the bustle and commotion and dishonesty within the temple courts caused Jesus to pick up a handy pile of cords, make a whip (John 2:15), and drive these distractions to worship from His Father's house.

Wednesday

Studying the Word
Luke 19:1–10

Do you know anyone as eager as Zacchaeus to meet Jesus? Are you ready to introduce that person to Jesus? Study the story of Zacchaeus and his trip up a tree in order to gain some tools for reaching others with the good news of salvation.

1. How did most Israelite tax collectors get their wealth (Luke 19:2, 8)? What did these common activities by tax collectors do for their general reputation?
2. Why couldn't Zacchaeus see Jesus (Luke 19:3)? What or who keeps people today from actually seeing Jesus?
3. What did Zacchaeus do about the problem (Luke 19:4)? What are some things people today might do in order to get a glimpse of Jesus?
4. When Jesus spotted Zacchaeus in the tree, what did He tell him to do? How quickly did He want him to do it (Luke 19:5)? What did Jesus' desire to go to Zacchaeus's house imply that Jesus wanted to do? What does that tell you about how you should begin to reach out to unbelievers?

5. How did Zacchaeus answer Jesus (Luke 19:6)?
6. What was the reaction of the crowd (Luke 19:7)? Why do you think they reacted this way? How do people react when you hang out with unbelievers? Why do you think this makes some uncomfortable?
7. What did Zacchaeus's actions reveal about his heart (Luke 19:8)? What sorts of actions could you look for today that would reveal heart changes in others?
8. What did Jesus say He saw in Zacchaeus (Luke 19:9)?

Thursday

Responding to the Word
John 13:1–17

Whose feet have you washed lately? Perhaps your toddlers' as you bathed them after a hard summer day of play? Or your elderly mother's or grandmother's, who can't reach her own calloused feet any longer? Or your husband's after he's spent a day working out in cold and wet weather?

When Jesus washed His disciples' feet, He performed the ultimate act of servanthood. When visitors entered a Jewish home, the lowest servant had the job of washing their dirty feet. Since people ordinarily wore open sandals, and removed them when entering a home, their feet were usually quite soiled and needed to be washed. The act also provided a comforting and relaxing welcome to visitors.

At the Last Supper, in a room with probably few if any servants present, the disciples neglected to wash feet, perhaps because they all felt they were above the job—too good to perform such a lowly act. Imagine the sight of Jesus—the One they knew was the Messiah, their Teacher and Lord (John 13:13), sent directly from God—getting up, removing His outer robe and covering His inner clothing with a towel, then kneeling down in front of each disciple to wash his feet.

Peter's reaction was a natural one. He pulled his feet away from Jesus, instinctively aware that this act was not a natural one. But Jesus had a lesson to teach with actions rather than words, so He drew Peter's feet toward Him and carefully, lovingly washed them. Leaving nothing to chance, Jesus explained clearly that He expected His disciples to do the same; that in order to be leaders, they must be servants.

Again, whose feet have you washed lately? Have you done anything you think might be "beneath" you? More important, have you done that act lovingly and carefully? Let's be real. Many of these jobs aren't easy. Washing floors or feet, cleaning up a baby or an incontinent older adult, filing information or folding clothes—you didn't go to school for this! But "this" may be just what God is calling you to do, may be just the act that breaks down the defenses of one resistant to God, may be just the act that allows you to show, and then receive, the love of God and the blessings Jesus promised (John 13:17).

Friday

Praying the Word
Mark 1:35–39

Banging, screeching, crying, yelling, pounding feet, repetitious toys, phones, washers and dryers, TV shows, computer games—the noise and commotion level in most households today would make your grandmother cover her ears in pain and take to the fields. Maybe you wish you could go with her at times. Jesus knew the value of time alone to meditate, revive, pray. Get as alone and quiet as you can in your prayer time today. You might have to get up early in the morning, "a long while before daylight." Or you might have to get even more creative. Spend the time you have thinking about God, not the next thing to be done. Such times will give you renewal and refreshing, just as they gave Jesus the energy and purpose He needed in order to continue His ministry.

Dear Lord, help me to be more like You. Help me to recognize the value in getting away alone to pray. My life is often so hectic, Lord, that I don't think about spending time alone with You until I'm lying exhausted in my bed at night. Change me, Lord. Make me so hungry for You that I must find time in my day to be alone with You. Amen.

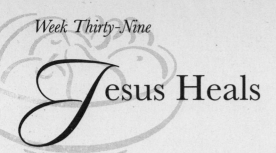

Week Thirty-Nine

Jesus Heals

Monday

Reading the Word
Matthew 9:27–33; Mark 1:40–2:12; 5:21–43; Luke 4:38–41;
9:37–43; 17:11–19; John 5:1–15; 11:1–44

THE STORY

The leper worked his way through the people who surrounded Jesus, careful to stay a few steps away from each, careful not to touch anyone and make him or her unclean. Each person he came close to drew back in disgust and fear, so a way was cleared almost automatically.

Jesus watched the leper make his way toward Him. He waited quietly, not drawing back as the others. When the leper was within a few steps, he collapsed to his knees and desperately begged Jesus to heal him. "Jesus, I know you can heal me. If only you would!" (Mark 1:40, author's paraphrase).

Jesus looked down at the man before Him, his clothing in rags, his face and form ravaged by the disease he suffered. And He was filled with sympathy and compassion for him. What a terrible thing leprosy was! Without a thought for clean and unclean rules and regulations, Jesus reached out and touched the sick man. He heard the gasps of some and the muttering of others. No Jewish person would willingly touch a leper. What was Jesus thinking?

But a touch was all it took. With a word and a touch, healing took place. The damage from the disease was gone in an instant, fresh skin replaced diseased, whole extremities replaced those deformed by the disease.

Instantly the leper knew what had happened. He felt it deep within, no need to look at the outward signs. With barely a moment to listen to Jesus' instructions about going to the priests and keeping quiet about how healing had come to him, he hurried off, eager to tell anyone who would listen how he had been miraculously healed by the Healer.

THE MESSAGE

Jesus performed many miracles during His ministry on earth. Some people followed Jesus only to get a chance to view His miracles, as though they were an exciting circus act. They were looking for excitement. Jesus' miracles, however, had much more power than just to thrill those who watched. They proved who Jesus is, the Son of God, One with power over illness, weather, even death.

THE MAIN POINT

John wrote that Jesus performed many more miracles than those He and the other gospel writers recorded (John 20:30). About forty are recorded in Matthew, Mark, Luke, and John. John also made it clear that the purpose of these miracles was to draw the spiritually hungry to Jesus, where they would find fulfillment and life (John 20:31).

TAKE NOTE

Mark 1:40—One of the most sinister and devastating of diseases described in the Bible, leprosy was a disease of the skin and tissue. Scholars now agree that the word refers to several skin diseases today, including leprosy, or what is now called Hanson's disease. Some of those skin diseases were infectious, some were not. God gave Moses strict and detailed laws for the containment of these diseases in Israelite communities. Those infected were considered ceremonially unclean and had to live in isolation outside of the towns and communities of Israel. They were also required to wear torn clothing, to keep their head uncovered (or their hair messy), and to call "Unclean!" to any who would come near them (Leviticus 13:44–46 NIV).

Tuesday

Angels stirring water. Pools for healing. Sick and diseased everywhere. Five covered porches surrounded the pool of Bethesda in Jerusalem, perfect locations for the ill to recline while waiting for the pool to be stirred. Imagine Jerusalem's sick and handicapped sitting around the pool day after day, waiting for the "certain time" (John 5:4 NKJV) when the angel whipped the water, the signal that healing was available to the first one in the pool. Pity the poor person who couldn't help him or herself. Sitting by a pool, waiting for healing, never to be healed.

For centuries the site of this pool was uncertain. The Scripture makes it clear it was in Jerusalem, near the Sheep Gate. But the exact location was disputed. Archaeologists are now quite certain that excavations of the remains of pools and porticoes near the Church of St. Anne reveal the location of this story. The Crusaders built this small church to commemorate the site where tradition says Mary, Jesus' mother, was born.

The invalid in John 5 had waited thirty-eight long years for healing. Now some rascal appeared and asked what appeared to be a foolish question: Do you want to be made well? Or perhaps it was not such a foolish question. Perhaps he had become complacent in his illness? Perhaps he would rather beg than work? Or perhaps he just simply wanted to get to the pool when the angel arrived but never managed it.

No matter now. The Great Healer was standing right in front of him. Jesus didn't ask anything else, just told the man to pick up his bed and walk. And he did. He found that he *could*. No stirred waters or racing involved.

Wednesday

Studying the Word
Mark 2:1–12

Check out this story of a few people determined to help their paralyzed friend. Then answer the following questions to digest the truths contained in the event.

1. What do you think all the people who crowded the house and the area around it were looking for (Mark 2:2)?

2. What had Jesus been doing a lot of (Mark 1)? Why do you think He *wasn't* doing miracles now (Mark 2:2)? What was He doing instead?

3. How determined were the paralyzed man's friends to get to Jesus (Mark 2:4)? Why do you think they were willing to go to such trouble? Picture the scene in your mind, from the sick person's perspective, then from the friends' perspective. What did they want Jesus to do for their friend?

4. What did Jesus offer instead (Mark 2:5)? What do you think Jesus saw as this man's deepest need? Being careful not to minimize disease and the pain it can cause in body, mind, and spirit, how does Jesus' action relate to sickness and suffering and people's needs today?

5. What truth about Jesus were the teachers of the law missing (Mark 2:6–7)?

6. How did Jesus answer them (Mark 2:8–10)? How did He prove His power (Mark 2:11)?

7. What was the most important thing Jesus taught the people in this story? How is that same truth important today? To you?

Thursday

Responding to the Word
Mark 5:24–34

Throughout the centuries women have suffered under the ministrations of doctors—until recently all were men—who often did not take female illnesses as seriously as they should have. And until recent time, not much was known about the causes and cures for the particular suffering of the woman in this story.

She had been bleeding for twelve long years. The monthly flow that would have been natural had turned into a daily, yearly torment that sapped strength and vitality, isolated her from family and friends because she was unclean, and emptied her purse. She had long ago lost hope for a cure. Except for now. Was relief within reach? With a surely shaking hand, she reached out to barely brush Jesus' robe.

With a rush that was so surprising it was almost painful, the woman felt her illness leave. She felt the vigorous, rich sensation of health enter her body. She trembled with the marvel of what had just happened—no, not just *marvel*, the *miracle*!

Did she now try to sneak away from Jesus as stealthily as she had sneaked toward Him? Did she raise her head in surprise and look around to see if anyone noticed what had happened? Did she wonder in her heart if even Jesus realized what had happened?

She didn't have to wonder for long. Jesus was not going to let the woman get away without acknowledging her and without giving her the opportunity to acknowledge Him. He knew immediately that someone had been healed. And despite His questions, He knew who. He wanted the woman to come forward, to openly admit her healing and her faith in the Healer.

Miraculous healing from illness still happens today. Sometimes it happens without the help of doctors, sometimes with the help of modern medicine and doctors, always with amazement and wonder at the beauty of a whole and healthy body. If you or someone you know has struggled for years with illness, whatever its source, whatever its symptoms, go to the Healer for help. Reach out and touch the hem of His robe in prayer, asking for healing, asking for strength when healing doesn't come for some reason, asking for grace to remember the ultimate healing that will be available to all when heaven's doors open.

Friday

Praying the Word
Luke 17:11–19

Only one returned to thank Jesus for healing. Pretty sad, right? How easy it is, and even understandable, to get caught up in the excitement of answered prayer but never stop to thank the One who answered. Review some of your recent prayer requests. How has God answered? Have you thanked Him? Spend your prayer time today in thanks to God.

I admit it, Lord. I'm usually more like the nine lepers in this story than the tenth. Forgive me. Teach me to be thankful to You for all You do, for all Your goodness, for Your loving answers to my prayers. Thank You most of all for being my God, my Savior, my Righteousness. Amen.

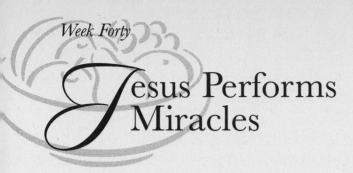

Week Forty

Jesus Performs Miracles

Monday

Reading the Word
Matthew 14:22–33; 17:24–27; Mark 4:35–41; Luke 5:1–11;
John 2:1–11; 6:1–14; 21:1–14

THE STORY

The sight of Jesus walking toward them on top of the water had astonished all of the disciples. But only Peter had the courage to try it too . . . to hop over the edge of the boat and walk toward Jesus. After a few unbelievable steps on top of the water, while watching Jesus, Peter looked down at his feet, amazed at his ability to walk on top of rather than sink into the water. And as soon as he thought it, he was sinking in it. The water, that is. With his mouth full and his arms flinging, Peter grabbed at Jesus and called His name, "Jesus! Save me!" Peter knew he was drowning in the huge waves and wind of the storm. Then he felt the strong hand of Jesus, pulling him to the surface, helping him into the boat and safety.

With a cough of seawater, Peter looked at this Jesus he and his friends were following, this One who could heal the sick and walk on water. In his still-wet robe and sandals, Peter fell to his knees and worshiped.

THE MESSAGE

Jesus' power over nature served to reinforce the message that He was not just another ordinary human being, He was sent from God, He was the "Son of God," as the disciples confessed after He and Peter walked on water. Jesus never performed a miracle for the dazzling effect it could have on the crowds who followed Him. He performed each miracle to prove one thing: He was the Messiah.

THE MAIN POINT

Don't you love Peter's impulsive eagerness to get involved? To get down into the nitty-gritty—or wet—reality of following Jesus? Peter was not one to stand back and watch the action from the sidelines. What made him think that because Jesus could walk on water, he could? One thing is certain: Peter entered this discipleship thing with every part of himself, holding nothing back. Which is exactly what Jesus is looking for today: disciples who are willing to throw caution to the wind, to follow Him no matter what the obstacle or danger.

TAKE NOTE

Matthew 14:25—The Jews kept time at night by the regular guard watch schedule of the Roman military. The first watch went from 6:00 p.m. to 9:00 p.m., the second from 9:00 p.m. to 12:00 a.m., and the third from 12:00 a.m. to 3:00 a.m. The fourth watch, the time when Jesus appeared, would have been sometime between 3:00 a.m. and 6:00 a.m.

Matthew 17:24—Jewish males were required to pay a tax for the upkeep of the temple. The tax had been instituted when the Israelites entered the Promised Land (Exodus 30:13). The tax was worth two days' wages, and all men over the age of twenty were required to pay it.

Tuesday

Reflecting on the Word
Mark 4:35–41

The stormy ride the disciples and a sleeping Jesus took was on the Sea of Galilee. This lake in northern Israel was the area where Jesus focused a good share of His ministry. His childhood town, Nazareth, was nearby. This sea was where some of Jesus' disciples did their fishing.

Therefore, this was nothing new or unknown to Jesus' disciples. A storm. Big deal. They had seen many storms. But not many like this one, obviously. They were certain they were going to die. And that Jesus guy was sleeping on a cushion right through it all.

The Sea of Galilee is fed on the north by the Jordan River, so it is made up of fresh waters, not salt. Storms come up quickly and violently on the lake. The cooler winds from the hill country sweep down to meet the warm air on the shores and over the waters of the lake, causing furious winds and waves—waves that even experienced fishermen feared, waves that broke over the top of the boat and threatened to fill it with water and sink it.

The passengers in these boats (there was more than one boat—see Mark 4:36) quickly realized the extreme danger they faced. Like frightened children, they unreasonably attacked the sleeping Jesus with their question: "Don't you care if we drown?" Their question clearly revealed the fact that they still didn't fully realize whom they were following. They knew He had power, they had seen it in healings already. But could He actually save them from this storm? Did He care enough to do it? Jesus' actions—talking the wind and the waves into quiet obedience—made them almost as afraid of Him as of the storm. Maybe now, finally, they understood. This Jesus was no ordinary man. He was the Son of God, come in power, to save not just these few disciples from the destruction of a storm but all those who would believe from the destruction of sin.

Wednesday

Studying the Word
John 6:1–14

Jesus fed five thousand men, plus women and children, and showed His followers more of His power and His compassion for their everyday needs. Read and study this passage to discover how much Jesus cares about you and your everyday needs.

1. This is the only miracle of Jesus that is recorded in all four gospels: Matthew 14:13–21; Mark 6:30–44; Luke 9:10–17; John 6:1–14. What does that tell you about its importance? Why do you think the Gospel writers thought it so significant?

2. Why did the people follow Jesus around the lake? What were they looking for (John 6:2)?

3. Why was Jesus interested in feeding the crowd (Matthew 14:15–16)?

4. When Jesus asked Philip for a solution, what was his response (John 6:7)? What does this tell you about Philip?

5. What does Andrew's response tell you about him (John 6:8–9)? How could you use Andrew's response to help you when you're in need?

6. What three things did Jesus do (John 6:10, 11a, 11*b*)? What significance is there in each of these steps?

7. How much was left after everyone had eaten (John 6:13)? What lesson does this teach you about Jesus' provision when you are in need?

Thursday

Responding to the Word
John 21:1–14

Peter, probably discouraged, decided to go fishing. For fish. Forgetting that he and the others had been commissioned to fish for people (Matthew 4:19), they instead headed out to fish for mere fish. And caught nothing.

Jesus had appeared to them several times since His resurrection (John 21:14), so they knew He was alive. He had made rather clear to them that their vocation was no longer that of fishermen (John 20:21–23). Perhaps they got impatient with waiting for Him to appear again. Or perhaps they just got bored. Or discouraged. Or perhaps they still didn't understand what was in their futures. So they went fishing.

When Jesus appeared, He told them to throw their nets on the other side of the boat. Sounded like a foolish proposition for a morning after catching no fish all night. But why not? What could it hurt? So they did. And the catch was so great they had to drag it to shore; the net full of fish was too heavy to haul into the boat.

The miracle opened John's eyes to who was on shore (John 21:7). Spontaneous Peter didn't wait one more second before jumping into the water and hurrying to the beach where Jesus waited. John and the others continued working with the boat and the fish. Before long, however, they all knew this was Jesus, come to Galilee to find them.

How easy it can be to get sidetracked! The mission you've been given in life, whatever it is, should always be your first priority. Maybe a time of discouragement or suffering has thrown you off track. Maybe just the busyness of living life in the twenty-first century has drawn you away from your true mission in life. Or maybe you're scared of what your mission will require from you. Take this story to heart! Jesus will provide all you need in order to complete your calling. More than you need! So much that you'll have trouble hauling it into your boat.

Friday

Praying the Word
Matthew 17:24–27

Imagine Peter's surprise when he opened the mouth of a fish he had just caught and found inside the exact amount of money needed to pay his and Jesus' temple tax. Have you ever been surprised by an answer to prayer? Because you weren't looking for it? Or because God answered in such a surprising way? Praise Him today for His remarkable and often unanticipated answers to your prayers.

Holy Father, You are my Provider. You know me and love me and give me what I need. Even so, I'm sometimes surprised at how generously or surprisingly You answer my prayers. Thank You for surprising me, Lord! Help me never to be complacent or think I know just how You will or how You should answer my prayers. Give me Your goodness in unexpected and surprising doses. I love You, Lord! Amen.

Jesus and the Pharisees

Monday

Reading the Word
Matthew 5:17–20; 15:1–20; 22:15–22; 23:1–39;
Mark 8:11–13; 12:28–31; Luke 6:1–11; 7:36–50;
16:13–15; 18:9–14; John 11:45–57

THE STORY

Jesus reclined quietly at Simon the Pharisee's table, the meal over, when He felt something drop on His bare foot. He turned to look and saw a woman leaning over His feet. She let her numerous tears fall to wet His feet. Not pulling His feet away or saying anything, Jesus let the woman wipe His feet with her unbound hair, let her kiss His feet lovingly, then let her pour a sweet smelling perfume on them. He saw into her heart, recognizing her love for Him and her desire to be forgiven of her sins. He saw her unexpected—and some might think undignified—act for what it was: an act of love.

THE MESSAGE

When Simon, Jesus' host, muttered his disgust at the woman's actions, Jesus quickly made it clear that those who had been forgiven much, loved much. Jesus' words and His actions revealed as much about His love for sinners as about the woman's need of forgiveness. His words and actions also revealed Simon the Pharisee's haughty legalism and lack of compassion.

THE MAIN POINT

Then and now, the heart of religion is not to perfectly follow a prescribed set of laws but to recognize that God is looking for inward faith and love exhibited in outward action. Throughout the Old and New Testaments, God has called for a people willing to respond to His love and follow Him with their whole hearts (Hosea 10:12; Micah 6:6–8; Matthew 22:37–40; 1 Timothy 1:12–14).

TAKE NOTE

Matthew 22:19—The coin Jesus asked for in this verse was the denarius, the most common Roman coin in circulation at the time. The coin was silver and was stamped with the head of the current Roman emperor. Archaeologists have discovered denarii stamped with the heads of twelve of the emperors of Rome who ruled during New Testament times.

Luke 7:37—The flask or jar of perfume that the sinful woman brought to anoint Jesus' feet was made from the soft, porous material called alabaster. The mineral could be carved easily into boxes and flasks. Most often white, but also available in reds and yellows, alabaster was found in the numerous caves of Israel's hill country.

Tuesday

With strict attention to every detail of Jewish religious law, with noses and attitudes raised against those who didn't keep those laws as vigilantly as they did, the Pharisees made living what they saw as a truly righteous life an unattainable goal for the Jewish people. Every law, oral and written, carefully interpreted and amplified, had to be strictly observed.

The Pharisees' origins can be found two centuries before Christ was born, or even further back to a similar sect formed after the Babylonian captivity. Their name, which has its roots in the word *separate,* came from their fierce opposition to anything not connected directly to Jewish law and life. They separated themselves from the influence of other cultures and religions, which was admirable. But their almost rabid legalism caused them to also separate themselves as a group from their own people. As their legalism and separatism grew, the religion they advocated gradually became more a matter of outward behavior than inward love for God.

No wonder then that the Pharisees in Jesus' time presented a perfect foil for Jesus' teachings about love and grace. With their haughty attitudes and judgmental statements and trick questions, they opened themselves up to Jesus' criticism. He could see clearly what others might miss: their behavior was impeccable, but their hearts were not. Jesus made it clear again and again that He was looking for those willing to follow the loving spirit of the law, willing to love God and others, not just those who could claim a clean record of outward obedience.

However, assuming all Pharisees were bad would be a bit like throwing the baby out with the bathwater. Some Pharisees were seekers after the truth (Nicodemus in John 3), some were careful in their approach to truth (Gamaliel in Acts 5:33–39), some were foundational members of the early church (Paul in Philippians 3:4–5).

Wednesday

Studying the Word
Matthew 15:1–20

Throughout His teachings Jesus worked to help the people understand that He was offering a refreshing and loving interpretation of God
and His laws. Read this denunciation of the Pharisees and examine your
own view of God's laws versus tradition and your need of cleansing
before God.

1. What did the Pharisees think the disciples should do (Matthew
   15:1–2)?
2. What did Jesus say was more important (Matthew 15:3)?
3. What specific way did Jesus point out the Pharisees' greater obedience to their own traditions than to God's laws (Matthew 15:4–6)?
   How might people today put tradition above the truth of God's
   Word?
4. What did He say is wrong with this (Matthew 15:7–9)? What was
   more important to the Pharisees according to Jesus?
5. What did Jesus mean when He talked about eating and being
   unclean (Matthew 15:10–11; 15:17–18)?
6. What did Jesus warn the disciples and the Pharisees of in Matthew
   15:13–14? What implications do His teachings have for religious
   leaders today?
7. Where did sin originate (Matthew 15:19?) What then is the issue
   between being clean and being unclean (Hebrews 10:22)?

Thursday

Responding to the Word
Mark 12:28–31

When one of the teachers of the law—Matthew identified him as a Pharisee (Matthew 22:41)—came and asked Jesus to identify which of God's commandments was most important, he got much more than he expected. Since the teachers in Jesus' day, the rabbis, had identified 613 individual laws for the people to obey, they were concerned with which were important and which were not so important. This teacher's question, then, appeared to be more sincere than merely an attempt to trick Jesus, like many other questions of the Pharisees.

Jesus began His answer by reciting the first words of the *shema*, words recited by all pious Jews morning and evening and found in Deuteronomy 6:4–5. He then added the words of Leviticus 19:18 as a second law, concluding that no commandment was greater than these.

Today, Jesus' words seem to be a statement of obvious fact, something no one should have difficulty believing as truth. However, the people of Jesus' time, especially the teachers of the law and the Pharisees, put obedience to the many laws of life and behavior right up alongside or equal to the laws of love. The Old Testament taught, and Jesus reiterated, that love was more important than any single law, love for God and love for others.

Let's get down to the nitty-gritty here. What's more important in your life? Love or doing what's expected of you? If you pass a woman having car trouble on your way to church, do you think: *Too bad, I'd stop but I'll be late for church*? Or, in the grocery line you see a mom struggling to pay for her groceries while keeping three preschoolers from man-handling the candy within reach—do you tap your foot or try to help? Look around you today for opportunities to show God's love to others, even if it might be inconvenient or might keep you from something "more important."

Friday

Jesus' story about the contrasting prayers of the Pharisee and the tax collector gave a clear image of the differing types and ways of praying. The Pharisee's prayer wasn't really a prayer at all, simply more obnoxious self-congratulations. The tax collector's prayer, however, was all about God and his need for God's love and mercy. As you pray today and at other times, carefully examine your motives and your approach to God, making sure you come in Jesus' righteousness rather than your own.

Dear God, I come before You humbled by my need for You, my unworthiness before You. Help me, Lord, to remember that only through Jesus' love and grace do I have any righteousness before You. Teach me to pray, Lord, as the tax collector prayed, with humility before You and love in my heart. In Jesus name I pray, Amen.

Jesus Is Tried and Crucified

Monday

Reading the Word

Luke 19:28–44; Matthew 26:1–16; Mark 14:12–16;
John 13:18–38; Mark 14:32–42; Luke 22:47–23:43;
John 19:25–27; Matthew 27:45–66

THE STORY

Mary's legs collapsed beneath her as she left the city and caught her first sight of the hill where they said her Son was being crucified. She covered her face and wouldn't have gone on except that the women with her lifted her up and almost carried her nearer the horrible sight. What had He done to deserve such treatment? Nothing, she knew, except anger those in authority with His goodness, teachings, and actions. She could barely lift her head to look up, terrified at what she'd see.

When she did raise her eyes, His eyes filled her vision, eyes filled with love for her, His mother. Looking at His disciple, John, who stood near where Mary knelt, Jesus turned His eyes back to His mother, telling her that John was now her son. Then He looked at John and told him, "My mother is now your mother." Implicit in the one-sided conversation was Jesus' love for His mother and desire that someone take good care of her. John, the disciple Jesus loved, was the perfect candidate.

THE MESSAGE

All of Jesus' actions and teachings have one thing at their foundation: love. His loving actions toward His mother while hanging on the cross, suffering, give a very personal glimpse of Jesus living what He taught: love God and others.

THE MAIN POINT

Love is the highest goal, no matter what the cost. Jesus' act of love toward His mother while suffering on the cross, Jesus' acts of love throughout His ministry, paint a portrait of love, one His true followers will want to imitate, painting their own portraits of love for others to see, beautiful enough for others to want such love as part of their lives too.

TAKE NOTE

Luke 23:33—The practice of putting criminals to death by crucifixion, either by nailing or tying on a cross, was reserved for the lowest criminals and most heinous crimes. Used by the governments of Greece and Rome, crucifixion caused tremendous suffering for hours before death came. The Romans continued to practice crucifixion until the conversion of Emperor Constantine, when the cross became a sacred symbol and its use as a means of torture and death was discontinued.

Tuesday

Reflecting on the Word
Mark 14:22–26

Jesus and His disciples celebrated the Passover meal together in an upper room in Jerusalem. The Passover, one of the most important feasts of the Jewish religion, commemorated the angel that "passed over" Israelite households in Egypt with the blood of a lamb spread on their doorposts. All those households without blood found the firstborn of the family dead the next morning. While Egypt mourned the loss of their family members, the Israelites left Egypt, freed at last from their slavery. So the Passover meal celebrated their deliverance from death and their deliverance from slavery.

Now Jesus took that same meal, offering the cup of wine and the bread, and made it a commemoration of the deliverance from death that every sinner deserves (Romans 6:23) and the deliverance from slavery to sin that is the curse of every human (Romans 6:6–7). Although those participating in this meal with Jesus didn't fully understand the significance of His gestures, before long comprehension came. Within just hours Jesus would die, would offer His body (the bread) and His blood (the wine) in order to pay fully for the sins of every person who would believe in Him (Romans 4:23–25; 8:1–4).

Still today, thousands of years later, believers across the world drink the wine or juice that symbolizes Jesus' blood and eat the bread that symbolizes His body. They recognize that their righteousness is not something they could ever gain on their own, but that they have gained it through Jesus' death as their substitute on the cross. When they observe what is now called the Lord's Supper, they celebrate and solemnly commemorate all that Christ did to save them.

Wednesday

Studying the Word
Matthew 27:45–54

Jesus suffered and died a criminal's death on the cross. But you knew that. Study these verses in Matthew for some unusual things that took place during Jesus' suffering and death and that give a deeper glimpse of the importance of this event.

1. What unusual event took place first (Matthew 27:45–46)? What was Jesus suffering besides the physical agony? Why do you think God might have caused it to be dark (the sixth to the ninth hour would be noon to 3:00 p.m.) while Jesus suffered the worst?
2. Since Elijah didn't die but went to heaven in a whirlwind (2 Kings 2:11), some thought he would come back to save righteous people when they were in trouble. Were these people at the crucifixion concerned with Jesus' suffering or mocking Him (Matthew 27:47–49)?
3. What did Jesus do just before He died (Matthew 27:50)? What does this tell you about His suffering?
4. What was the second unusual event (Matthew 27:51a)? What is unusual or difficult about the way the curtain was torn? This curtain separated the Holy Place in the temple from the Most Holy Place. What do you think its tearing signified?
5. What was the third unusual event (Matthew 27:51b)? Why do you think this would take place at Jesus' death? What might God have been trying to say through nature?
6. What was the fourth unusual event (Matthew 27:52–53)? Amazing, huh? What might these dead coming back to life be foretelling? (See 1 Corinthians 15:20 and 1 Thessalonians 4:16–17 for a hint.)
7. How did those present at the crucifixion respond to these unusual events (Matthew 27:54)? What does that tell you about your possible response to Jesus' crucifixion and the events surrounding it?

Thursday

Responding to the Word
Luke 19:37–40

Can you believe it? Even rocks got what the Pharisees didn't!

When Jesus came into Jerusalem for the last time before His death, His entrance was one of glory and praise. He rode the colt of a donkey, a sign that He came as a king of peace. Riding a horse was reserved for warriors. Those who witnessed this parade threw down their cloaks for Him to ride over, a custom at that time that showed respect and admiration for a king or general. They also cut branches from the area trees and threw them along His path. As He passed, the people began to shout their praise of this man who had been teaching and preaching and healing in their midst. They called Him their king, which quickly got the attention of the local Pharisees. "Jesus," they whined, "tell these people to stop!" (Luke 19:39, author's paraphrase).

Jesus then delivered His famous few-word homily on praise. "If these people don't praise Me," He told the Pharisees, "the rocks *will*" (Luke 19:40, author's paraphrase). Can't you just see the Pharisees, some angry at Jesus' audacity, some probably sniggering at His assumption that rocks would praise Him if people wouldn't?

Jesus was serious, you know. There are still rocks around, ready to take up the slack if His people don't praise Him. Carefully examine your praise life today. How much of your time with Jesus is spent asking and talking about your needs and others' needs? And how much of your time is spent in praise? If your praise quotient is off-kilter, spend time today praising Jesus for all He is and all He's done in your life. He deserves every minute of it.

Friday

Praying the Word
Mark 13:32–37

Ever fall asleep while praying? Not such a bad thing if you happen to be praying while you're falling asleep at night. Not such a good thing if you happen to be sleeping while you're in the middle of a regular prayer time. Notice that Jesus didn't reject His disciples because they couldn't stay awake. But He was disappointed in them. In your prayer time today, confess those times when sleep or distractions or busyness or whatever have gotten in the way of your time with God. Ask Him to help you make prayer a priority.

Dear Jesus, forgive me when I'm like the disciples, too sleepy or busy or distracted to be aware of the situation around me and the need for prayer. Help me to realize the privilege I have of being able to come to You, my holy God and Savior, with nothing holding me back, nothing in between. Give me a clear understanding of how important prayer needs to be in my life, Lord. I love You and I praise You for Your love for me and Your saving work on the cross. Amen.

$\mathcal{J}$esus' Resurrection and Ascension

Monday

Reading the Word
Matthew 28:1–20; Mark 16:1–20; Luke 24:1–53;
John 20:1–21:25; Acts 1:1–11

THE STORY

Peter hopped along the road on one foot, trying to dislodge a stone that had gotten into his sandal. Just as the stone fell to the ground, the disciple John flew past him, robes flapping, arms pumping. Peter started to run again toward Jesus' tomb, which Mary Magdalene said was empty. Rounding a turn in the road, Peter slowed when he saw that John had already arrived at the tomb and was bent over to look inside. Peter came up behind him, then bent over himself and walked into the tomb.

Mary was right! It was empty! The cloths in which they had wrapped Jesus' body after that horrible day were laying there. The napkin they had put over His face was folded neatly and rested near them. Strange. If robbers had stolen the body, they would have just grabbed Jesus, grave clothes and all. Wouldn't they? Heart and lungs pumping as much from running as from shock, Peter turned to look at John, who had followed him into the tomb. Their eyes communicated what their mouths could not. Was this what Jesus had meant with some of His strange teachings? Was He truly risen from the dead?

THE MESSAGE

Jesus' resurrection is the pivotal point of the salvation story. If He had died for the sins of the world and remained dead, His death would have had no power, would have accomplished nothing. But He rose again, revealing His power over even that most unbeatable foe, the grave.

THE MAIN POINT

On that Sunday—now called Easter—Jesus rose, conquering not only sin by His crucifixion but also death by His resurrection. As all humans died because of Adam's sin, that is, they all became sinful with the grave as their natural end, now in Christ those who believe in His work as Savior are offered not only deliverance from sin, but also everlasting life (1 Corinthians 15:22).

TAKE NOTE

John 20:6–7—In Jesus' day it was common practice to first wash a dead body, then wrap it in long strips of cloth, including spices as the fabric was wound. The entire body would be wrapped except the head, which instead received a separate piece of cloth put over the face.

Tuesday

Reflecting on the Word
Matthew 28:2–3

When you think of angels, what comes to your mind? Pictures of chubby cherubs flitting on their wings? Visions of powerful angels flying to someone's rescue? Statues of colorless angels with wire wings? Contrary to what some might think, angels are *not* human beings who have died and "gained their wings." Fact is, angels probably don't even have wings. The only mention of wings on heavenly creatures in the Bible is on cherubim, who appeared on the Ark of the Covenant and in embroidery and carvings in the tabernacle and the temple (Exodus 25:18; 26:1; 1 Kings 6:23–28), and on seraphim, who appeared to Isaiah in his vision (Isaiah 6:1–7).

Angels made appearances in many of Scripture's most dazzling stories. An angel rescued Hagar (Genesis 16:7), Lot (Genesis 19:15), and Daniel's three friends (Daniel 3:28). Although Balaam missed the angel standing in the road, his donkey didn't (Numbers 22:22–23). An angel announced the upcoming birth of Samson (Judges 13:2–3), John the Baptist (Luke 1:11), and Jesus (Matthew 1:20; Luke 1:26–28). An angel offered help to Elijah when he was tired and discouraged (1 Kings 19:3–7). An angel killed 185,000 Assyrian soldiers (Isaiah 37:36). An angel freed some of the disciples (Acts 5:19) and Peter (Acts 12:7) from jail. An angel told Philip to go to the desert where he met up with an Ethiopian who was seeking salvation (Acts 8:26). Angels by the thousands worship God in heaven (Revelation 5:11). And these are only a sampling of the almost three hundred times angels are mentioned in the Bible.

God created the angels specifically for His use and glory. Everything the angels do—all the help they offer, the messages they bring, the appearances they make—is done in response to God's direction. Angels are spiritual beings, sometimes taking on physical form when appearing to human beings. They are superior to humans in power and intelligence (Hebrews

2:7; 2 Peter 2:11) but not all-powerful—operating only under God's direction and guidance (Psalm 103:20). The Bible actually names only two angels: Michael, guardian of God's people (Daniel 12:1; Revelation 12:7), and Gabriel, who announced the coming birth of Jesus (Luke 1:26).

Angels were created before human beings, and at some point, a number of them rebelled against God (2 Peter 2:4; Jude 6). These fallen angels are called demons, the chief of which is Satan (Revelation 12:7–9). Their goal is to frustrate God's plans, including trying to draw people away from relationship with God.

Did you know that the angels have had a party because of you? If you've received Christ as your Savior, they have (Luke 15:10)! Amazing, isn't it? Your salvation caused a party in heaven with angels shouting for joy.

Wednesday

Studying the Word
John 20:10–18

Of all the people Jesus could have appeared to first after His resurrection, He chose a woman, Mary Magdalene. His choice has definite significance. Read the story and answer the following questions to discover the beauty behind Jesus' appearance to this faithful female follower.

1. Who was Mary Magdalene (Mark 16:9)?
2. What do you think the disciples thought about Jesus' disappearance (John 20:10; also John 20:8–9)?
3. Why do you think Mary might have stayed behind (John 20:11)?
4. Why was she crying? What did she think had happened to Jesus (John 20:13)?
5. Mary Magdalene appeared to know Jesus well. Why didn't she recognize Him at this point (John 20:14–15)?
6. What did Jesus do that made Mary recognize Him (John 20:16)? Why do you think this one small thing changed her perspective? What does this tell you about Mary's relationship with Jesus? About Jesus' love for Mary?
7. Why did Jesus tell Mary not to hold on to Him? What had changed (John 20:17)?
8. What did Mary do immediately after seeing Jesus (John 20:18)? Describe what you think she might have been feeling. Describe how you think the disciples might have reacted to her news. Why would they or wouldn't they believe her over some other witness?
9. Given the lowly position of women in society in Jesus' day, what does His resurrection appearance to a woman first tell you about His understanding of the position and importance of women? How does that relate to your position as a woman in your culture today? In your church today?

Thursday

Responding to the Word
Acts 1:1–11

Picture yourself at the scene of Jesus' ascension, with His disciples, with a crook in your neck just like theirs, watching Jesus ascend into heaven. Can't you just picture it? Heads bent back, eyes on the skies, mouths open, stunned at what they were seeing, what they had heard, what they had experienced the last few years. With Jesus gone, their last hopes for an earthly kingdom died (Acts 1:6), and only now would they begin to realize that what Jesus offered them was something much different, much better.

Two angels appeared to help them get their eyes off the skies, looking instead toward a future of serving Jesus and awaiting His return. They had the honor of being God's agents here on earth. With a serving of power in the form of the Holy Spirit, the disciples were given the task of bringing the good news to Jerusalem. (No problem!) To Judea. (OK, not too difficult.) To Samaria. (Possible but not so easy.) And to the whole earth. (What? To everyone everywhere? Really?)

You have a job and a career. You have to make a living, after all. But you also have a commission, and that goes way beyond your profession. You have the honor of being Jesus' agent here on earth, wherever you live, wherever you travel, wherever you're called. Are you making the best of it? Take every opportunity (Colossians 4:5) to tell others of the salvation Jesus freely offers. Your friends, coworkers, and neighbors, your local store clerks and car attendants and government officials, your family members—all those you know and come into contact with—have a need for what Jesus offers. Be sure you're ready, willing, and eager to fulfill your part of the Great Commission, reaching your _____, your _____, your _____, and your *world* for Christ.

Friday

Praying the Word
Matthew 28:20

What comfort and courage is found in this verse! You have Jesus with you, through the person of the Holy Spirit. He's with you always—not just in church, not just in prayer times, not just during Bible reading—*always*. Spend some time in prayer today, specifically acknowledging God's ever-present presence in your life.

Father, Son, Holy Spirit, I gratefully acknowledge all You are and do in my life. I'm thankful You accompany me wherever I go. Help me to be blessedly aware of Your presence with me, Lord, knowing that You will help and guide and comfort—that You will be there and be aware of what I need. With a thankful heart, I praise You! Amen.

The Holy Spirit Arrives

Monday

Reading the Word
Acts 2

THE STORY

Peter felt inside himself as much as heard the sound of the wind. It sounded off in the distance at first but then exploded within the room where he had gathered with his disciple friends. With eyes wide, however, Peter realized that it was sound only, no sensation of wind. He watched as tongues of fire appeared and separated to rest on each of those present. Without even being able to see it, Peter knew one of those tongues of fire rested over his own head. He felt within himself a sense of fulfillment and power, an understanding of what Jesus had come to accomplish, and a need to stand and shout the truth from the rooftops. Breathing heavily, with excitement as much as fear or awe, Peter moved out of the room. He stood on some outside steps overlooking the gathering crowd. Barely realizing what he was doing, Peter began to speak.

THE MESSAGE

The Holy Spirit had arrived, just as Jesus had promised (Acts 1:4–5). He came in a blaze of power and revolutionized the lives of those who received Him. All that didn't make sense before began to make sense. Those who couldn't speak any language but their own communicated in other tongues. Those who were quiet and uneducated got up to speak with power and authority in front of thousands. With the arrival of the Holy Spirit, God changed His location from the temple in Jerusalem to take up residence within His people. The Holy Spirit provided the final link in the chain of events that had been building link by link since Adam's fall. Salvation through Christ's blood had been accomplished. Now the Holy Spirit would lend power to all those who would spread that good news.

THE MAIN POINT

That same Holy Spirit is just as available today as He was on the day of Pentecost. He may not arrive in your life in exactly the same manner, but His power and presence are as available (Titus 3:5–6). He will take up residence in any willing heart, including your own.

TAKE NOTE

Acts 2:1—The Holy Spirit arrived on the Jewish festival day known as Pentecost. Originally called the Feast of Harvest (Exodus 23:16), it celebrated the harvesting of grains, when the people presented the firstfruits of the grain harvest. With Passover and the Feast of Tabernacles, it was one of the three feasts for which Jewish males would travel to Jerusalem.

Tuesday

Reflecting on the Word
Acts 2:5

People from nations encircling Israel arrived in Jerusalem by the hundreds, ready to celebrate Pentecost, an important feast on the Jewish calendar. They came from Rome and the island of Crete in the northeast, from Mesopotamia in the north, from Arabia to the southeast, and from Egypt to the southwest. Many probably spoke Aramaic, the language of Israel at that time. But many also spoke the languages of the countries they were from.

Jews were dispersed from Israel throughout other geographic areas during the Assyrian and Babylonian captivities in the Old Testament. While some returned to Israel, many did not, but continued to live out their faith in these places that had been foreign but were now home. While Greeks like Alexander the Great ruled the world and Palestine, many Jews emigrated to other countries in order to expand the businesses of Israel. By the time of the New Testament many more Jews lived outside of Israel than within its borders.

Now, thousands of these Jews from other parts of the world had gathered in Jerusalem for the Feast of Pentecost. They worshiped in the temple and fulfilled the ceremonial requirements of the festival. In the middle of it all, the sound of wind and the spectacle of uneducated Galileans (Acts 2:7) speaking in their own languages aroused their curiosity.

The Holy Spirit had arrived and they were fortunate enough to be eyewitnesses to His coming. They heard the wind, they saw the flames of fire, and they heard the apostles preach the truth about Jesus in their own languages.

Wednesday

Studying the Word
Acts 2:42–47

This short description of life in the early days of the church provides a great recipe for life as believers today. Read through these verses, and then answer the following questions to uncover the riches of a life of fellowship with other believers.

1. What three things distinguished believers in the early church (Acts 2:42)? Describe how these three things might have looked in the life of an early believer, then how they can or should look in the life of a believer today.

2. Why do you think those watching what was going on were fearful or, in more contemporary terms, in awe (Acts 2:43)? What were they seeing? What did these amazing acts of the apostles reveal about them and their relationship with Jesus?

3. What sort of living arrangement does Acts 2:44 describe? Why do you think early church believers chose to live this way? Why would or wouldn't today's believers choose to live this way? What might be some advantages? Disadvantages?

4. What did the early church believers share (Acts 2:44*b*–45)? What prompted them to do this? What benefit would such actions have for those involved? How would such a way of life affect the church as a whole today?

5. Where did early church believers meet? What did they do in each location? Where do believers meet today? What benefits would be found in meeting in homes as well as in churches?

6. How did the early church believers' lifestyle benefit others? What do you think attracted others so that they decided to seek salvation? What would attract unbelievers today to your church? To you personally?

The Women's Devotional Guide to the Bible

Thursday

Responding to the Word
Acts 2:21, 38

Wouldn't you have liked to have been in Jerusalem on the day of Pentecost? Hearing the good news of salvation in Jesus preached for the very first time? Watching and listening as rough-around-the-edges Peter fluently and eloquently outlined the truth of what had been happening through Jesus' death and resurrection? What incredibly good news! In his sermon, Peter urged his listeners to do three things: call on the name of Jesus, repent, and be baptized.

When you call on Jesus' name, you recognize that only He has the power to help you. You could call on a friend or another god or your own inner power or whatever—but none of those has the power to free you from yourself or from your sin. Only Jesus has that power. He lived and died and rose again to prove it.

Repentance is the act of turning away from your sins. Peter was calling for more than a light oopsy-daisy-I'm-a-sinner response. He was urging those listening to go deep, to recognize their sin and their need to be forgiven. And to turn their backs on that sin.

Then Peter called his listeners to be baptized. John the Baptist had already been baptizing. Now Peter encouraged those who responded to be baptized in Jesus' name, as an act of recognition that Jesus had saved them.

All three of those actions are still appropriate today: call on Jesus' name, repent, be baptized. As you examine your heart today, call to Jesus for help in dealing with any sinfulness you find there, telling Him that your deepest desire is to turn away from that sin to follow Him. Then, if you have never been baptized, consider it. Baptism is an act of obedience and testimony that has significance far beyond the mere ritual itself. Your baptism speaks to others of your salvation and decision to follow Christ. Your baptism speaks to you personally of your newfound cleansing from sin through Jesus and your status as a new person in Christ (2 Corinthians 5:17).

Friday

Praying the Word
Acts 2:37

If you go to church or participate in Christian activities regularly, it's pretty easy to become immune to the beauty and depth of what Christ has made possible through His death and resurrection. You've heard it all before. The words and actions are so familiar that they lose their power to touch you. Those who heard Peter on the day of Pentecost were "cut to the heart" by what he said. Today, ask God to make your heart and mind receptive to the truths of Scripture whenever you hear or read them.

Dear God, may I never grow so accustomed to truth that it no longer has the power to touch my heart and mind. Keep my heart tender, Lord, to You and to what You've done in my life. May I always be keenly aware of my need for You. Amen.

Peter and John's Ministry

Monday

Reading the Word
Acts 3:1–6:7; 10:1–12:19

THE STORY

Peter and John both turned as the beggar reached out his cup and asked them for money. They knew begging provided this man's only income. His feet and legs crippled from birth, he couldn't work as others did. "Look at us" (Acts 3:4*b* NKJV). Peter laughed. He knew if the man only looked, he would realize they had no money. They were just poor fishermen after all. But they did have something to offer. Something better than money. Reaching out to grasp the man's hand, Peter declared, "I don't have any silver or gold to give you. But what I do have, I give. In Jesus' name, walk!" (Acts 3:6–7, author's paraphrase). He pulled the beggar up to his feet, and for the first time in his life, the man not only walked, he danced. Peter and John grinned and laughed and praised God with the others around them, telling the crowd that this man, disabled from birth, could walk because of the power of faith in Jesus.

THE MESSAGE

Peter and John, fishermen from Galilee turned preachers and teachers, worked on the front lines of the early church, when the truth of what Jesus had come to accomplish was just being fully understood. When the

Holy Spirit arrived, He produced a power and authority in them that could only be supernatural.

THE MAIN POINT

Jesus still needs people to work on the front lines, to preach and teach and minister. Only when believers speak does the good news get told. God has no other vessel or means to get the word out. He needs Peters and Johns and Marys today as much as He did in the time of the early church.

TAKE NOTE

Acts 4:5—The group of leaders that interrogated Peter and John were known as the Sanhedrin. Seventy members composed this governmental council, led by the high priest, in this case Annas (Acts 4:6). The seventy members were drawn from three distinct groups of men: chief priests, which included the high priest as well as other distinguished priests; teachers of the law or scribes, which included the Pharisees; and elders, heads of leading families in Judea (Matthew 16:21). As a body the Sanhedrin had considerable power to rule Israel, even during Greek and Roman occupation. They had complete power to rule on issues of religious law. Their civil power, however, went only as far as the government of the time would allow.

Acts 11:26—If you call yourself a Christian, you follow in the footsteps of early believers in Antioch. Previously, early church believers called themselves disciples or saints or brothers and sisters. But in Antioch the tag "Christian" took hold, meaning someone who was like or who followed Christ.

Tuesday

Reflecting on the Word
Acts 11:19–21

Serious persecution began with the stoning of the disciple Stephen in Jerusalem (Acts 7:54–60). This is when Saul did his most destructive work, dragging believers, men and women alike, from their homes and putting them in prison. Herod joined the game when he had James, one of the twelve disciples, killed (Acts 12:2). James was the first of Jesus' disciples to be martyred.

In order to escape, believing Jews fled Jerusalem and settled in other areas, including Phoenicia, an area along the coast of the Mediterranean Sea north of Israel; Cyprus, a Mediterranean island north and east of Israel; and Antioch, a city north of Israel. Everywhere these believers went, they carried the good news, telling it primarily to other Jews, but then also expanding their reach to Greeks.

Christians have been persecuted somewhere in the world throughout the history of the church. The early persecution of believers in Jerusalem spread across the Roman world, where Christians were imprisoned and put to death because of their refusal to worship the current emperor. Those of Islamic faith have persecuted Christians in their nations for centuries. Communist rulers of the Soviet Union as well as China and other countries have attempted to eradicate the Christian religion by persecution as well as indoctrination. Believers in many countries today still must meet in secret and live under the constant possibility of discovery and imprisonment for their faith.

The beautiful thing about persecution, if one can be found, is the way it has continually and consistently grown the church wherever it has occurred. When believing Jews left Jerusalem, they didn't leave their faith behind but took it with them and spread it wherever they settled. "A great number" (Acts 11:21 NKJV) were saved. The same is still happening today. In countries where believers face great oppression, the church continues to grow, often at a greater rate than in those places where Christians practice their faith freely. Jesus taught that believers could expect to be persecuted (Matthew 5:12) and that they are blessed because of it (Matthew 5:10).

Wednesday

Studying the Word
Acts 5:1–11

The story of Ananias and Sapphira is one that makes many uncomfortable with its quick punishment for a sin that doesn't seem so bad. Read the story and answer these questions to discover its significance.

1. What did Ananias and Sapphira decide to do with the money they made from selling their field (Acts 5:2)?
2. What did Peter say about what they did? What other options did they have for using the money? What was wrong with the option they chose?
3. Why do you think punishment was so immediate and so severe (Acts 5:5*b*)?
4. Why do you think Peter asked Sapphira this question (Acts 5:8)? What were her options for answering?
5. What was the effect of their deaths on the church (Acts 5:11)? Was this a good thing or a bad thing? Explain your answer.
6. What is one great lesson to be gained from Ananias and Sapphira's actions?

Thursday

Responding to the Word
Acts 4:5–13

The leaders of the people paid Peter and John the ultimate compliment for any believer: they recognized that Peter and John had been with Jesus.

Peter and John's rough hands and clothing and Galilean speech gave them away as uneducated fishermen. Their background had nothing in it to explain their eloquence, their knowledge, the miracles they performed. When questioned by what power they had healed the man in the temple, they answered with little hesitation and much conviction, "By the power of Jesus, whom you crucified" (Acts 4:7–10, author's paraphrase).

Talk about brave! It's one thing to proclaim the good news of salvation to crowds eager to hear. It's another to proclaim Him to those involved in His crucifixion. But Peter's words held more than accusation. He let these leaders know that God used that gruesome act of crucifixion for good, that Jesus' death and resurrection had provided a way of salvation that had not been available to anyone before.

As the leaders watched and listened, their amazement grew. Unfortunately, it only grew so far. They were amazed enough to recognize that these men had been revolutionized by being with Jesus. But not enough to recognize who Jesus really was and what He offered.

As you study Peter and John this week, remember: those in contact with these men could readily see they had been with Jesus. What does your life or character or demeanor or actions reveal about you? When others look at you, who do they see? Only little you? Or can they see that you've been with Jesus?

Friday

Praying the Word
Acts 4:23–31

After being grilled and threatened by the Sanhedrin, Peter and John went to their fellow believers, related what had happened, then did the very thing they had been told not to do. Under the power and conviction of the Holy Spirit, "they spoke the word of God with boldness" (Acts 4:31 NKJV). If you're a knee-shaking, dry-mouthed, empty-minded witness for Christ, you can get the boldness you need to speak for Him just where Peter and John got it: from the Holy Spirit's presence in your life. In your prayers today, ask God to give you that fearlessness to speak for Him whenever the opportunity arises.

Dear God, how I'd like to be as bold and brave as Peter and John, willing to speak about You even under threat of death or imprisonment. Fill me with Your Spirit, Lord, so that I can speak of You to my friends who don't know You, to acquaintances who ask about You, to unsaved family members who wonder about You. Steady my knees and fill my mind and mouth with the words You would have me speak, Lord Jesus. Amen.

Stephen and Philip's Ministry

Monday

Reading the Word
Acts 6:8–8:40

THE STORY

Philip's legs felt strong and steady as he ran to catch up to the chariot he saw ahead of him. As he got closer, he could hear the Ethiopian in the chariot reading from the book of Isaiah. Philip recognized the words as a prophecy about Jesus. When he got close to the chariot, he asked the man, "Do you understand what you're reading?" The look on the Ethiopian's face told Philip the same thing as his words: "If someone doesn't explain this to me, I won't understand." Philip didn't wait for a second, but willingly jumped up into the chariot at the man's invitation. He started with the very passage the man was reading and eagerly explained the good news to him.

THE MESSAGE

The disciples had been preaching the salvation of Jesus in Jerusalem and Judea. Now Philip, a man who had been chosen to help the disciples serve the believers in Jerusalem, spread the word farther (Acts 8:2–5). He preached in the towns of Samaria. Then, acting on the prompting of the Holy Spirit, he told an Ethiopian official about Jesus (Acts 8:26–40). Philip was the first to begin to fulfill the Great Commission Jesus had given just before He went back to heaven: you will be my witnesses in Jerusalem, Judea, Samaria, and the ends of the earth (Acts 1:8).

THE MAIN POINT

The gospel began to spread throughout the known world at that time. With one person obeying the prompting of the Holy Spirit and reaching one person, the word spread to Ethiopia. One by one, little by little, the good news still spreads today, with believers who willingly follow the prompting of the Spirit to speak.

TAKE NOTE

Acts 8:27—Ethiopia, a country in Africa south of Egypt, was formed from the descendants of Cush, son of Ham, one of Noah's sons (Genesis 10:6). The nation is sometimes called Cush in the Bible (Genesis 2:13). In the time of the New Testament, the nation was ruled by a powerful woman, Candace. The Nile River and its tributaries originate in Ethiopia and flow from there through Egypt to the Mediterranean Sea.

Tuesday

Reflecting on the Word
Acts 7:54–60

When Stephen claimed to look into heaven and see Jesus standing with God, the men of the Sanhedrin could stand no more. To name God and claim to see Him, to claim Jesus as His Son—both were blasphemy to their ears. Without further discussion or proceedings, like madmen they hauled Stephen outside of the city and killed him.

Stoning was the usual Hebrew punishment for blasphemy against God (Leviticus 24:16). The action had to take place outside of the city walls (Leviticus 24:14). The first stones were to be thrown by the person's accusers, and then the entire community was to participate (Deuteronomy 17:7). The abundance of stones in Israel, cleared from farming fields as well as handy along the side of any road, made them common for use as a tool of punishment and as a weapon in war (Judges 20:16). The accusers and the community members present at the punishment would pick up large stones and hurl them at the offender until he or she died, a horrific sight, and one designed to prevent further crimes.

In the Old Testament, stoning was the accepted form of capital punishment. Achan was stoned for stealing from God (Joshua 7:25), David's men talked of stoning him in their discouragement over losses (1 Samuel 30:6), and Ahab had Naboth stoned under trumped-up charges (1 Kings 21:11–14). In the New Testament, Jesus prevented a woman's stoning (John 8:3–10) and stole away from His own probable stoning (John 8:59). Saul/Paul, who was present at Stephen's stoning, was himself stoned and left for dead (Acts 14:19–20).

Most cultures today view this particular form of punishment as barbaric. However, a few countries still practice stoning for certain crimes, including adultery.

Wednesday

Studying the Word
Acts 7:51–53

Stephen didn't mince words at the end of his speech. Read these verses, these last words before he died, then answer the following questions.

1. How were the people Stephen was talking to like their ancestors (Acts 7:51)?
2. How were they resisting the Holy Spirit?
3. Look up the story of Elijah, one of the most famous Old Testament prophets, and describe how he was persecuted (1 Kings 16:29–19:18). How are God's prophets and preachers persecuted yet today?
4. Whom might Stephen have been talking about in Acts 7:52*b* (Matthew 14:6–11)?
5. Why do you think Stephen spoke so forcefully, even harshly?

Thursday

Responding to the Word
Acts 7:2–50

Stephen's speech to the Sanhedrin was a twelve-hundred-word lesson in the history of the Hebrew people and God's work in and through them. He wasn't telling his audience anything they didn't know. They had heard and studied the history of their people thoroughly. What they didn't get, however, was what it all meant.

For centuries, God had been slowly working in His people, building them as a nation set apart from all other nations, urging them to worship Him only. But as Stephen recounts, they continually turned away from God, worshiping idols and persecuting the prophets sent to bring them God's messages. Through the beginnings of the nation in Abraham through their stay and growth as a people in Egypt, under Moses' leadership leaving Egypt, rebelling and spending forty years wandering in the desert, then finally settling in the Promised Land, Stephen builds to the climax of his lesson. Not only did they reject God in the past, they were rejecting Him and His Son in the present.

As you read through Stephen's history lesson, recall the history of your own life, how God has been working and how you have been responding. Is there anything that requires change? As you reflect, be sure to respond to what the Holy Spirit is telling you.

Friday

Praying the Word
Acts 7:60

Stephen's prayer of complete selflessness, spoken as he died, makes many prayers seem trite and trivial, doesn't it? Today, examine your prayer life for selfishness. How much of yourself is embedded in what you pray and how much of others? Ask God to give you more and more compassion for the needs of others.

Father, how often I have prayed to You and asked only for myself! Make me ever more sensitive to the needs of others near me and around the world. Give me a passion in praying for them. Make me like Stephen and Jesus, who both prayed for their executioners as they died. Amen.

*P*aul's Conversion and Ministry

Monday

Reading the Word
Acts 9:1–31; 13–14; 15:36–28:31

THE STORY

His legs and arms weak and tired from swimming in the churning waters, Paul collapsed on the rocks of the shoreline. He watched as one person after another from the ship made it safely to shore, some swimming, some floating on pieces of the ship. He took a shaky breath, his stomach churning as heavily as the waves, his eyes burning from the salty water. The soldier in charge of Paul stepped from rock to rock in order to get near him after swimming ashore. They looked at each other, the soldier amazed that what Paul had predicted had actually happened—everyone from the shipwrecked boat had made it safely to shore.

THE MESSAGE

With action that reads much like fiction, Paul went from city to city telling the Jews and the Gentiles alike about the salvation that was available to them through the work of Jesus. Whippings, stonings, visions, healings, and shipwrecks dotted his ministry and travels. But he never wavered in his mission.

THE MAIN POINT

How often are you tempted to just give up when the going gets too hard? Each person faces a unique set of circumstances, unique difficulties in life, unique victories as well as hardships. Whatever you face personally, remember Paul and keep on keeping on, knowing that nothing in life is worth more than finishing well (Acts 20:24).

TAKE NOTE

Acts 13:9—Many Jews in the time of the book of Acts had two names. Saul/Paul was no exception. Saul was his Jewish name, Paul was his name as a citizen of Rome. As his ministry moved toward reaching the Gentiles of the world, he began to use and be referred to exclusively by his Greek name, Paul.

Tuesday

Reflecting on the Word
Acts 13:2–3

Paul's missionary journeys began not with a board meeting and fund-raising or brainstorming a way to reach others. His ministry began with praying and fasting. The best start for any ministry, even today.

Paul had been hidden away in Tarsus for a time, safe from those who wished to kill him (Acts 9:20–30), when his friend and mentor, Barnabas (Acts 9:27), left his ministry in Antioch, traveled to Tarsus, found Paul, and brought him back to Antioch. Many had already believed in Jesus under good Barnabas's ministry (Acts 11:21), and now, with Paul's help, they taught the people the truths of Jesus' life and work. Barnabas clearly saw Paul's sincerity and potential when everyone else was still fearful of him.

During a time of worship and fasting, an integral part of early church life, the Holy Spirit gave instructions for Barnabas and Paul to be sent out from there as missionaries. Their first stop? Cyprus, an island in the Mediterranean with a large population of Jews. From there they traveled to Perga, Pisidian Antioch, Lystra, and Derbe—all prominent cities—before returning to their starting point in Antioch.

After that first journey Paul and Barnabas had an argument about whether John Mark should go with them on another journey. Mark had left them for some unknown reason before completing the first missionary journey (Acts 13:13), and Paul was unwilling to take him along again. So Paul and Barnabas split up, which was not necessarily good for them but was good for the spread of the gospel. Paul struck out with Silas, heading for Cyprus; and Barnabas left with Mark, heading for Syria. This second journey took Paul to Philippi, Thessalonica, and Corinth, all cities to whom he later wrote letters that became part of the New Testament. He ended this second journey back in Antioch.

From Antioch, Paul set out on his third missionary journey, revisiting some earlier churches then traveling on to Ephesus, the major emphasis of this third trip. After traveling through Macedonia and Greece, Paul began the long journey to Jerusalem, a trip some urged him not to make because of the dangers involved (Acts 21:10–12).

True to the prophecies of danger in Jerusalem, the Jews arrested Paul there shortly after his arrival. After appearing before the Jewish councils as well as local government officials, Paul appealed his case to Caesar, the right of all Roman citizens (Acts 22:27; 25:11). In order for his appeal to be met, he had to travel to Rome. That last journey makes up the final verses of the book of Acts. Even while a prisoner in Rome, Paul continued his work as a missionary, spreading the good news to all who came to see him (Acts 28:30–31).

Wednesday

Studying the Word
Acts 9:1–19

Rather like the shot that was heard around the world (from Emerson's poem about the Revolutionary War), Saul's conversion was the salvation story heard around the world. Read about that event and then answer these questions to discover its significance.

1. What was Saul busy doing (Acts 9:1–2)? Why do you think he was so militant in his hatred of the followers of Jesus?
2. What happened on the way to Damascus? Who spoke to him (Acts 9:3–5)?
3. What did the voice tell him to do (Acts 9:6)?
4. How did those with Saul react to what they saw (Acts 9:7–8)?
5. What was the immediate result of this experience (Acts 9:9)? Why do you think Saul's sight was taken away? What would/could this accomplish?
6. Why did Ananias object when told to go to Saul (Acts 9:13–14)? Was his objection legitimate?
7. What did Ananias call Saul when he saw him (Acts 9:17)? What does this tell you about Ananias's response to what God had told him in Acts 9:15?
8. Why do you think God chose someone like Saul, the believers' worst enemy, to save and use as a missionary?

Thursday

How do you respond to difficult situations in your life? Moan and groan? Pick yourself up and grimly force your way forward? Limp along? Whatever your usual response to difficulty, you can learn a lot from reading about Paul and Silas's reaction to imprisonment.

Try to picture the scene. Stripped and whipped until almost dead, their feet in stocks, sitting in an inner cell, probably without windows and only a small door, what did Paul and Silas do? Whimper and cry? No. Pray for release? Maybe. As unlikely as it might seem, they sat there together, in the dark, perhaps shivering from cold and very likely in pain from the flogging, and sang hymns together. That had to be one of the most beautiful and stirring duets you'd ever be likely to hear.

Hard times come to everyone at some point in life. Some situations are worse than others. Some can bring believers to the breaking point, crushing their spirits, making them cry out to God for relief. Others cause quiet desperation and prayers of intense longing. Some are quick and sharp. Others are like a persistent and annoying drip of water. All can cause believers to crumble beneath the load of grief or pain.

There is definite value in reading through Scripture to find out how others have faced the difficulties common to living in this broken world. But few will lift your battered spirit like reading of Paul and Silas belting out their favorite hymns while in a dank, dark prison.

Friday

Praying the Word
Acts 20:32

Paul's prayer for the believers at Ephesus, who came to see him when he was on his way to Jerusalem, is one you can pray for anyone in your life—children, family members, friends—releasing them to God and His power. Today, pick a few people to pray these words of truth over.

Father, I give _____ to Your loving care and teaching, knowing that only You can do what I cannot do for them. Build them up, Father, hold them close, keep them on the path of following You, help them to realize the security and love they can find in You and in their fellow believers. These are people I love, Lord, and I entrust them to You. Amen.

$\mathcal{P}$aul's Letters to Rome and Corinth

Monday

Reading the Word
Romans 3; 5; 7:7–8:39; 12; 1 Corinthians 1; 12–13; 15;
2 Corinthians 1; 4–5; 9:6–15; 12:1–10

THE STORY

With challenges and judgments, gentle criticisms and thorough discourses, Paul wrote these longer letters, one to the church he longed to visit in Rome and two to the church he had founded in Corinth. While these books contain some heady theological data, they also offer practical insight for living the Christian life in any culture or time.

THE MESSAGE

These letters of Paul cover specific problems and questions that had arisen in these churches. Paul wrote to the believers in Rome to help them identify and defend what they believed about the gospel. He wrote to the Corinthian church for very different reasons. He had heard troublesome news about divisions and misbehavior, not just in isolated cases but rampant in the church. He wrote to correct them and to help them better understand basic Christian truth.

THE MAIN POINT

If you have ever wondered about the essential truths of your faith, these books are excellent starting points. Romans communicates clear teaching on grace and righteousness gained by faith in Christ. Corinthians swings along from chapter to chapter with information on how the church and believers should look and act, not just in the first century but in the twenty-first century. Carefully study both and you'll gather one nugget of truth after another.

TAKE NOTE

Romans 1:7—From humble beginnings as a defendable stockade for area shepherds, the city of Rome grew through the centuries to become the capital of the Roman Empire. The building projects of one emperor after another made the city one of beautiful temples, aqueducts, palaces, and baths. The emperor Augustus claimed that he came to a "city built of brick and left it built of marble."[1] By the time of Paul and the early church, the city's population numbered about a million, and many historians believe that at least a fifth of those were Christians.

1 Corinthians 1:2—The city of Corinth, a regional capital of the Roman empire, was a city with three harbors, forming an important business and shipping link between Rome and cities to the east. A Roman city of luxury, riches, and depravity, Corinthians worshiped Poseidon, god of the sea, Aphrodite, goddess of love, as well as a myriad of other gods. At its largest, Corinth had a population of about two hundred thousand free people as well as nearly five hundred thousand slaves.

---

[1]Suetonius, The Lives of the Twelve Caesars (121 AD). For more information, visit http://en.wikipedia.org/wiki/Lives_of_the_Twelve_Caesars..

Tuesday

Reflecting on the Word
1 Corinthians 12

Everyone likes gifts. And this chapter of Paul's letter to the church in Corinth offers a series of gifts that are available to every believer through the work of the Holy Spirit.

Paul began his discussion of spiritual gifts in 1 Corinthians 12:1 with the words, "Now concerning" (NKJV) or "Now about"(NIV) suggesting that this information was being given in response to a question posed by the Corinthian believers. As usual for him, Paul's answer was detailed, precise, and clear. And his answer would be the same to you today if you could ask him the same question the Corinthian church asked so long ago.

First, spiritual gifts are given to believers by the Holy Spirit. Each gift is a manifestation of the Spirit's work in that believer's life, given to him or her to benefit the church. Just as there are many different people, there are many different gifts.

Paul listed a number of the gifts in the following verses, beginning with those most important to the growth and development of the church, gifts of communication. The first gift he mentioned is the gift of wisdom, the ability to discern and convey the truths of the Bible. The second, the gift of knowledge, is the Spirit-given ability to clearly teach the way of faith in Jesus. Paul then went on to list the gift of faith, that is, not merely faith to believe in Jesus but faith to endure hardship and perhaps even persecution and martyrdom. Next appeared the gifts of healing and miracles, those spectacular evidences of the Spirit's work. Paul ended his list with four related gifts: prophecy, discernment, tongues, and the ability to interpret tongues.

Given the divisions that the Corinthian church was experiencing, it's no surprise that Paul went on to emphasize that even though there were many gifts and many different people, all of them came from the same Spirit, one was not more worthy or less worthy than another. Paul built on this topic by comparing the church to a body, that one part of a body couldn't operate without another, just as all the diverse gifts are necessary for the best functioning church.

And since division has at its core a lack of love, Paul finished his discourse on spiritual gifts by proposing that love is the best gift of all, what he called a "more excellent way" (1 Corinthians 12:31 NKJV). Finish your day of studying the spiritual gifts by reading 1 Corinthians 13, remembering that without love, all the gifts and miracles and preaching and teaching are like ashes, worth less than nothing.

Wednesday

Studying the Word
Romans 7:15–25; 8:37–39

Paul's lessons on sin and the struggle believers can have with it will provide a dose of reality for those who study them. Read these verses, and then answer the following questions for your own reality check and reassurance.

1. What did Paul mean by all these *do* and *do not* words (Romans 7:15–16)? How do you identify with Paul?
2. Who was actually sinning according to Paul (Romans 7:17)? Wasn't this a bit of an evasion on his part? Explain your answer.
3. Why do you think Paul repeated his argument in Romans 7:18–20? What does this accomplish?
4. How did Paul express his relationship with sin (Romans 7:23)? How are you a captive or prisoner of sin?
5. How did Paul answer his own question in Romans 7:24 (Romans 7:25)?
6. Only a short chapter later, Paul expressed a similar but yet very different reaction. How are the two passages related (Romans 8:37)?
7. What sort of comfort can you receive from the words of Romans 8:38–39?

The Women's Devotional Guide to the Bible

Thursday

Responding to the Word
1 Corinthians 1:26–31

Without apology, Paul expressed what God was doing through His people, using those who had little going for them to bring about great things in the church and the world. He chose those who weren't the smartest or the wisest or the best looking or the richest or the "–est" anything in order to accomplish His work. Instead, He chose to use those who were ordinary, weak, and not so great.

That's us, of course.

God used Paul, the one who had been out to murder believers, to reach the Gentile world. He chose Peter, that impetuous, act-before-thinking disciple, to preach the first salvation sermon. In the Old Testament, He chose prostitutes, murderers, and moral weaklings to do His work.

And He's still in the same business today. The business of using ordinary, less-than-perfect people to get His work done, His good news out. If your pastor isn't the best in one area or another, perhaps you should rejoice instead of criticizing. If the missionary you support doesn't have the gifts to get part of the job done, maybe you should thank God. If you feel like you have little to offer the kingdom, maybe you should celebrate.

That might be going a bit far, but not by much. God has been using ordinary people since the beginning of time to get extraordinary things accomplished. He can get more done through those who are weak in their own strength, who recognize their lack of ability, than through those who think they have it all together. He's always looking for workers who know they can't get the job done, so they let God get it done through them.

Today, as you read these words, examine yourself. What do you have to boast about? Something you've accomplished on your own, through your own ability? Or something that only God could accomplish through you?

Friday

Praying the Word
2 Corinthians 9:6–8

In your prayer time today, concentrate on your giving, not just on how much you give, but on *how* you give it. Ask God to not only make you a generous giver but a jolly giver, one who delights in giving back to God and sharing with others.

Faithful God, show me today how I can give generously and with a truly cheerful attitude. Help me to never hold so tightly to the things I own that I can't happily share them with others. Make me aware of the needs of others that I can meet with the plenty You've given me. And over it all, Lord, help me to realize that none of it really belongs to me anyway—it's all a gift from Your hand. In the name of Jesus, the greatest gift of all, Amen.

Paul's Other Letters

Monday

Reading the Word
Galatians 3–6; Ephesians 4–6; Philippians 1–4;
Colossians 3; 1 Thessalonians 4; 2 Thessalonians 2;
1 Timothy 4; 6; 2 Timothy 1; Titus 3; Philemon

THE STORY

Paul wrote the majority of these shorter letters while he was in prison. His remarkable ability to look beyond his own difficult circumstances to the needs of others comes through clearly in these short missives. These letters read like personal notes to personal friends.

THE MESSAGE

Each of these short books contains vital instruction for living the Christian life well in any time or culture. Paul's letters offer practical, nononsense guidelines for life as well as treatises on points of theology. While he doesn't put theology in place of or higher than the realistic standards of living every day for Jesus, theology and life are intricately tied together in Paul's writings.

THE MAIN POINT

Your understanding of Paul's teachings in these books has implications for how you live your life. Purely reading and gaining insight into the truth is only half the picture, and not a very clear one if your lifestyle is unaffected. Read these sweet little letters from Paul, and you'll gain not only truth but a changed life.

TAKE NOTE

Galatians 1:2—Galatia was a province of Rome in the area where Turkey is today. Paul and Barnabas had established churches there on their first missionary journey.

Ephesians 1:1—Ephesus was a port city and a frequent destination for religious pilgrims, who came to worship the goddess Artemis (Greek) or Diana (Roman). Many who came purchased souvenirs of their visit, which made silversmithing one of the primary trades of the city. Paul visited the city on his third missionary journey.

Philippians 1:1—Philippi, the Roman gateway to the east, was the first European church established by Paul. In this city, Paul and Silas were miraculously freed from prison, resulting in the salvation of their jail keeper (Acts 16:16–40).

Colossians 1:2—Colosse, a small town in what is now Turkey, had a church that was established by a coworker of Paul while he was working in Ephesus (Colossians 1:7).

1 Thessalonians 1:1—Thessalonica was a city in Macedonia with a large number of Jewish inhabitants. Paul's two little letters to this church are perhaps his earliest surviving letters. He visited Thessalonica on his second missionary journey.

Tuesday

Reflecting on the Word
Galatians 3

The relationship between the Old Testament law and the grace available through Jesus Christ has been a topic of debate and discussion since the time when Paul wrote this letter to the churches in Galatia. The Jewish believers in Galatia argued about whether Gentile believers were required to keep the ritual laws of the Jewish religion, such as circumcision. Paul wrote to try to clear up the disagreement.

Is a person justified before God by observing the laws, or by faith? That was Paul's basic question to the believers in Galatia. He carefully built the argument that the law without faith accomplishes nothing. The law points out sin more effectively than it saves from sin. Trying to gain righteousness through obedience to a set of laws was, as Paul could tell from personal experience, an exercise in futility. When he realized that only through the grace of Christ could he gain righteousness, he stopped relying on the law. And he wanted the Galatians to understand and do the same.

Does this mean that all Old Testament laws can be thrown out? Ignored? Not quite. Many of the laws of the Old Testament are excellent guidelines for living a holy, moral life. Many of the principles outlined in the laws are timeless and just as applicable today as they were when they were given to Moses and the Israelites in the desert.

The important thing to remember, according to Paul, is that the law is totally ineffective if it's used to try to gain salvation. No one can be good enough. The only effective means to gain salvation is to accept Christ's work on the cross. What freedom Paul's words offer to anyone who has tried—and failed—to be good enough to earn God's favor! Paul urged the believers in Galatia not to give up that freedom ever again for the burden of slavery to the law (Galatians 5:1).

Wednesday

Studying the Word
Philippians 4:4–8

Words worth remembering during the everydayness of life are found in these few captivating verses in Philippians. They are superior as a guideline for living life well. Read them, maybe memorize them, then answer these questions to dig a bit deeper and find application for your life.

1. How in the world are people supposed to rejoice "always" (Philippians 4:4 NKJV)? Even in the hardest, toughest, saddest times? Is this realistic? What does Paul mean?

2. Compare the prophet's words in Habakkuk 3:17–18. (Remember that Habakkuk wrote when his country was under siege, and Paul wrote while imprisoned in Rome.) Where does Habakkuk suggest you find strength to live this way (Habakkuk 3:19)?

3. How in the world are people supposed to be anxious about "nothing" (Philippians 4:6 NKJV)? What recipe for ridding yourself of anxiety is found in this verse?

4. What does Paul promise you'll gain (Philippians 4:7)?

5. What does Paul suggest you focus your mind on (Philippians 4:8)? What sorts of things does this include? What might it *not* include? Is this realistic? How can you go about meditating on these good things in everyday life?

Thursday

Responding to the Word
Ephesians 6:10–18

In his letter to the Ephesians, Paul urged the believers in that church to dance to a new tune. Whereas before they had worshiped idols and been involved in sexual immorality, he now wanted them to think of themselves in a very different way: dead to sin and alive in Christ (Ephesians 2:1, 5), children of light rather than darkness (Ephesians 4:18, 24). In order to live this new life, Paul gave them a word picture for their new way of living—wearing new clothing, the armor of God. Your new life in Christ requires new clothing also. Check out your new wardrobe as a believer.

Begin by putting the truth as a belt around your waist. Truth implies knowledge; know what is true and what is not, in order to defend yourself against the devil's lies. Add to that the breastplate of righteousness, the metal plate of armor that covered an ancient soldier from neck to thighs. Both your good character and the righteousness you gain by faith in Jesus offer a defense against the enemy. Next put the gospel of peace on your feet. Soldiers need good footwear in order to succeed in battle. Just as a good pair of boots provides a good foundation for a soldier, a knowledge and dependence on the peace of God provides a good foundation for a believer. Now, pick up the shield of faith, your handheld protection against whatever the devil throws at you, and then put on the helmet of salvation to protect your mind. Next pick up the sword of the Spirit, which is God's Word, your only offensive weapon. But what a weapon it is, as Jesus demonstrated during His own time of temptation (Matthew 4:1–11).

Just as a soldier prepares for battle by dressing properly, a believer can grow strong and prepare to do battle with the evil one by dressing properly. When you get up in the morning and get ready for the day, don't just put on your makeup and jewelry and clothing and shoes, put on your armor. Only then will you truly be ready to face whatever the day brings.

Friday

Praying the Word
1 Thessalonians 5:17

What could Paul possibly have meant when he told the Thessalonians to "pray without ceasing" (NKJV)? Impossible to do in this busy, noisy, distracting culture? The goal is to have a mind of prayer, one that grasps that all of today's business is dependent on God. Praying without ceasing or continually doesn't necessarily look like an over-pious person who causes an accident at a red light because he or she is praying. Rather, it's an attitude, an outlook that keeps life in balance, that remembers who's in charge, that breathes a prayer—silent, quick, often.

Father, I admit that I don't really fully understand how to pray without ceasing. Will You teach me? Will You make my mind and heart so aware of Your presence even in the mediocre and mundane parts of my life that I can't help but keep the lines of communication open with You? I love You, Lord! Amen.

The Letter to the Hebrews

Monday

Reading the Word
Hebrews 3–7; 10–13

THE STORY

The letter to the Hebrews (its authorship is uncertain) was written to remind early Jewish believers of their heritage, their foundation for faith, their roots. Tempted to go back to their Old Testament ways because of hardship and persecution, this letter urged them to stick with this superior way, this new covenant of faith in Jesus Christ.

THE MESSAGE

The Christian life has its difficulties, its hardships, its ups and downs. The book of Hebrews acknowledges that and urges readers not to give up but to keep the faith. It's that simple—and that difficult.

THE MAIN POINT

Whatever you face as a believer, wherever your journey takes you, don't turn away from your faith in Christ. All the parts and pieces of life—those disciplines Hebrews 12 talks about—will bring you to greater faith and a deeper relationship with Jesus, if you stick with Him throughout.

TAKE NOTE

Hebrews 7:1—Melchizedek was a priest and the king of Salem—later known as Jerusalem—during the time of Abraham. Abraham met Melchizedek after winning a great battle and offered him 10 percent of the spoils (Genesis 14:18–20). David mentioned him in Psalm 110 as a prototype of the Messiah.

Tuesday

Reflecting on the Word
Hebrews 11

This chapter of the book of Hebrews is rather like visiting a museum or hall of fame. The writer honored those heroes from the Old Testament who were justified by their faith, faith in promises that had yet to be fulfilled. In spite of hardship beyond what many today are called to endure (Hebrews 11:36–38), they didn't give up but remained faithful.

The writer of this book began by defining faith as believing in things that can't be seen or proven. Faith has a life-giving quality to it; it's not something insubstantial or fragile or only the concern of mystics. Faith is lived out in everyday life, revealed through obedience, and unveiled in an individual sense through each person listed in this hall of fame of faith.

Faith can, according to this author, have two different concentrations. The first is a focus on what the believer hopes for. The second is what the believer can't see. Neither can be verified by visual or scientific evidence. Both must be accepted by faith in God, a trust that God knows what He's doing and is in ultimate control.

The writer went on to identify these heroes and their actions or reactions. From Abel and Enoch to Abraham and Joseph, from Moses and Rahab to David and Samuel, from named to unnamed, these men and women didn't merely believe in God but acted on their belief, sometimes with miraculous results, sometimes with pain or death as a result.

Read through this moving register of individuals who faced life with faith, recognizing as you read that these were not perfect people without sin or failings. They were faithful people, who believed in a God big enough to do what He had promised He would do.

Wednesday

Studying the Word
Hebrews 12:1–3, 9–11

Nobody much likes being disciplined. Parents didn't like being disciplined when they were children, and they don't enjoy having to discipline their children now. Believers don't enjoy discipline itself but can enjoy its results. Read these verses and then answer the following questions to discover the benefits of discipline.

1. What "great . . . cloud of witnesses" (Hebrews 12:1 NKJV) surrounds you today? (Hebrews 11 is a clue.)
2. What effect does/could/should this audience have on you (Hebrews 12:1)?
3. Where can you look for courage to face your faith journey (Hebrews 12:2)? What has Jesus done that qualifies Him as One worthy of your gaze (Hebrews 12:2–3)?
4. How were you disciplined as a child (Hebrews 12:9)? What effect did discipline have on your relationship with your parents?
5. Why does God discipline believers (Hebrews 12:10)?
6. What does discipline accomplish in the life of a believer (Hebrews 12:11)? How does it accomplish this?
7. What discipline or chastening have you experienced in recent years? What has that discipline accomplished in your life?

Thursday

Responding to the Word
Hebrews 10:25

Here's the church.
Here's the steeple.
Open the doors.
See all the people.

OK, maybe not always a steeple today. But God's people still gather together for worship and fellowship across the world, in homes and restaurants and malls and tents and hiding places. The writer to the Hebrews recognized the importance of regular association with fellow believers and urged his readers to continue to gather. He saw grave danger in trying to live the Christian life in isolation, then and now.

Hebrews 10:25 is linked to the previous verse and provides the good logic behind the writer's directive to continue to get together. Only in association with other believers could one be stirred up to acts of "love and good works." Not a bad goal. Those sorts of actions have a way of dissolving, disappearing when life is lived alone.

Then (and now also), some believers for some reason didn't think it important to get together with other believers on a regular basis. But the truths of Scripture are truths lived out in community, not in isolation. Getting together to worship, to encourage each other, to teach and to learn, to offer help and comfort and guidance—all are aspects of the Christian life that only take place in community.

What does your community look like? Is it a mega-church atmosphere? A tiny country church or an urban church with few members? A house church or small group? Whatever your community, don't give up meeting together with them. They need you. And you need them.

Friday

This verse makes it abundantly clear where your confidence for the future lies. Not in your savings or your ability to earn or your inheritance or in getting more. God has and will continue to provide for His people. In your prayer time today, ask God to reveal where you are depending on your bank account or abilities rather than on Him.

Father who owns all, I put every part of my life into Your hands. I confess that at times I think more about my money situation and my abilities than about Your ability to provide what I need. Help me, Lord, to recognize that You will never leave me, that I will only find true contentment when I trust in Your willingness and ability to provide. In Jesus' name, Amen.

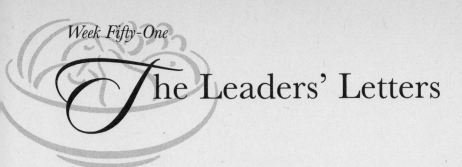

The Leaders' Letters

Monday

Reading the Word
James 1–5; 1 Peter 1; 3–4; 2 Peter 1;
1 John 2:28–4:21; 2 John; 3 John; Jude

THE STORY

Little letters all, but they pack a big punch. The church leaders—James, Peter, John, and Jude—wrote these short letters to address a particular issue in the church. Don't let their brevity fool you into thinking they're not valuable or significant. Read each one to discover the concerns of the early church and how these leaders addressed those concerns.

THE MESSAGE

Jesus' half-brothers, James and Jude, and Jesus' disciples, Peter and John, wrote these missives to encourage the early church and to teach some principles of living that are as applicable today as they were in the first century.

THE MAIN POINT

From James's taming of the tongue to the hope and holiness that Peter claimed suffering accomplishes to John's living a life of love, enjoy each slice of truth as the writers present them. You'll find teaching, encouragement, correction, and a passion for Christ that will pierce your heart as you read. As with all of Scripture, these words are "God-breathed" (2 Timothy 3:16 NIV) and will send a breath of fresh air into your life and study.

Tuesday

Reflecting on the Word
1 Peter 1:6–7

Peter wrote his two little letters to the believers who were scattered throughout the area now known as Turkey. He calls them the "pilgrims of the Dispersion" (1 Peter 1:1 NKJV), in other words, believing Jews who lived in places other than Israel.

When the early church was established, the Roman government treated Christians much the same as those of other religions, offering them freedom to express their religious beliefs. But the tolerance of the government faded as religious Jews and Christians argued and as believers gained influence and power. Anything that threatened the stability of the empire was suspect; therefore, later in the first century Christians came under attack. Their property was taken away, they were imprisoned, and some were martyred.

Peter recognized that these persecutions would severely test the faith of some, so he addressed their troubles right from the start in his first letter. He spoke from experience, having been beaten and imprisoned (Acts 12:1–19). He told his readers that their trials had a purpose.

The troubles that believers faced then and still face today work to strengthen and prove the genuineness of their faith. When gold is heated, everything that is impure in it floats away. When faith is heated, put to the test, everything that is unnecessary and tainted fades away. What is left is pure gold or pure, robust faith. Then, wonderful thought, that faith results in praise and honor and glory for Jesus!

Easier said than done, of course. Which was Peter's point. He urged the persecuted believers to hang on, to suffer "for a little while" (1 Peter 1:6 NKJV) because of the glory their suffering would produce. He even went so far as to say they could *rejoice* in their sufferings because of what those difficulties would generate in them and offer to Jesus.

Wednesday

Studying the Word
James 2:14–24

James, who was probably one of Jesus' half-brothers, is best known for his teaching on taming the tongue (James 3:1–12) and his teaching on the relationship between faith and works. As you answer the following questions, find your way to a better understanding of the relationship between your faith and your deeds.

1. How would you answer James's question in James 2:14?
2. How did he answer the question (James 2:15–17)?
3. Does this mean that you need works in order to be saved? How does this relate to Paul's teaching that you're saved by grace alone (Ephesians 2:8–9)?
4. Explain what you think James meant when he said he'll show you his faith by what he does (James 2:18). How can you personally show your faith by what you do?
5. How did James say Abraham's faith was made perfect (James 2:20–23)?
6. If you don't need anything but faith to be made righteous, what does James mean by saying that you are justified by your works as well as your faith (James 2:24)? How would you describe the relationship between your faith and your works?

Thursday

Responding to the Word
1 John 4:7–21

The apostle John, known as the disciple whom Jesus loved (John 13:23), appropriately wrote this passage on love. Given his past history and relationship with Jesus, he obviously knew something about this characteristic.

John began by tying the love of Christians for each other to God's love. Because believers are loved by God, they have a special, increased capacity to love others. At least they *should*. Because God's love for believers is so undeserved, they have a special, increased capacity to love those who might be less than lovable. At least they *should*.

If you're wondering how exactly you should be living this life of love, what it might look like, you have the perfect example to follow, according to John. He had watched as Jesus selflessly gave His life away because of His love for sinners. He watched as Jesus depleted His own strength and ignored His own needs in order to meet the needs of others. And he urged his readers to follow Jesus' example.

The natural tendency of human beings is to live life rather—or sometimes more than rather—selfishly, tending to our own needs before worrying or dealing with the needs of others. John's little letter urges you to live very differently. The best response to Jesus' love for you is to let that love flow through you to others.

While that might not be much of a problem when dealing with some people, it might be a bit more difficult when dealing with the cantankerous, the difficult, the socially inept, or the less-than-pleasing people you meet each day. John noted no differentiation between loving the lovable and the not-so-lovable. He stated it simply and clearly: if you say you love God, you'd better be loving others. He went even further and said that if you say you love God then *don't* love others, you're a liar.

Obviously, this love thing was pretty important to John. And to God.

Today, spend some time examining your love levels. Start with your love for God, thanking Him for His love for you. Then work your way through the love you have for others—your family, your friends, your neighbors, the girl who delivers your paper, the young man who fixes your car—all those lovable and not-so-lovable people in your everyday life.

Friday

Praying the Word
Jude 3

The devil would like nothing better than for believers to become complacent and self-satisfied. Jude urged believers to "contend earnestly" (NKJV) for the faith. In your prayer time today, ask God to reveal areas where you may be complacent and then ask Him to show you where you need to declare firmly your allegiance to Christ.

Lord of all, I know that I am at times less than eager to protect and affirm the faith I have in You. Show me the areas where I need to change and grow. Then help me to be one of Your front line defenders of the faith. I love You, Lord, and my heart's desire is to serve You wholeheartedly. Amen.

Week Fifty-Two

The Coming Victory

Monday

Reading the Word
Revelation 1–5; 19–22

THE STORY

Like science fiction or fantasy, the images and symbols and visions of the book of Revelation amaze and confound those who read them. While some are sure of their meanings, others debate and doubt. Some see these events as having been fulfilled in the first century; others see a fulfillment that is still in the future; still others see fulfillment both ways. But the central message of the book is easily deciphered even if you don't understand one of the signs or symbols: Jesus wins!

THE MESSAGE

Evil and good have warred throughout history, starting at the very beginning in the Garden of Eden, when the serpent convinced Eve to eat forbidden fruit. It would be easy to be discouraged and think that the war will continue forever or that evil will finally win. But just the opposite is true. Revelation, with pictures and symbols and catastrophes and battles, tells the all-important story of the victory that Christ the King will win over evil.

THE MAIN POINT

You don't need to fear. Ultimate victory belongs to Jesus. He will destroy Satan and his cohorts and will reign forever as King of kings and Lord of lords!

TAKE NOTE

Revelation 2:1, 8, 12, 18; 3:1, 7, 14—The book of Revelation begins with letters written to seven churches in the Roman province of Asia, alternately complimenting and denouncing them for their successes and problems. It is likely that John, who wrote the book of Revelation, ministered in these churches.

Revelation 19:1—The word *hallelujah* (NCV) is really two Hebrew words, which mean "praise the Lord," or "praise Yahweh." When you say, "Hallelujah," you're sort of speaking Hebrew.

The Women's Devotional Guide to the Bible

Tuesday

Reflecting on the Word
Revelation 3:15–16

These verses record some of the harshest words in Scripture, a denunciation of those whose faith is only "lukewarm" (Revelation 3:16 NKJV), causing God to "vomit" (NKJV) them out of His mouth. Strong words, ugly picture. The church in Laodicea had it all, except what really counted.

Laodicea was a prosperous town on the Roman road, along the way from Ephesus to Asia. With large wool and banking industries, as well as the commerce that was a natural part of being central on the trade routes, Laodicea acquired enormous wealth and self-sufficiency. Which was ultimately the reason for the condemnation they received. Its inhabitants were self-reliant, self-contained, and selfish. Their middle names were compromise and concession. They stood for nothing. They were lukewarm. The description would have been one the church there understood completely, since for all its wealth, Laodicea had poor water, which was piped from hot springs and entered the city warm rather than cool and refreshing.

The people's relationship with Jesus was so thin, so inadequate, that the writer of Revelation knew they were in danger of missing Jesus altogether. While being spiritually cold is not something Jesus would want, at least those people know where they stand. They don't act like they have it all together when they don't. Being hot is the same. Those people know they believe, act like they believe, stand firm in their belief. About those who are lukewarm, however, no one can be certain. And therein resides the danger, a danger so real that Jesus made His famous offer to knock on the door and to enter and give them something about which to be passionate—hot rather than lukewarm.

Wednesday

Studying the Word
Revelation 4; 21:1–4

Want a glimpse of heaven? Read these passages in Revelation, then answer the following questions for a hint of what that place will be like.

1. Since John saw it first, what must be most important in heaven (Revelation 4:2)?

2. How did John try to describe the one who sat on this throne (Revelation 4:3)?

3. We won't bother to ask who the twenty-four elders were (Revelation 4:4), since not even Bible scholars can agree. Some say they are angelic beings representing Israel's twelve tribes and Jesus' twelve disciples. But whoever they are, what was their role (Revelation 4:10)? Why do you think they laid their crowns down before the throne?

4. What other creatures surrounded the throne (Revelation 4:5–8)? What was their primary role (Revelation 4:8)? Try to describe what you think this scene might look like, what emotions it might produce in you if you were there.

5. Who was the One on the throne being worshiped? Why does He deserve worship (Revelation 4:8*b*, 11)?

6. You may not be able to decipher who and what the creatures in this chapter are. But beyond those details, what picture of heaven do you gain by reading this chapter?

7. What does Revelation 21:1–2 say about what heaven will be like? What one word does John use to describe heaven and earth and Jerusalem? Why is that word a good description?

8. Who will be heaven's most important inhabitant (Revelation 21:3)?

9. What will *not* be in heaven (Revelation 21:4)?

10. What about heaven intrigues or excites you?

Thursday

Responding to the Word
Revelation 19

How adept are you at praising God? You might want to use this chapter to get in some praise practice. You can be sure that you'll be doing a lot of it in heaven. Depending on what you read about heaven, you might be doing other things as well, but praise will likely be one of your primary activities. After all, the God of all of heaven and earth sent His Son to die so that you could live forever. He deserves your praise.

The battle between good and evil has reached its final climax. Jesus has won! And all of heaven bursts into praise with a "roar" (Revelation 19:1 NIV). Aren't you eager to be a part of that assembly? Watching the final battle, then seeing Jesus emerge triumphant? Like a great victory at a sporting event, the entire audience will jump up in spontaneous cheering and shouting and praise. The praises will be so overwhelming and loud that Revelation says they'll sound like the roar of water and like peals of thunder (Revelation 19:6). If you've ever been part of a huge multitude that cheered something, whether a team or God, you have a small peek at what that praise in heaven will be like.

All of heaven's beings have reason to praise God. But only the redeemed can praise Him for salvation, for the reality of what the Son's death on the cross accomplished. That will be your privilege in heaven, to praise Jesus and bow before Him as your King of kings and Lord of lords.

Friday

Praying the Word
Revelation 22:20–21

The final words of the Bible form your final prayer of this study. Use them to pray for Jesus' quick return and for the church to remain faithful to the end.

Lord Jesus, Maranatha! *Come quickly! I look for You to return soon, to redeem Your people who have remained faithful to You by Your grace, and to establish Your holy and victorious kingdom. I love and serve You, my King of kings, my Lord of lords. Amen.*

Index of Scriptures Used in Weekly Themes

Topical Index

Women of the Bible
A One-Year Devotional Study of Women in Scripture
By Ann Spangler and Jean E. Syswerda

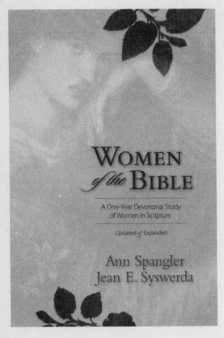

Hardcover, Jacketed
0-310-27055-3

Women of the Bible focuses on fifty-two remarkable women in Scripture—women whose struggles to live with faith and courage are not unlike your own. And now this bestselling devotional study book has been updated and expanded to enhance its flexibility, usefulness, and relevance for both individuals and groups.

Small groups will especially welcome the way the Bible studies have been streamlined to fit the unique needs of the group setting. Other important changes include:

- A list of all the women of the Bible keyed to Scripture
- Timeline A timeline of the foremost women of the Bible
- A list of women in Jesus' family tree
- A list of women in Jesus' life and ministry

Vital and deeply human, the women in this book encourage you through their failures as well as their successes. You'll see how God acted in surprising and wonderful ways to draw them—and you—to himself. This year-long devotional offers a unique method to help you slow down and savor the story of God's unrelenting love for his people, offering a fresh perspective that will nourish and strengthen your personal communion with him.

Pick up a copy at your favorite bookstore!

ZONDERVAN™